I0893885

ANTI-CATHOLICISM IN ARKANSAS

Anti-Catholicism in Arkansas

How Politicians, the Press, the Klan, and Religious Leaders Imagined an Enemy, 1910–1960

KENNETH C. BARNES

The University of Arkansas Press • Fayetteville • 2016

Manufactured in the United States of America
ISBN: 978-1-68226-016-6
e-ISBN: 978-1-61075-599-3

20 19 18 17 16 5 4 3 2 1

Designed by Liz Lester

∞ The paper used in this publication meets the minimum requirements of the American National Standard for Permanence of Paper for Printed Library Materials Z39.48-1984.

Library of Congress Control Number: 2016947889

For John and Lynda, my favorite Arkansas Catholics

CONTENTS

ACKNOWLEDGMENTS

This book stems from an intersection of my professional and personal lives. While I have written in the past about religion, prejudice, and Arkansas, this book about anti-Catholicism in Arkansas combines these themes. My initial interest in this project stems from my own biography. I grew up in a Baptist family in rural Arkansas in the 1960s. In an environment that was hostile to Roman Catholicism, my older brother, my only sibling, converted to the Catholic faith while in high school. The experience of overhearing angry religious debates constitutes the only traumatic event of my childhood. This book has allowed me to explore the origins of my parents' prejudices against Roman Catholicism.

As always, librarians and archivists have assisted my work in valuable ways. Elizabeth DiPrince, Tim Purkiss, Amanda Bryant, and Rosalie Lovelace, of the interlibrary loan office of Torreyson Library of the University of Central Arkansas, have brought obscure and remote material for my convenient use. Aryn Denette, of the university's archives, helped me process illustrations for this book. I thank Timothy Nutt and the gracious staff of the Special Collections Department, the University of Arkansas Libraries. I especially note archivist Todd Lewis, whose stimulating conversation and many suggestions about sources made my time in Fayetteville more productive. The administration and library staff of the Missionary Baptist Seminary in Little Rock, particularly Mark Harris and Gerald Cronan, graciously opened their collection to me. I also thank Hannah Wood, librarian of Archives and Special Collections at Harding University; Susan H. Brosnan, archivist at the Knights of Columbus Museum in New Haven, Connecticut; Janice L. Cantrell, archivist at the Archives of the Diocese of Fort Wayne/South Bend in Fort Wayne, Indiana; and Gail Hennagin and Phyllis Kinnison of the Special Collections Department of the Riley-Hickingbotham Library of Ouachita Baptist University.

Dr. Ray Granade gave me valuable advice on Arkansas Baptist Convention records. Kathy Fairchild provided advice and information about the *Menace* and resources in Aurora, Missouri. Dr. James Willis advised me about the history of Magnolia, Arkansas, and the Reverend

Joseph A. Scarboro. The Reverend Steve Norris educated me about the traditions and theology of the Churches of Christ.

I thank D. S. Cunningham, my editor at the University of Arkansas Press, for his interest in this project and assistance in moving along the publication process.

I have been fortunate to have support from the University of Central Arkansas. A grant from the university's Research Council funded travel to archives. A sabbatical leave enabled me to complete the initial draft of this book. Administrative assistance from Judy Huff and Sam VanHouten helped in many ways.

I thank Jeannie Whayne and James Woods for their perceptive readings and many suggestions stemming from their vast knowledge of Arkansas history. My colleagues at the University of Central Arkansas, Mike Rosenow, Jim Brodman, and Debbie Barnes, read drafts of this book and provided valuable advice. Mike gave me the insights of a specialist in the Progressive Era of American history and warded me away from the naïveté of an interloper to the field. Jim gave me the insights of a scholar with expertise in the history and culture of Roman Catholicism. Debbie helped me excise and edit passages that strained the interest and comprehension of a non-specialist. In addition, Debbie, as my life partner, has cheerfully endured my musings about this project and my considerable investment of time.

I dedicate this book to my brother, John, whose courageous and sometimes painful experiences inspired me to write this book, and his wife, Lynda, whose career has been spent in service to her parish church.

ANTI-CATHOLICISM IN ARKANSAS

Image from masthead of the *Liberator*.

CHAPTER 1

Prelude: Before 1913

ATOP THE MASTHEAD of the *Liberator*, an anti-Catholic weekly newspaper published in Magnolia, Arkansas, from 1912 to 1915, an image of the "Whore of Babylon" represented the Roman Catholic Church. The editor, Joseph A. Scarboro, pastor of Magnolia's First Baptist Church, was referring to the passage in Revelations 17 that described a woman sitting on a seven-headed, seven-horned beast, holding a golden cup full of abominations and the filth of her fornications. The cup looks very much like a communion chalice or perhaps a glass popular in the early 1900s for champagne and cocktails, said to be inspired by the shape of a woman's breast.[1]

This sort of titillating sexual imagery and a deluge of misleading reporting whipped white Protestants in small-town and rural Arkansas into a frenzy of anti-Catholicism in the 1910s and 1920s. The antipathy toward the institutions of the Roman Catholic Church, more so than to actual Catholic neighbors, connected Protestants to broader fears of immigration, opposition to liquor, and, eventually, anxiety over a war against Germany. In the 1920s, anti-Catholicism became subsumed into the new Ku Klux Klan, which loudly proclaimed that Roman Catholics were not real Americans. The prejudice against Catholics began to fade after 1928, when Joe T. Robinson, the Methodist senator from Arkansas, teamed as vice presidential running mate with the Catholic governor of New York, Al Smith, in the presidential race. The 1960 campaign of John Fitzgerald Kennedy motivated a last gasp of anti-Catholicism, although some would argue it has never completely gone away.

Two books have provided the author with the greatest intellectual inheritance in preparing this work, John Higham's *Strangers in the Land: Patterns of American Nativism* and Justin Nordstrom's *Danger on the*

Doorstep: Anti-Catholicism and American Print Culture in the Progressive Era.[2] For a publication first appearing in 1955, Higham's book has had a long shelf life because of the way he so defines nativism as a subject and thoroughly relates different forms of nativism to each other and to the historical context. Nordstrom provides a close reading of anti-Catholic newspapers, pamphlets, and books of the early twentieth century. He correlates anti-Catholicism with geography, class, social psychology, and American culture. Higham rightfully presents anti-Catholicism as a key manifestation of nativism, but he sees Catholicism essentially as a marker for ethnicity. In contrast, Nordstrom views anti-Catholicism more as a prejudice against a particular religion than against immigrants and foreigners. Like Nordstrom, I see anti-Catholicism as essentially about a religion. But this study takes a closer look at the religious sentiments of anti-Catholics and explains why certain evangelical groups, such as Baptists, expressed anti-Catholic views stridently and consistently.

In the 1910s many white Protestants in Arkansas imagined Roman Catholics as an immoral "other" against whom they affirmed their own moral identity and community mores, particularly concerning sex and alcohol. In the 1920s Catholics became the foil as white Protestants defined the authentic American identity. With the presidential politicking of 1924 and 1928, and then again with the John Kennedy election of 1960, some white evangelical voters raised the specter of a Catholic plot to take over the United States and its institutions. This book shows us how a dominant group can project a cultural minority as a feared or despised other and how prejudice waxes and wanes over time. Arkansas, a largely Protestant state in the Upper South, was the type of environment where anti-Catholic sentiments were most intense in the twentieth century. This study of one extended community allows us to see how prejudice against Catholics grew, operated, and declined in a specific social, political, and cultural context.[3]

Anti-Catholicism has deep roots in American history. Going back to colonial days, Protestant settlers in many parts of the English colonies feared a Stuart restoration and considered threats from France to the west and Spain to the south to have counter-Reformation overtones. For educated colonials in the 1700s, Catholicism appeared to embody the sort of superstition the Enlightenment opposed. In the mid-nineteenth century, the wave of immigration from Ireland and German states led to a nativist anti-Catholic movement that culminated in the American Party, more often called the Know-Nothing Party because members were expected, when asked about their affiliation, to answer that they knew nothing. Know-Nothing leaders opposed Catholicism on religious and political grounds, insisting that those loyal to a pope's authoritarian rule over the church could not truly support American democracy.[4] In the 1890s another wave of anti-Catholicism organized as the American Protective Association, which opposed unrestricted immigration, parochial schools, and the holding of public offices by Roman Catholics. The movement was particularly strong in the Northeast and Midwest. The American Protective Association had close ties with the Republican Party, which made it less attractive in the Democratic South. It may have had some presence in Arkansas.[5]

Ironically, the earliest expressions of Christianity in what would become Arkansas were Roman Catholic. On June 21, 1541, the expedition of Spanish explorer Hernando de Soto, including several priests by then in tattered robes, crossed the Mississippi River into what would later be Arkansas. A few days later, De Soto's men erected a large wooden cross atop an Indian mound in the village of Casqui, and the entire company sang the Latin chant, the *Te Deum Laudemus*. This was the first recorded Christian ceremony in Arkansas. More than one hundred years later, in 1673, a French Jesuit priest, Father Jacques Marquette, and his partner, Louis Joliet, travelled down the Mississippi and explored parts of eastern Arkansas. Another French explorer, Robert Cavelier de La Salle, accompanied by priest missionaries, formally claimed the region in March 1682 for King Louis XIV. A few years later, the French established the small fort and trading post of Arkansas Post, near the confluence of the Arkansas and Mississippi Rivers.[6] From 1686 until 1803, when the United States purchased Louisiana from the French emperor Napoleon Bonaparte, Arkansas Post was a small outpost of European culture in the wilderness that was Arkansas. While no dedicated church was erected there, Catholic priests were resident at the post at various intervals, saying mass, performing marriages and baptisms, and reaching out unsuccessfully to the local Quapaw Indian population.[7]

After 1803, the small French Catholic population would be overwhelmed by the arrival of English-speaking Protestant settlers. The first Catholic church constructed in Arkansas was in 1834 near Pine

Bluff, where descendants of earlier French settlers around Arkansas Post had dispersed. In 1843, just seven years after Arkansas became a state, Catholic authorities created the diocese of Little Rock, which included the entirety of the state. Arkansas's first bishop, Irish-born Andrew Byrne, presided over just a handful of parishes that composed the diocese. By mid-century less than 1 percent of Arkansas's population was Catholic.[8]

In the last half of the nineteenth century, substantial immigration brought more Catholics to Arkansas. In rural Franklin County in the late 1870s, the Benedictine Order founded Subiaco Abbey for men and St. Scholastica Monastery for women in nearby Shoal Creek. Both institutions established academies, and the sisters provided health care in a number of towns in the Arkansas River Valley. Benedictines recruited settlers from German-speaking Europe to come to the area. Similarly, the Holy Ghost Order recruited German-speaking immigrants to settle further east along the Arkansas River. This order established parishes from Atkins to Conway and set up a monastery and seminary in Morrilton. One of the Benedictine priests at Subiaco, Father Eugene John Weibel, journeyed to northeastern Arkansas, where he founded several parishes and built a convent, school, and hospital in Jonesboro. Despite this growth, the percentage Catholic within Arkansas remained near 1 percent.[9]

The presence of Catholicism in the United States changed tremendously by the beginning of the twentieth century. The last great manifestation of anti-Catholicism, in fact, would begin after vast numbers of Catholic immigrants from eastern and southern Europe poured into the United States in the early 1900s. The population of the United States grew from roughly 76 million in 1880 to 92 million in 1910, but fully 10 million of this 16 million in population growth was Roman Catholic. The percentage of Americans who were Roman Catholics rose from 8 percent in 1880 to 18 percent in 1910, with no sign that the number of Catholic immigrants arriving through Ellis Island was abating.[10] The immigrant flood caused such concern that in 1907 the US Congress convened a special committee, usually called the Dillingham Commission after its chair, Senator William P. Dillingham of Vermont, to investigate the immigration issue. The commission issued its forty-one-volume report in 1911, complete with voluminous statistics and analysis. The report confirmed what many native-born Americans already believed:

that immigrants from southern and eastern Europe were indeed arriving at an alarming rate, and that the country should restrict immigration to preserve American culture. The largest number of new immigrants was settling in the country's biggest cities, primarily in the North and the East. The Dillingham report, in fact, noted that the larger the city, the greater the percentage of disparity between foreign-born and native-born populations.[11]

Residents of Arkansas, one of the nation's most rural states, reasonably had little to fear concerning an inundation of foreigners and Roman Catholics. Only 1.1 percent of the state's population in the censuses of both 1900 and 1910 were foreign-born white, with the highest percentage in Sebastian County (4.8 percent) and with Columbia, Howard, and Izard Counties vying for the lowest proportion at 0.1 percent.[12] Similarly, the proportion of Arkansas church members who were Roman Catholic was among the lowest in the United States. Just 3.6 percent of reported church members in Arkansas in 1916 were Roman Catholic. Only Georgia, Tennessee, and North Carolina had a smaller proportion of Roman Catholics. Moreover, the percentage of Catholics within Arkansas's population had declined from the previous report of 1906.[13] Arkansas's Catholic population was not dispersed throughout the state but concentrated in the larger towns, such as Little Rock, Fort Smith, and Pine Bluff, and in rural communities where German and Swiss-German Catholic emigrants had settled in the Arkansas River Valley in the late 1880s. A community of Italians settled in Lake Village in southeastern Arkansas, and then a group of them left the swampy mosquito-plagued region to establish Tontitown in the northwestern corner of the state. Smaller groups of Italian immigrants founded Little Italy, west of Little Rock, and Catholic Point, a rural community in Conway County. These German- and Italian-speaking communities tended to stick together, intermarry, or send for brides from the old country, and they had little contact with their Protestant neighbors. The large majority of Arkansans in 1910 probably did not even know personally a Roman Catholic.

The relationship between Catholics and Protestants in Arkansas, moreover, was showing positive signs in 1910. The Arkansas General Assembly met for the first time in the newly constructed capitol building in 1911 and passed an act to make October 12 a state holiday in Arkansas, Columbus Day. The Catholic fraternal order, the Knights of Columbus, had led the movement in Arkansas and elsewhere for a Columbus Day holiday to provide recognition of the role that Roman Catholics played in American history and culture. Arkansas joined thirty-four other states in recognizing Columbus Day. The author of the Arkansas bill was E. J. Kerwin, a Catholic attorney and Knight, who represented Jefferson County in the Arkansas House. The bill appeared to have passed through with little discussion—it was not even reported in the state's leading paper, the *Arkansas Gazette*—and became law as Arkansas Act 443. October 12, 1911, saw the first official celebration of Columbus Day as a state holiday. The day began with mass at St. Andrew's Cathedral and then a banquet at the Capital Hotel presided over by Bishop John Morris. Governor George Donaghey, who signed the bill into law, gave a toast, followed by the rector of Little Rock College, a seminary for priests, who gave a talk entitled "The Influence of Catholicity on American Progress." The crowd of more than two hundred sang "America" before Bishop Morris dismissed the group.[14]

Ironically, in the amicable glow of goodwill toward Catholics in Arkansas, the wheels began moving for the most intense phase of anti-Catholic prejudice in the United States since the Know-Nothing cause of the 1850s. Unlike earlier anti-Catholic movements in American history, which had their greatest strength in urban areas of the Northeast and Midwest, the anti-Catholic campaign that began in 1910 was strongest in rural areas of the Midwest and the South, particularly the Upper South, far from the largest number of new Catholic immigrants.[15] The beginning moment of this renewed anti-Catholicism was in the fall of 1910 when Tom Watson, the former populist politician of Thomson, Georgia, began musing against Catholics in his monthly mouthpiece, *Watson's Jeffersonian Magazine*.

Watson by 1910 might appear to be a washed-up politician. He had achieved a national stage in the 1890s as the champion for the little man, attacking big business, railroads, bankers, and big-city newspapers. As a US congressman, he defected from the Democratic Party to help found the People's Party in 1892. At various times in the 1890s and early 1900s, he ran for the Populist vote as a vice presidential and presidential candidate. With the collapse of the People's Party in the 1908 election, Watson looked like a political has-been. By 1910, he had returned to Hickory Hill, his Georgia farmhouse, and concentrated on a writing career. While he had shot arrows occasionally at the papacy in previous years, he now largely abandoned his tirade against the wealthy to battle the Roman Catholic Church.[16] In August 1910, Watson launched a series of blistering attacks entitled "The Roman Catholic Hierarchy: The Deadliest Menace to Our Liberties and Our Civilization" in *Watson's Jeffersonian Magazine*. The series continued through twenty-seven monthly chapters, finally concluding in late 1912. In what his biographer, C. Vann Woodward, called "a curious mixture of erudition and sensationalism bordering on the pathological," Watson covered much of the ground that would be the substance of anti-Catholic rhetoric in the coming years.[17]

Clearly, Watson articulated an argument at precisely the time when a large portion of the reading public was prepared to receive it eagerly. The impact of Watson's articles was enormous and almost immediate. Earnest E. Tuggle, an insurance agent in Little Rock, wrote the magazine, saying, "It is with trembling heart and tear-dimmed eyes that I lay aside the latest issue." He praised Watson for being a modern-day revelator in speaking out against the "Bloody Whore Romen [*sic*] Church."[18] Many readers apparently had the same reaction as Tuggle. Before Watson finished his anti-Catholic series, several newspapers began to appear that were devoted specifically to the anti-Catholic cause: the *Menace* (Aurora, Missouri), the *Silverton Journal* (Silverton, Oregon), and the *Liberator* (Magnolia, Arkansas). Other newspapers would follow later in the 1910s, such as the *Rail Splitter* (Milan, Illinois), the *Crusader* (Iola, Kansas), and the *Peril* (Wilkesboro, North Carolina). Other existing small-town newspapers morphed into anti-Catholic papers, such as the *Yellow Jacket* (Moravian Falls, North Carolina) and the *Mountain Advocate* (Barbourville, Kentucky).[19]

The most widely distributed and well-known anti-Catholic paper was the *Menace*, published in Aurora, in the Missouri Ozarks just thirty miles north of the Arkansas line. The editor of Aurora's local newspaper, Wilbur F. Phelps, along with Theodore Walker, a Congregationalist minister, founded the *Menace* in April 1911. In an effort to capitalize on the popularity of Watson's articles, they named their paper the *Menace* after the anti-Catholic series title in *Watson's Jeffersonian Magazine*. A young Tennessee native, Marvin Brown, became managing editor. In contrast to Brown's benign demeanor, the *Menace* printed stories in an angry sensationalistic tone that would strain credibility for an educated person.

Within a year the *Menace* had 120,000 subscribers nationwide. In two years more than a million readers subscribed to the weekly newspaper, with circulation peaking at a million and a half in April 1915. A year's subscription cost just fifty cents, and the paper made most of its revenue through advertisements. The *Menace* also published anti-Catholic books and arranged schedules for a number of professional anti-Catholic lecturers.[20]

With the *Menace* and *Watson's Jeffersonian Magazine* providing material to excerpt and use for editorials, small-town Arkansas newspapers in 1911 and 1912 began to beat the drum against Rome. The editor of the *Glenwood News*, W. E. Whitford, in August 1911 claimed nuns were "concubines locked behind prison bars in the convents" and their children, "the offspring of the priests[,] are murdered and their bones covered with lime."[21] In June 1912 the *Huntingdon Herald*, edited by Dan Hogan in southern Sebastian County, ran the article "Will Rome Rule America?" decrying so-called Catholic attempts to defy the separation of church and state. A couple of months later the *Wilmot Weekly*, in south-central Arkansas, accused the Roman Catholic Church of fighting the public school system, controlling political parties, debauching municipal governments, and resting a heavy hand over the White House for years.[22] The *Sheridan Headlight*, edited by father and son team Robert and Britt Adams, would take a strong anti-Catholic stance throughout the 1910s. The *Southern Guardian*, the Catholic weekly published by the diocese in Little Rock, charged that the local papers in Greenwood, Wilmot, and Sheridan were in fact subsidized by, and received much of their content from, the Guardians of Liberty, an anti-Catholic organization founded in 1911 by Tom Watson and three other men. Father J. M. Lucey, a priest in Pine Bluff, even suggested that a warning be issued to prospective Catholic immigrants to "avoid places like Glenwood, Wilmot, and Sheridan and their vicinities," where Catholics were not wanted.[23]

While the views of these Arkansas editors are known primarily through references in the *Menace*, issues of one small-town newspaper, the *Gravette News Herald*, have survived to show when anti-Catholic writing appeared. Herbert (Herb) P. Lewis, who had moved with his family to Arkansas from Minnesota when he was seventeen, purchased the newspaper in his hometown, Gravette, in far northwestern Arkansas in 1908. He edited the weekly *News Herald* through 1925 and then again from 1935 until his death in 1938. Herb Lewis was a community booster and a member of the Knights of Pythias, the Independent Order of Oddfellows, and the local Christian (Disciples of Christ) congregation. He eventually became mayor of Gravette. Herb had bought the *News Herald* from Averel C. Veach, who sold the weekly paper so he could concentrate on two monthly papers he was publishing for fraternal groups on a national level: the *Globe*, a Masonic magazine, and the *Sovereign Odd Fellow*, published on behalf of the International Order of Odd Fellows. Veach also would take a strong anti-Catholic position in his two monthly papers, and the two men probably shared coffee, conversation, and content. Gravette, a small town with less than a thousand inhabitants, thus was unusual in having three newspapers, all taking a strong anti-Catholic position.[24]

A man who never failed to mince words on the editorial page, Herb Lewis gave his first denunciation of "the gang of priests and cohorts behind Catholicism" in July 1911. By late 1911 the anti-Catholic attacks were occasional, through early 1912 they were frequent, and by later 1912 and 1913 they appeared weekly. Early in 1912 Lewis had discovered the *Menace*, and thereafter he quoted and excerpted it profusely. He also bought, read, and reviewed anti-Catholic books the *Menace* published and disseminated. By May he also had subscribed to the *Liberator*, Arkansas's own anti-Catholic weekly. From the *Liberator* he received anti-Catholic news with a local theme, learning that "even Arkansas is contaminated with Romanism, Rum, and Rottenness." Lewis promoted to his readers a meeting in Little Rock planned for May 8, 1912, by the *Liberator* for the purpose of forming an organization with the goal of "putting down Romanism in this country."[25]

Herb's anti-Catholicism by August 1912 was in full form, having educated himself through the *Menace* and the *Liberator,* and he dared his readers to deny any of the following propositions:

> That every Roman Catholic is, first, under subjective allegiance to a sovereign power, the Pope, above allegiance to our government;
>
> That the Knights of Columbus is an armed military organization subject to beck and call of the Pope, and under oath to DO ANYTHING to exterminate any but Roman Catholics.
>
> That the Pope declares anyone married outside the R.C. church to be living in adultery.

> That the monks (he-nuns) manufacture the vilest liquor (knockout dope) for sale in many saloons—and that many Roman Catholics are in the saloon business.
>
> [That] The nunneries, "Houses of Good Shepherd," etc., are conducted behind closed doors and high walls without license or inspection, in violation of law and that boys and girls are kept there against their will, at hard labor (and for other purposes) to the financial gain of the hierarchy.
>
> That the hierarchy is bending every effort to control political parties, the court and legislation, favorable to making America Catholic.
>
> That a large percent of Roman priests are boozers and anything but "celibates."[26]

Lewis would address all of his listed points in great detail in the years that followed. He went on to claim that Catholics were behind the assassinations of Presidents Abraham Lincoln, James Garfield, and William McKinley and the shooting of Theodore Roosevelt. He also protested President Woodrow Wilson's choice of a Roman Catholic, Joseph Patrick Tumulty, as his personal secretary when he entered the White House, saying Tumulty would be a spy for the pope.[27]

Herb Lewis took boilerplate material freely from the *Menace* and the *Liberator*, but both papers also quoted him and recommended his paper to their readers. The *Liberator* excerpted one of his long editorials and cheered "Hurrah for Lewis and the News Herald" and complimented Lewis for having "a backbone like a telephone pole." The *Menace* endorsed his candidacy in January 1914 when he announced a bid for a seat in the Arkansas House of Representatives, headlining "Friends, Elect This Man."[28] But Lewis's weekly and the papers in Glenwood, Wilmot, Sheridan, and Huntingdon that staked out anti-Catholic editorial stances were multipurpose small-town newspapers. The *Menace* and the *Liberator* were dedicated exclusively to the anti-Catholic message and had wide audiences in Arkansas. The *Menace* reported 4,870 subscriptions in Arkansas in January 1913, 6,305 by August, and 10,407 by November 1913, the last time it reported subscriptions by state. Arkansas had a greater number of *Menace* subscriptions than other southern state except Texas. The largest numbers of *Menace* subscribers, however, were in Missouri, Illinois, Ohio, and Pennsylvania. The *Liberator* appeared on the scene in March 1912, and the editor claimed to have 15,000 sub-

Herb Lewis, from Fred W. Allsopp, *History of the Arkansas Press for a Hundred Years and More.*

scribers in forty-six states by September 1914. Most of these subscribers were in the South and West, Joseph A. Scarboro said, but undoubtedly many of them were in Arkansas.[29]

The Reverend Scarboro's *Liberator* reflects a more self-consciously religious version of anti-Catholicism than that of the more secular *Menace*. This religiously motivated antipathy toward Catholicism resonated in Arkansas, especially within the Baptist churches. Baptists were by far the largest number of Arkansans who claimed membership in a religious organization, composing almost half of the church membership of the state in 1916. Methodists had another quarter, with other denominations together making up the rest.[30]

The numerically largest Baptist denomination in Arkansas in the early 1900s was an African American body, the National Baptist Convention (NBC), which is today the largest black Christian denomination in the United States. The NBC's first president, from its founding in 1895 to his death in 1922, was the Reverend Elias Camp Morris of Helena, Arkansas. It is difficult to assess attitudes of black Baptists toward Catholics because of the paucity of evidence. However, in 1911 the Reverend J. P. Robinson, who had been pastor of Little Rock's black First Baptist Church since 1887, published a small book entitled *Why Believers Should Be Baptised and Catholicism Exposed.* Robinson suggested the need to inform ministers of his church about the inroads of Catholicism in recent years. Heretofore, he said Catholics had not done much among the Negro people in this country, but they had begun to erect schools and churches. He warned readers to "Beware these leeches of Romanism." The Catholic Church, he said, did not teach men to read and obey the Bible, but instead to be obedient to the priest. Thus, he claimed, "Roman Catholicism is a church of slavery," and the black race especially should stay away.[31]

White Baptists in Arkansas left behind a much greater body of written evidence. However, they were in a state of turmoil in the early 1900s as the conservative wing of a conservative church was in the process of seceding and forming a new denomination. The largest white Baptist church body, the Arkansas Baptist Convention was part of the Southern Baptist Convention. The conservatives who were splitting away were variously called "Landmark" or "Associational" or "Missionary" Baptists. Hereafter, the term Missionary Baptist will be used, the name by which this Baptist group is commonly called today. While Baptists in general were stridently anti-Catholic, the Missionary Baptists were especially so. Moreover, Missionary Baptists throughout the twentieth century have had their greatest concentration in Arkansas. Two of the founding figures of the Missionary Baptist movement, the *Liberator*'s editor, Reverend Scarboro, and Dr. Ben Bogard, would lead the charge in Arkansas against Roman Catholicism in the 1910s and 1920s, respectively.

Southern Baptists began to take a strong anti-Catholic position as 1911 went on. Catholicism did not appear on the radar of the Arkansas Convention's weekly paper, the *Baptist Advance*, in the first three-quarters of the year, but by October the paper began reprinting articles from the *Menace* and other sources. In 1912 the anti-Catholic pieces appeared regularly, along with articles denouncing Mormonism and Russellism (the Jehovah's Witnesses).[32] One particularly scathing piece, published in February 1912, "Romanism, an American Peril," was excerpted from a book, *Warning Signals or Romanism, an American Peril,* published the year before by one of the state's leading Southern Baptist pastors and an associate editor of the *Baptist Advance,* Allen Hill Autry of Nashville, Arkansas.

Autry had grown up in western Arkansas, began preaching at nineteen, and attended Buckner College, a Baptist school in Sebastian County, and then William Jewell College in Missouri. He served as pastor at Booneville, Magazine, Dardanelle, Springdale, and Hope before arriving in Nashville, in southwestern Arkansas.[33] Without an academic library in Nashville, Autry must have had his own small collection of anti-Catholic literature that he used to prepare a thorough exposé of the theological, social, and political dangers of Roman Catholicism. Autry laid out an elaborate exegesis of Old and New Testament scriptures that he said prophesized how Romanism would become a corrupt priesthood that would debase Christianity. Autry decried doctrines of purgatory, transubstantiation, sacramentalism, and papal infallibility, and he criticized the hierarchical authority structure of the Roman Catholic Church. He suggested that the church sheltered public immorality, including offenses ranging from drunkenness to swearing, adultery, gambling, and even murder. He cited the St. Bartholomew Day's Massacre in sixteenth-century France as an example of Catholic murder. He charged priests with corrupting young women in the confessional, using nuns in convents as sexual slaves, and then murdering the infants conceived from their illicit unions. Autry moved back and forth between the religious and moral critique but ended with the theme of a political threat posed by Catholicism in America. For Autry, Catholics could not be loyal Americans because their attachment to Rome trumped any other political identity. Moreover, Autry believed Catholics were out to destroy public education in the United States and replace public schools with parochial ones. To reinforce his attack on Catholic education, he noted that Catholic countries of Europe, such as Italy, Portugal, and Spain, had the highest illiteracy rates. Protestant ones, he said, such as Germany, Denmark, and Sweden, had the lowest levels. Autry's anti-Catholic tirade in *Warning Signals* may appear to reflect the thinking of a small-town Southern Baptist preacher, but from Nashville, Arkansas, Autry would go on to pastor the prosperous congregation of Pulaski Heights Baptist Church in Little Rock by 1917. He would serve as president of the Arkansas Baptist Convention on three occasions.[34] His book of 1911 summarized the corpus of anti-Catholic rhetoric that would prevail in Arkansas over the next seventeen years.

While Southern Baptists would take a strong stand against Catholicism, the Missionary Baptists in Arkansas were the real crusaders. Missionary Baptists were in the process of becoming a separate Baptist denomination in the early 1900s. The secession of a large number of Arkansas congregations from the Southern Baptist Convention in 1905 had its roots in theological and social factors. In the mid-1800s James Robinson Graves, a Baptist preacher in Nashville, Tennessee, and some followers began calling themselves Landmark Baptists because they believed that they held to the "landmarks" of authentic Christianity as established by Jesus Christ himself. Baptists, Landmarkers argued, descended in a direct line from the early Church and pre-figured the founding of Roman Catholicism by five hundred years. Thus Landmarkers believed that authentic Baptists were not Protestants in the sense of being an offshoot of the Reformation; they were the original Christians. Landmarkers also emphasized the total sovereignty of individual congregations, arguing that only a congregation could train and ordain a clergyman or missionary. Landmarkers supported associations, gatherings of like-minded congregations that made joint decisions, but opposed centralized administrative authority. This position brought Landmarkers increasingly into conflict with other Southern Baptists as the denomination acquired the administrative bureaucracy to conduct educational work, publications, and missionary endeavors. The Landmark view was most represented among Southern Baptists in Arkansas, Texas, Tennessee, Kentucky, and Missouri.[35]

Landmarkers in Arkansas clashed with other Southern Baptists in what became a classic power struggle over control of the church organization. Dr. William A. Clark, the editor of the Arkansas Convention's newspaper, the *Arkansas Baptist*, spoke against the trend of growing centralization at the expense of congregational sovereignty. At the 1900 Arkansas Convention in Hope, the body approved a plan by a corresponding secretary, the Reverend Arthur J. Barton, for broader supervision of missionary work under a mission secretary. Clark and other Landmarkers insisted that individual congregations should have full control over the sending of missionaries. Southern Baptists would claim that Dr. Clark's opposition was motivated by the fact that he was passed over for the post of corresponding secretary in 1899. Nonetheless, battle lines were drawn for the 1901 state convention in November at the Opera House in Paragould. Before the meeting, the president of the convention, former Arkansas governor James P. Eagle, used a plan to configure representation that favored large congregations in towns over small churches in rural areas, where Landmarkers had their strength. Dr. Clark and the Reverend Ben Bogard, a charismatic preacher in Searcy, led the charge on behalf of the Landmark faction. Complicating matters even further, Jeff Davis, the sitting governor of Arkansas, was elected vice president of the convention. Davis, a populist-style politician who appealed to the common folk of Arkansas and eschewed the Democratic establishment, promoted the Landmark view, countering former governor Eagle's leadership on the other side. When the vote took place on abolition of the mission secretary, Landmarkers failed by a vote of 148 to 151. Several Landmarkers walked out at this point. Later in the evening a vote to censure Dr. Clark passed by one vote, 37 to 36. A permanent schism resulted.[36]

Representatives of Landmark congregations met April 10–11, 1902, at Antioch Baptist Church in Little Rock and organized the State Association of Missionary Baptist Churches, with Ben Bogard as the dominant leader of the emerging denomination. The Southern Baptists started their own publication, the *Baptist Advance,* in 1902, given that the *Arkansas Baptist* was controlled by Landmarkers. The Missionary Baptists would have their own annual associations thereafter, but for the next few years they sent representatives to the Arkansas Convention. In 1905 a last effort to bring the two groups back together failed when the Missionary Baptists refused a compromise settlement. They then joined with a group of Landmarkers in northeastern Texas to launch officially the denomination, the General Association of Missionary Baptist Churches. Southern Baptists for years to come seemed uncertain if the division was a permanent one, but from the Missionary Baptist side it was a done deal. Perhaps more than half of Arkansas's Southern Baptists, especially in rural congregations, left the denomination to become Missionary Baptists. Christopher Bart Barber, whose doctoral dissertation dissected the schism of 1901–1905, concluded that the social differences were far more significant than theological ones in determining the split. The most reliable predictor for whether a congregation would stay Southern Baptist or go with the Missionary Baptists, Barber said, "was a particular church's distance from a railhead."[37]

The two key figures who worked publicly to defame Catholicism in Arkansas were leaders of this new Missionary Baptist Church, Ben Bogard and Joseph Scarboro.[38] Benjamin Marcus Bogard was the son of a Confederate veteran living in poverty as a tobacco tenant farmer in central Kentucky. Bogard was baptized in February 1885 at the age of sixteen, immersed in a hole hacked through six inches of ice in a frozen pond. Two years later he acquired his license to preach the Gospel. He attended Bethel College and Georgetown College in Kentucky but never earned a degree. In 1894 he became pastor of a Baptist church in Fulton in southwestern Kentucky, a town that was emerging, like Arkansas, as one of the nerve centers of the Landmark movement. After moving on to Wingo, Kentucky, and then a church in Charleston in the Missouri Bootheel, he came to Arkansas as pastor of the Baptist church in Searcy in 1899. Bogard began to contribute to Clark's *Arkansas Baptist*, becoming joint editor in 1901. With Clark and other Landmarkers he began to make war against the Arkansas Convention leaders of the denomination. Bogard's forceful personality and powerful voice and pen made him the indisputable leader of the new church association as the Missionary Baptists organized themselves between 1902 and 1905 and thereafter.[39]

Bogard would dominate the anti-Catholic crusade of the 1920s, but in the early 1910s the key figure was the *Liberator*'s editor, Joseph Addison Scarboro. Born in Georgia in 1857, Scarboro was largely self-educated and was ordained a Baptist minister in 1876. Scarboro made a name for himself in Landmark circles in 1904 when he authored a book, *The Bible, The Baptists, and the Board System*, which opposed the missionary boards as the epitome of evil denominational centralization. The Reverend Scarboro moved closer to the hearth of the Missionary Baptist movement in 1909 when he became pastor of First Baptist Church of Magnolia, the county seat of Columbia County, Arkansas. In the next year he began publishing a monthly magazine, the *Plain Truth*, in which, he said, "the Romish question came up for discussion." In 1910 Scarboro contributed an article to *Watson's Jeffersonian Magazine* and advertised his *Plain Truth* there. In the next year, his article, "Romanism Ruling and Ruining" from the *Plain Truth*, was reprinted by *Watson's Jeffersonian*

Magazine. In the article, Scarboro decried the Catholic influence on American politics, particularly frothing over a meeting in June 1911 in Baltimore where President William Howard Taft, Vice President Charles W. Fairbanks, and ex-president Theodore Roosevelt, along with the chief justice of the Supreme Court, Speakers of the House and Senate, and the governor of Maryland, all shared the stage with Baltimore's Cardinal James Gibbons in his scarlet robes. By March 1912, Scarboro converted the *Plain Truth* magazine into a weekly paper, the *Liberator*, which was devoted specifically to the anti-Catholic crusade.[40]

In comparison to *Watson's Jeffersonian Magazine*, the *Menace*, and the *Gravette News Herald*, the Reverend Scarboro's newspaper took a self-consciously religious approach in its anti-Catholicism. While only two issues are known to have survived, for October 2 and 16, 1913, additional glimpses of the contents of the weekly for other dates are known

The Reverend Joseph A. Scarboro, from his 1904 book, *The Bible, Baptists, and the Board System.*

from quotes and references in other newspapers. In the two surviving issues, Scarboro devoted about half of his space to in-depth theological interpretations of Catholicism as the incarnation of the satanic beast described in biblical prophecy. Yet while he carved a more specifically religious niche within anti-Catholic literature, some of Scarboro's language appears especially vicious and mean-spirited. In the October 2, 1913, issue he advised, "Preacher, load your gun and go after Romanism. The hunting season is now and the game is plentiful." In 1912, Scarboro devoted two pages of an issue to cover reports of a break-in of a small Catholic church in Stamps, twenty-five miles west of Magnolia. Scarboro apparently suggested that violence and vandalism were justified because it was a Catholic church. The editor of the Stamps newspaper, who insisted he was not, nor ever had been, a Catholic, feuded with Scarboro. He said that the *Liberator* had gone one step past the normal kind of anti-Catholic "rabid, fire-eating attacks" and advocated mob action against Catholic institutions.[41]

Beyond the theological attacks on Rome, Scarboro's material was boilerplate anti-Catholicism. In a box on the front page of the four-page weekly he listed the twelve principles of the *Liberator*:

I. Liberty of Conscience, Speech and Press.

II. Complete Separation of Church and State.

III. No Public Funds or Property to Religious Institutions.

IV. Denial of Citizenship, Office and the Franchise to all who are under oath of allegiance to any foreign power, real or assumed.

V. Support of the Public Schools as the Bulwark of our Liberties.

VI. No enemy of the Public Schools to be allowed to teach in them.

VII. All efforts to subvert the government and overthrow this Republic is treason, whether concealed under religious disguise or otherwise, and should be punished as such.

VIII. Since Romanism seeks to establish itself as the one religion of the state, no Romanist should be allowed to vote or hold office of any kind.

IX. We demand that the political history of Romanism should be taught in the Public Schools as a necessary part of a true education.

X. Pre-election pledges made to Romanists or other enemies of this Republic to bestow office or favors upon them as such, to constitute a prima facie betrayal of trust and disqualify of office.

XI. The Inspection by government officials of all Convents, Houses of the Good Shepherd, Nunneries or other sectarian or private institutions that have the custody of persons or asking contributions of the public.

XII. The Incarceration of persons against their own choice in any place or under any guise by others than parents, guardians, or officers of the government to be prima facie evidence of slavery, and the crime a felony under national and state laws.[42]

These twelve points, like Autry's book *Warning Signals* and Herb Lewis's propositions, were a summary of the anti-Catholic positions articulated in the 1910s.

Single-handedly, the Reverend Scarboro edited and wrote content for the *Liberator*, with the assistance of his son, J. A. Scarboro Jr., as linotype operator. An annual subscription cost fifty cents, the same as the *Menace*, or twenty-five cents if readers were in a club of four or more. He said he would gladly send the paper to any Missionary Baptist for twenty-five cents. Subscriptions would not keep the paper afloat, however, and Scarboro constantly tried to raise money. By 1913, he was selling stock in the paper for five dollars a share. He said he even "had no objection to women stockholders." In 1912 and early 1913 he edited the paper in addition to his pastoral duties at First Baptist Church. Later in 1913, he gave up his pastorate for the publishing work, supplemented by a $600 salary he received for serving as treasurer for the General Association of Missionary Baptist Churches. Scarboro also did some lecturing on "Romanism" at churches and associational meetings in Arkansas, Missouri, Illinois, Indiana, Kentucky, and Louisiana. He was also a frequent contributor to the *Baptist*, the Missionary Baptist weekly newspaper published in Little Rock.[43]

Besides the newspapers and Baptist pulpits, another piece of the anti-Catholic movement involved professional anti-Catholic lecturers who travelled the country, but especially the South and Midwest.[44] In early January 1912, William Lloyd Clark, an anti-Catholic lecturer from Milan, Illinois, arrived in Hope, in southwestern Arkansas, to follow-up several weeks of sermons on Romanism by the local Baptist pastor, the Reverend William M. Bostick. Some Hope residents apparently had been stirred by a number of Protestant children attending a Catholic school and by efforts to solicit subscriptions from Protestants to support construction of a new Catholic church building in the town. Clark held forth for a week at Bostick's church, his speeches moving from the Dark Ages and Inquisition to present-day problems of Catholic meddling in the national government. He also exposed the high rates of illiteracy in Catholic countries and frequent sexual abuses by priests of women in the confessional and nuns in their convents. The local priest, Father P. J. Higgins, pastor of Our Lady of Hope, reported to Little Rock's weekly Catholic paper, the *Southern Guardian*, that Clark was really just there for the money, to sell subscriptions to the *Menace* and hawk his anti-Catholic books. Besides his lecturing, Clark was the author of many anti-Catholic pamphlets with titles such as *Washington in the Grasp of Rome, The Devil's Prayer Book, Roman Oaths and Papal Curses,* and *Beyond Convent Bars.* The *Menace* sold his books and Mrs. William Lloyd Clark's pamphlet, *Priest and Woman—The Confessional Unmasked,* for the price of twenty-five cents each. Clark's lectures clearly resulted in heightened strife between Protestants and Catholics in Hope. Some Protestants were pulling their children out of the Catholic school and cancelling their subscriptions to support the church building. Catholics reportedly threatened to boycott Protestant businesses as a result.[45]

Three months later, in April 1912, Clark returned to southwestern Arkansas to lecture in Scarboro's hometown, Magnolia. This time, Father Higgins followed from Hope, and the priest lectured on Catholicism on two nights to large audiences in the Columbia County courthouse. He criticized the *Liberator* for giving a black eye to the entire state of Arkansas.[46] When Clark moved on to lecture in Mena, Catholics reported that placards blanketed the town, filled with insulting sayings about priests and nuns. Someone stole the picture of Mena's priest, Father A. P. Gallagher, from a gallery of founders of the town. Gallagher had established St. Agnes Church in Mena in 1897, a year after the town was settled and incorporated.[47] By early 1913, Clark was back in Arkansas, lecturing in Piggott and Marmaduke in the northeastern corner of the state. The local Baptist pastor Butler in Piggott reported to the *Menace* that Clark's series of lectures "took like a wild fire with our people." The Reverend Butler pledged that he was working to deliver subscriptions to the *Menace* and the *Liberator* and any others who were fighting Rome.[48]

William Lloyd Clark, from his book *Reminiscences of a Reformer's Life, Or Twenty-Five Years on the Skirmish Line Against Political Romanism.*

The renewed bout of anti-Catholicism triggered by Tom Watson's attacks on Rome in late 1910 had by 1913 become a full-blown mainstream movement in many parts of the United States, but especially so in Arkansas. The state was typical of the environment most amenable to anti-Catholic sentiments, a mostly rural and small-town state in the Upper South with a high percentage of evangelical Protestants, especially Baptists. In the first decade of the twentieth century, Arkansas was the birthplace of the Missionary Baptist denomination, a group that particularly espoused anti-Catholic views. In 1913, the state as a community began to engage anti-Catholicism through legislation proposed to the Arkansas General Assembly. The issue that would work anti-Catholics into a lather over the next few years would be the association of Roman Catholic priests with sexual abuse committed against innocent females. The reverends Scarboro and Autry and editor Lewis, echoing the *Menace*'s many articles, had suggested sexual improprieties of supposedly celibate priests and nuns. These word pictures would work powerfully on the imagination of some Arkansans, including legislators.

CHAPTER 2

Sex and the Sisters, 1913–1915

ON THE EVENING of May 13, 1892, a mob of approximately five hundred white men bearing sledgehammers broke down the gates of a prison in Little Rock and forcibly took an African American man, Henry James, from his cell. James had been accused of raping a five-year-old white girl in the house where he worked as a handyman. The mob hanged James from a telegraph pole at Fifth and Main Streets, just a few blocks from the state capitol. Thousands of spectators reportedly filed by for a look and even braved a thunderstorm that tossed the dead body around at the end of the rope. A photographer took pictures. Some members of the crowd cut into pieces the 125-foot-long rope and noose to keep as souvenirs.[1] In the heyday of lynching in the American South in the late 1800s and early 1900s, white men seemed to have an irrational fear of black male sexuality. As they imagined black men as oversexed beasts, they postulated their own responsibility to "protect" white females. In a similar way, in the early 1910s white men asserted a view of Catholic priests as sexual predators, alleging that priests sexually abused nuns, schoolgirls, and their own housekeepers. In addition, anti-Catholics argued that the confessional was a dark private space in which so-called celibate priests could recruit men's wives and daughters as their lovers. The subject of sex, so rarely discussed in public, energized the anti-Catholic movement in the early and mid-1910s.

By early 1913 this sex fixation began to bear fruit in legislation deliberated in both chambers of the Arkansas General Assembly. The elected representative from Grant County, Robert Randolph Posey of Sheridan, introduced a convent inspection bill that would require religious institutions such as convents, monasteries, hospitals, orphanages, asylums, seminaries, or schools to submit to an inspection by the county sheriff or

Representative Robert Posey. *Courtesy of Special Collections, University of Arkansas Libraries, Fayetteville.*

a grand jury upon the request of a judge or a petition of twenty citizens. Posey, a thirty-year-old school teacher by training who had passed the bar and become a lawyer, should have had little concern, for there was no Catholic church in all of Grant County, much less any convents or monasteries. He apparently got the language of the bill from the *Menace*, for the paper ran an article about Posey's planned bill well before the Arkansas legislature even convened.[2] State senator James T. M. Holt, who represented Hempstead and Nevada Counties in southwestern Arkansas, introduced in the Senate a similar inspection bill. Holt's bill added a provision that a blood relative within a fourth degree of affinity to a person under age twenty-one in an institution could also petition a judge to inspect the institution. The bill also would give any member of the Arkansas General Assembly the right to inspect any institution covered by the bill.[3]

By later standards one wonders what the fuss was about that led to a call for "inspection." The anti-Catholic press, from *Watson's Jeffersonian Magazine* to the *Menace*, had been recycling sensationalistic nineteen-century tales of young girls in sexual slavery in Catholic boarding schools or convents. One such story was *The Awful Disclosures of Maria Monk*, a book first published in 1836 but reprinted, republished, and augmented dozens of time, well into the twentieth century. As measured by number of books sold, *Maria Monk* ranked second to *Uncle Tom's Cabin* as the most popular book in antebellum America.[4] William Lloyd Clark had retold the sad tale of Maria Monk at his lectures in Hope in 1912. Maria's story is indeed an awful one. Raised Protestant, Maria had been educated in a convent school and then entered the Hotel Dieu convent in Montreal to become a nun. Maria quickly learned that the convent was complete with hidden doors and a secret passageway to the seminary to facilitate sexual liaisons with clergy. For nuns who did not willingly submit to priests' sexual demands, there were hidden prison cells and torture chambers. When sisters became pregnant, babies were killed and buried in a mass grave sprinkled with lime in the basement. As the story went, Maria escaped the convent when she became pregnant. She gave birth to her baby, married, and moved to the United States where she wrote her book to expose the abuses of the convent. Maria Monk was indeed a real person, but her own mother said she had never lived in a convent and that her story was a fantasy of a girl whose brain had been injured in infancy when she ran a slate pencil into her head. After its initial publication in 1836, Catholic authors have repeatedly refuted the account. Scholars believed it was actually written by a group of Protestant clergymen in New York who profited financially from Maria's wild tale. Nonetheless, the story of Maria Monk still now gets republished as anti-Catholic propaganda.[5]

In fact, the credibility of such stories provided a main topic for debate on the floors of the Arkansas House and Senate. The Senate discussed the Holt bill on Thursday afternoon, February 20. Senator Charles Jacobson of Pulaski County asked supporters of the bill to name specific instances where inspection was warranted or when a relative was denied access to an underage person in an institution. Supporters of the bill could not provide any evidence. But Senator James Wood of Ashley County responded that if all were good, what was wrong with an inspection? Senator Webb Covington of Johnson County countered that prejudice, specifically against Catholic institutions, made this a "damnable bill." Jacobsen agreed, denouncing the Holt bill as being "as vicious a piece of legislation as ever came before this body." Covington and Jacobson won the day, and the bill went down by a vote of twenty to ten.[6] A similar debate unfolded in the much larger House on Saturday, March 1. Supporters of the Posey bill explained that something was being kept under cover and Catholics did not want the cover pulled off. When challenged to substantiate such claims, no one could do so, beyond reading excerpts from various anti-Catholic newspapers. One of the bill's leading supporters, Wesley Davis, a Missionary Baptist minister from Lafayette County, simply made the general assertion that celibates should neither have control over children nor keep doors barred from any investigations. The lone Roman Catholic member of the House, John Willems of Logan County, paced up and down the aisles during the discussion, taking the bill as a personal insult and an attack on Catholics in general. The Posey bill passed the House by a vote of fifty to eighteen. The bill died when the Senate, having already defeated the similar Holt bill, failed to even bring it up before adjourning on March 13.[7]

The yeas and nays in the roll call votes for both the Holt and Posey bills did not correspond to an identifiable regional or urban-rural pattern. But the leaders who supported the bills, the sponsors, Representative Posey and Senator Holt, and James R. Woods from Ashley County, Senator Thomas E. Toler from Grant County, Representative Wesley M. Davis (a Missionary Baptist preacher) of Lafayette County, and Representative Jefferson D. Doyle of Lawrence County, were from areas of Arkansas with few Roman Catholics. These areas were also the location of anti-Catholic newspapers (in Magnolia, Wilmot, Glenwood, Sheridan). The political leaders who spoke out against the bills came from localities with Roman Catholic constituents and neighbors: Senator L. Clyde Going from Poinsett County, Senator Webb Covington from Johnson County, Senator Charles Jacobson from Pulaski County, Representative Heartsill H. Ragon of Johnson County, Lewis E. Sawyer of Garland County, and Representative Louis Joseph of Texarkana. Senator Jacobson and Representative Joseph had additional motivations to oppose legislation discriminating against a religious minority, for both were Jewish.[8]

The discussion surrounding the anti-Catholic bills spilled beyond the walls of the legislature. The Reverend Scarboro, editor of the *Liberator*, came to Little Rock during the session to lecture on Catholicism at Central Baptist Church at Thirteenth and Chester Streets. He and other preachers and editors of Protestant papers attended the Senate committee hearing about the Holt bill on Saturday, February 15. Herb Lewis editorialized about the bill, "OPEN ROME'S PENS, ARKANSAS, OR REMOVE THEM FROM THE STATE," and lamented that other legislators "sat like clams" instead of defending the bill.[9] The Catholic paper, the *Southern Guardian*, and Little Rock's weekly *Baptist Advance* provided lively commentary about the bills and even sparred directly with each other. As one might expect, the editors of the diocesan paper railed against the Holt and Posey bills as expressing prejudice and bigotry.

The *Baptist Advance*, edited by E.J.A. McKinney, was the mouthpiece of the Arkansas Baptist Convention, and it campaigned for the inspection bills throughout February and March. McKinney frequently excerpted material from the *Menace* and kept a running campaign against Catholicism on several fronts. Through the early part of 1913, McKinney and writers of the *Southern Guardian* feuded after McKinney printed a purported oath of the Catholic fraternal organization the Knights of Columbus. The Knights had been organized in New Haven, Connecticut, in 1882 to provide Catholic men an alternative to the era's burgeoning secret societies, many of which excluded Catholics from membership. Father Thomas Tobin, the rector of St. Andrews Cathedral in Little Rock, argued that the purported oath, which McKinney admitted he had taken from *Watson's Magazine*, was a hoax. Tobin, a member of the Knights of Columbus, said he had never taken such an oath and that it had been repeatedly exposed as a fraud by the Catholic Church. The Knights of Columbus, in fact, had been founded as a way for Catholic men to show their loyalty and patriotism. McKinney went on to reprint another oath published in the *Menace* provided by an ex-priest and anti-Catholic lecturer, Peter A. Seguin. This one claimed to "disown any allegiance as due to any Protestant king, prince or state, or obedience to any of their inferior officers."[10]

Besides feuding with the *Baptist Advance*, the *Southern Guardian* mixed it up with the other anti-Catholic papers. In a July headline the *Guardian* labeled Herb Lewis's *Gravette News Herald* as another anti-Catholic paper after receiving some of Lewis's editorials. A Catholic man from Little Rock, apparently on behalf of the *Guardian*, showed up at the office of the Gravette newspaper and asked for evidence of the charges Lewis made about the Catholic Church. Lewis reported the visit by an agent of the pope, a man he said was shaped like a beer-keg and who denounced Arkansas governor George Washington Hays because he was a Baptist. Not one to back down from a fight, Lewis insisted that as a Protestant and an editor he had the liberty to protest "such institutions as Romanism, Mormonism, and other un-American things . . . and do so vigorously."[11]

The Catholic weekly also tackled Representative Posey's hometown newspaper, the *Sheridan Headlight*, whose editors, Robert and Britt Adams, had announced that "Catholics who acknowledge the Pope of Rome as the head of their church are not wanted in Grant county." The *Southern Guardian* asked the Knights of Columbus and the German *Staatsverband*, an association of German Catholic immigrants, to investigate whether the businessmen of Sheridan endorsed the anti-Catholic position taken by the community's paper. The Catholic paper threatened to exert economic pressure by steering prospective settlers away from Grant County. The *Guardian* proudly announced that two of the most prominent landowners in the county, who controlled more than half of the available land for settlers, were indignant about the *Sheridan Headlight*'s vilification of the Roman Catholic Church. Catholics, these men said, would be welcomed to Grant County with open arms.[12] Similarly, the Knights of Columbus at its annual convention in Pine Bluff formed a committee to investigate business and community leaders in towns with anti-Catholic newspapers. The *Menace* condemned Pine Bluff Knights, whom it called "the Arkansas Boycotters," for "defending Satan and his angels, the priests." The paper warned Arkansas readers: "If you are deceived by them you are simply allowing them to discredit your intelligence and make an ass of you for the benefit of their damnable system and the glory of the pope."[13]

In this combative environment following the failed legislation, Father Boniface Spanke, a priest at Subiaco Abbey, came up with a plan to combat anti-Catholic prejudice on a grass-roots level. To his abbot, Ignatius Conrad, and to Bishop John B. Morris, Father Boniface proposed to build a portable chapel to travel through rural Arkansas to teach people about Catholicism and dispel the many myths and misconceptions about the church. Two years before, when Boniface was pastor of St. Boniface Church in Fort Smith, he had clashed with Bishop Morris over a plan to borrow twelve thousand dollars to build a new school, and he was transferred to a parish in Nevada, Missouri, for nineteen months. By the summer of 1913 he was back at Subiaco, and with the bishop's approval he set to work constructing what he called his "Gospel Wagon."[14]

Indefatigable, charismatic, even ornery—Father Boniface Spanke was just the man to take up the sword against anti-Catholic prejudice. Born Anton Spanke in Westphalia, Germany, in 1873, he emigrated with his family when he was nine, coming to the German Catholic settlement of Hartman, in Johnson County, Arkansas, in 1881. He became a student at neighboring Subiaco in the opening year of the abbey's academy for young men, and he was the first graduate of the academy to enter the monastery, choosing the name of Boniface in 1893. He took holy orders as a priest in 1897. Father Boniface served several parishes before coming back to Logan County in 1912 as pastor to the St. Scholastica Church and Convent, a few miles east of Subiaco in Shoal Creek.[15]

Through the summer of 1913 Boniface worked on constructing his Gospel Wagon. In the late 1800s and early 1900s several denominations had constructed "chapel cars," railway carriages outfitted as mobile churches that could take Christianity to areas lacking organized congregations. The Catholic Church Extension Society, an evangelizing movement with its headquarters in Chicago, in 1907 dedicated its first chapel car, a renovated Pullman car christened the St. Anthony. In the years following, the St. Anthony made extended tours through the far West and Midwest and one tour through Mississippi. The society had a second chapel car, the St. Peter, built by the Barney and Smith Car Company in 1912.[16] By early 1913, the Catholic Church Extension Society had constructed its first "motor chapel," a two-ton automotive vehicle to penetrate areas that the rail chapel cars would not reach. The motor chapel set out in March from Brownsville, Texas, accompanied by two priests, to work the Rio Grande Valley.[17]

Father Boniface's Gospel Wagon, an adaptation of the mobile chapel to fit the muddy byways of rural Arkansas, was placed on a wagon pulled by two horses. Father Boniface drew up a design of his Gospel Wagon, which he sent to Bishop Morris and to the Catholic Church Extension Society for approval. In the summer heat in 1913 and with the help of two other monks, Father Anton and Frater Hugo, Boniface constructed the wagon. On top of a rolling carriage base, donated by a local German Catholic layman, Conrad Elsken, they built a wooden box, twenty feet long, six feet wide, and seven feet high. The entire structure was covered with tin, donated by a manufacturing company in St. Louis. Five windows on each side allowed natural light into the two-room structure. A smaller room at the back of the structure contained a kitchen to the left and toilet to the right. The larger front room served as a chapel with a moveable altar on the forward left wall and benches on the side walls to seat up to fifteen people. After mass was said, the altar could be moved to the back wall and the room became a living and dining room. In the evening two cots could swing down from the walls for Father Boniface and his driver to sleep. Underneath the wagon was a water tank to service the kitchen and toilet. The wagon was finished by July 19 and weighed in at 2,900 pounds, 4,500 pounds when fully furnished. There was space underneath the wagon to store about forty-five folding camp chairs and a 22-by-42-foot tarpaulin for outdoor meetings. In early August Father Boniface bought two horses in Fort Smith for $250, provided by Bishop Morris, buying them from a Knight of Columbus who sold them at cost. Gifts from Knights of Columbus chapters provided the religious equipment—vestments, chalice, linens, missals, and other items. The Catholic Church Extension Society funded the purchase of kitchen equipment, complete with a coal oil stove, and other miscellaneous items for the wagon. The Reynolds and Davis firm of Fort Smith donated a supply of canned food. An alumnus of Subiaco Academy from Memphis purchased a large phonograph and a stereopticon slide projector, which Father Boniface would use for his "magic lantern" show, the slides ordered all the way from Paris, France. The machine used an acetylene gas generator to provide light and illuminate the pictures—all very high tech for 1913.[18]

The Gospel Wagon was dedicated in a ceremony at the city park of Subiaco on Sunday morning, August 10. Besides the locals, special trains brought guests from Charleston, Paris, and Fort Smith. Estimates of the crowd ranged from one thousand to twenty-five hundred. Three brass bands performed. A collection was taken producing fifty dollars. Prior

The Gospel Wagon on dedication day, with Father Boniface on the steps. *Courtesy of Joyce Friddle and the Logan County Historical Society.*

Augustine Stocker presided over a high mass with the Paris church choir leading the liturgical music. Sporting a tan from his summer's work in the sun, Father Boniface spoke from the rear platform of the wagon, comparing himself to Noah, saying, "When he built the ark, several of the bystanders made fun of him, and I have lacked no critics who made a joke of this wagon." Father Boniface gave tours of the wagon, and the abbey opened its buildings and grounds for tours as well.[19]

Word of Boniface's plans prompted a response in the anti-Catholic press even before he began his missionary journey. Herb Lewis subscribed to the *Southern Guardian* so he could keep tabs on his enemies, and he explained to his readers that the "Celibate Daddy—the Rivrent Father Bony face" was setting out to convert Arkansas to popery, with his wagon, religious services, and "probably a beer garden." With fanfare Lewis concluded: "It will include a moving picture show, to show the pope in his 'nighty,' and a talking machine, which may be used to repeat the orders of the 'inquisition,' or the order of the pope who ordered all 'heretics' in America exterminated. Yes, get ready to meet Daddy and have your coin ready to pay purgatorial fees, buy a string of 'blessed' beads, or some 'holy water for family use.'"[20]

On Saturday, September 7, Father Boniface began his crusade, accompanied by a young seminarian, Peter Illigen, who had emigrated from Germany just two years before, and a layman from nearby Morrison Bluff, who managed the horses.[21] They started off in the friendly environment of Shoal Creek, where Father Boniface's parishioners had been encouraged to bring out their "American" neighbors to the Peedee School House, which had been secured for the event. At the first gathering more than a hundred people showed up on a rainy day. Father Boniface illuminated the schoolhouse with his acetylene gas lamp and played music on his Victrola for forty-five minutes. Then he spoke on this topic: "What do Catholics believe about the forgiveness of sins?" He closed with his magic lantern, showing thirty illustrations from the catechism, followed by a final recording of a quartet singing "God be with you 'til we meet again."

The meetings continued for seven consecutive evenings with bigger crowds each night. Boniface worked his way through other Catholic teachings, from veneration of saints to communion to purgatory, with the slide programs changing also each night. His final program concerned the "falsehoods circulated about the Catholic Church by the *Menace* and other vile publications and about the unwarranted attempt of our last legislature to foist on our state a law in opposition to the constitution of the United States." He took the opportunity to point out that John Willems, "our representative" in the state legislature, had offered fifty dollars to anyone who could prove immorality and white slavery in Catholic institutions. He added that Father John Frances Noll, a priest in Huntingdon, Indiana, had placed a thousand dollars at Boniface's disposal for anyone who could prove these scandalous accusations. Father Noll had in the previous year founded a Catholic paper, *Our Sunday Visitor*, to counter the anti-Catholic lies of the *Menace*. The office of *Our Sunday Visitor* would be a nerve center of opposition to anti-Catholicism for years to come.[22]

From Shoal Creek the missionaries set out for the rural community of Blaine, a Protestant area several miles to the east. Here they made camp in a cemetery and tried out cooking and dining in the wagon. The next morning Boniface celebrated mass on the wagon's altar, the first time a mass was ever said in the neighborhood. Getting permission to use a public school building, Boniface repeated the programs as he had done before with smaller crowds owing to bad weather, heavy rain cancelling the mission entirely on one evening. But on the last evening, Boniface reported, the schoolhouse was packed. From Blaine, they went on to Delaware, on the eastern edge of Logan County, then to Bethel School in Yell County, near Dardanelle, where the crowds became so large that they pulled out the camp chairs to accommodate the overflow. Father Boniface's acolyte created drama one evening in Delaware when he failed to close one of the valves on the acetylene generator and later lit a match. A gas explosion resulted with flames that shot up to the ceiling and emptied the school room. After he repaired the machine, people returned, and Boniface resumed his presentation. Boniface even admitted that some of the crowds attended for the sheer entertainment value of his sight-and-sound show and from curiosity about the rolling chapel and new gadgets like the generator. One woman in Yell County even said that had people known that he was a priest, no one would have shown up on the first night. One man there forbade his family to attend, but on seeing "nearly all the neighbors go and report a fine time he decided to relent in his opposition."[23]

It was at Delaware that Father Boniface's mission encountered the first overt anti-Catholic opposition. A man walked up after Boniface's address, refused his outstretched hand, and asked if he had permission from all the school directors to use the facility. Boniface responded that he had talked to three directors and phoned the fourth, a Mr. Johnson, who was not at home, but Mrs. Johnson indicated it would be alright with her husband. The man was Mr. Johnson, and he denied that his wife had given any permission. He said that several people had complained about granting access of the school, and he personally did not "believe in holding up the Catholic belief in this community." Boniface learned that another director had argued with Johnson, telling him there was no reason to fuss, for Boniface had brought a tent and would just move outside for the meeting if they denied him the schoolhouse. Similarly, in his mission at Sunny Point, in Pope County just south of Russellville, Father Boniface was approached by a school director on the second night of the mission who insisted that the schoolhouse could not be used for Catholic services. He returned a few nights later with two other directors and demanded that the priest remove himself and his equipment from the school. Boniface responded that the directors gave use of the school to "every Tom, Dick, and Harry, but you discriminate against Catholics. That is what I call mixing up religion and politics which is un-American." Boniface packed up his equipment and moved to a nearby miners' union hall, owned by a Catholic man named Gillespie. He set up his Victrola and cranked the volume up loud for the music to pour through the open door to the ears of the school board. The next morning Boniface placed a large sign on his wagon announcing that because the school directors had discriminated against Catholics in using a public building, he had decided to stay in Sunny Point and "hold forth for another week at Gillespie's Hall, every body invited. Fr. Boniface, O.S.B." Now that he extended his stay, he squeezed in an extra presentation at the Butler Theatre in downtown Russellville. In his extra week in Pope County, he claimed three "converts," of whom one was a member of the Methodist Church.[24]

From Sunny Point the missionaries made their way by the end of October to Atkins, where they boarded at the rectory of the local Catholic church. Father Boniface claimed it was his first night to sleep in a house in two months. Then Boniface was off to Morrilton, where the two men parked the wagon in front of the rectory of the Sacred Heart Church and contracted a school auditorium that could seat five hundred people. The room had electricity and could project a figure of Jesus in his slide show to a height of twelve feet. Boniface claimed that his lecture there on Sunday evening, November 16, combatting the lies of the *Menace*, had the largest attendance of his entire mission. From Morrilton the pair headed north into the hills to the small community of Solgohachia, where one local man at the general store asked, through a mouthful of chewing tobacco, if he was about to begin the examinations, evidently mistaking Father Boniface for the travelling hookworm doctor who was at that time making the rounds of Conway County. One member of the audience took copious notes and turned out to be a Presbyterian minister who was there intending to give a counter presentation. He held forth to the crowd at the general store about the immorality of the Catholic Church. He had told of a girl who had been in a convent in Hope, Arkansas, until age fifteen, at which time a priest made sexual advances toward her in the confessional. When she refused she was shut up in a dungeon and maltreated. Boniface told the Solgohachia men that he would gladly give a hundred dollars if they could produce any evidence of this story. Another local man at the general store argued with Boniface in unvarnished language that the horned beast spoken of in Revelation was indeed the Roman Catholic Church. Perhaps this man had seen the masthead of the *Liberator*. When Boniface and Peter Illigen packed their gear underneath the wagon to leave Solgohachia, they found "some smart youngster had tried to play us a prank by taking the nut off one of the wheels."[25]

Almost as much as the anti-Catholic prejudice, Boniface was challenged by the difficulties of travel over the country roads of rural Arkansas. It was a rainy fall, and Boniface constantly complained of the muddy roads and the difficulty of fording creeks and climbing hills in a 4,500-pound wagon. The soil of Yell County, he said, was a "sticky gumbo," and of Conway County he said he could not understand how so rich a county could have roads so poor. For most of his journey he depended upon local Catholic laymen who would hitch an extra team of mules to the two horses in order to pull through the mud and up the hills. Even in dry conditions Boniface complained about the rocky roads of Faulkner County that bounced him out of his seat to bump his head and sent Peter out of his seat to the floor of the wagon.[26]

What turned out to be the last leg of the Gospel Wagon's mission was its easternmost stop in late November in Conway. As elsewhere, local Catholics had made arrangements in advance, and the county judge, J. W. Holt, had allowed use of the circuit court room in the Faulkner County courthouse for Father Boniface's talks. Some local folks complained to Judge Holt for allowing Catholics to use the courthouse. He responded that a Holiness group had been allowed to use the room for a revival a short while before and that, although he was a Protestant, his position was that Catholics should have the same rights as anyone else. Boniface proceeded to give his presentations, albeit to small crowds.[27]

At his Friday night presentation, someone gave Father Boniface a handbill announcing that anti-Catholic speaker Otis L. Spurgeon was speaking that Friday, Saturday, and Sunday in the auditorium in Morrilton. Spurgeon had been a Baptist preacher in Nashua, Iowa, and had made a reputation for anti-Catholic preaching. Then in 1912 he gave up the pulpit and moved his family to Des Moines, where he began full-time work as an organizer for an anti-Catholic organization, the Knights of Luther, and lectured as time permitted.[28] He also edited the question-and-answer column for the *Menace*. Spurgeon had apparently been invited by Morrilton's Presbyterian pastor, the Reverend John P. Kidd, after Boniface had given his Catholic presentations in the town. Spurgeon's three lecture topics were entitled "The Roman Catholic Priesthood and White Slavery (For Men Only)," "To Make America Catholic," and "The Beast of the Apocalypse." Unfortunately, Boniface had already missed the titillating first lecture, but he cancelled his Conway programs for the weekend so he could hasten to Morrilton for Spurgeon's Saturday presentation.

Otis Spurgeon was apparently surprised to find Father Boniface in the fourth row of the same auditorium where the priest had held forth just a month before. Spurgeon had earlier called Boniface a coward and said he would eat his hat if the priest showed up. Boniface was ready with pencil and notebook as Spurgeon began. When he finished the presentation and as a collection was taken, Boniface stood and challenged the fifth point of Spurgeon's lecture, that "the Catholic Priesthood is a lecherous bunch of White Slavers." Boniface announced that he would deposit five hundred dollars in a Morrilton bank to be given to Spurgeon if he could successfully prove this charge to a jury, saying, "Our constitution says that no one shall be condemned unless a jury of twelve men unite in declaring him guilty. If the case with individuals, how much more should it be the case with 15,000,000 people." Boniface proposed that Spurgeon deposit a hundred dollars as security for a debate and that each of them would choose one person and these two men would then appoint ten more citizens of Morrilton to form the jury, all to be non-Catholics. Spurgeon agreed and specified the second week of January as the time for the debate. Spurgeon proposed that he would talk one night, then Boniface another, and so on. Boniface said no, he wished to answer Spurgeon on the same night that he spoke, for he "believed in eating biscuits when they were hot." To this the auditorium burst into laughter, and Spurgeon accepted the terms.

Boniface stayed for more fireworks on Sunday. In the afternoon, Spurgeon repeated his "White Slavery" talk from Friday night. Boniface pointed out after the talk that although the lecture was advertised "For Men Only" he had seen boys with short pants in the auditorium and was concerned that Spurgeon had "contaminated the minds of these boys with the filth he has produced." Boniface reminded listeners that

Protestant and Catholic residents of Morrilton had lived as neighbors and friends for thirty years. He encouraged the men present to ask their wives to inquire of their female Catholic friends, since men could not freely speak of such matters to female neighbors, whether priests have indeed preyed upon women in the manner that Spurgeon described. Boniface went on to debunk the story of Maria Monk, which had been part of Spurgeon's "evidence" about white slavery. Boniface was back for the evening lecture, "Rome as the Beast of the Apocalypse." This time he did not wait politely to speak but interrupted Spurgeon to say, "This is not so!" when he made the claim that at one point in history the pope was a woman. To this, a voice from behind told Boniface, "Shut up!" Boniface noted that Spurgeon had the city marshal escort him back to his hotel each evening after his presentation.[29]

On Monday morning, Boniface met with Spurgeon to work out the details of the upcoming debate. Spurgeon and Boniface had originally agreed that a jury of twelve non-Catholic citizens of Morrilton would judge the debate. But Spurgeon tried to broaden the jury to twelve such citizens of Conway County. According to Boniface, Spurgeon was trying to organize a chapter of the Knights of Luther, and he was finding it easier to find likeminded citizens "in the backwoods of the county." Many of the Morrilton folks, Boniface said, were "too broadminded to join his 'Menace' organization." Boniface secured the agreement in writing, and the two men went to the Bank of Morrilton to sign before a notary public and deposit their money as a forfeit in case either failed to return in January for the debate. Spurgeon had received a hundred dollars, wired from the *Menace* Saturday evening. They shook hands and parted ways. Boniface determined to make one more rebuttal to Spurgeon before he left Morrilton. He telephoned the business manager of the *Southern Guardian* in Little Rock and ordered the printing of two thousand posters to be sent from Little Rock to Morrilton by train, with the following wording: "Tuesday night at the auditorium Father Boniface will speak on the Beast of the Apocalypse. Will prove by Spurgeon's own reasoning that Brother Spurgeon is the beast of the Apocalypse. Spurgeon is invited to speak provided he will come on the stage without the escort of the city marshal." Boniface found that several of his signs were torn down and burned. He admitted criticism from some quarters for speaking about someone after the person had gone (Spurgeon had left Morrilton the day before). Others suggested it would be better to ignore Spurgeon altogether. Nonetheless, Boniface gave his talk, which he claimed was to a large audience, and returned to Conway on Wednesday to finish his interrupted mission. There on Thursday, Saturday, and Sunday he lectured to a small audience that he complained was mostly local Catholics, for few Protestants came out.[30] From Conway, Boniface took the Gospel Wagon on to Pulaski County, where he took refuge at the bishop's orphanage in North Little Rock.[31]

Diocesan authorities evidently shifted their position regarding Boniface. While Boniface's Gospel Wagon had headlined the *Southern Guardian* with top-to-bottom articles weekly for three months, by late December, the paper almost entirely dropped Boniface from the news. As Boniface was putting on his boxing gloves, evidently Bishop Morris questioned the benefits of the publicity that Boniface was bringing to the Catholic Church. Earlier in his mission Boniface had been challenged to a debate by a subscriber of the *Menace* in Logan County but had responded that he was opposed to debates and that "they created only hard feelings and had no good results." Perhaps the attention of the auditorium crowds and the power of his eloquent pen went to his head, and he embraced the role of attack dog for the church. Boniface later claimed to have Bishop Morris's approval to conduct the debate, but clearly Catholic authorities, if not the lay folk and local priests, were turning against him.[32]

Meanwhile, over the holiday season, the people of Morrilton were getting ready for the debate. A tent was ordered from Kansas City with a seating capacity of 1,500 to 2,000 people, complete with lights and heat, to be erected on a vacant lot. Advance publicity appeared in newspapers in Arkansas and outside the state. The Reverend Kidd and Reverend Johnson, of the Presbyterian Church and Baptist Church, respectively, handled much of the local arrangements before and during the debate. On opening day, January 13, trains were crowded and hotels full. Newspaper reporters, representatives of Protestant churches, and some Catholic leaders were there. Father Boniface received assistance from the local priest, Father Haas, and a Catholic layman, Will Drilling. The *Menace* sent a correspondent and an editor, and the Reverend Scarboro of the *Liberator* came up from Magnolia to cover the event, along with the editor and a reporter from the *Sentinel of Liberty*, an anti-Catholic weekly in Grand Saline, Texas. A reporter for the *Arkansas Gazette* sent daily accounts back to Little Rock. Some of the professional lecturers, such as William Lloyd Clark, were there to support Spurgeon. The anti-Catholic editors and lecturers led meetings in local churches in afternoons, which Boniface suggested were designed to prejudice the jury. The *Menace* reported that visitors from various parts of Arkansas as well as Iowa, Missouri, Oklahoma, Tennessee, and Texas had come to Morrilton for the debate. The paper complemented the fine people of Morrilton for taking the visitors into their homes. The *Arkansas Gazette* reported that 3,000 people attended the opening session of the debate, and that the closing session, ten days later, had an even larger crowd—this in a town whose population at the 1910 census was only 2,424.[33]

One reason for the large crowd may have been that the real focus of the debate concerned SEX. How would a jury of twelve Protestant men rule on Spurgeon's proposition that Catholic priests were a bunch of white sex slavers?[34] As Spurgeon and Boniface unpacked this subject over eight evenings in a ten-day period, plenty of titillating anecdotes, accusations, and denials kept the attention of listeners. None of the debates was designated "for men only," although women were warned not to attend if they would be offended "by plain language." Evidently women had little fear, for the *Arkansas Gazette* estimated the female proportion of the audience at a third in the second debate, growing to half by the fourth evening. After a couple of evenings the presentations became somewhat repetitive, and the last evening was a summation of the whole.[35]

To make his case on the lecherous priesthood, Spurgeon opened with an anthropological, theological, and historical critique of clerical celibacy. Priests are human beings, he said, and humanity is pretty much the same everywhere. Celibacy was against all the laws of human nature. While celibacy may have been possible for Jesus Christ and the Apostle Paul, it was an unattainable goal for ordinary men. To this Boniface returned that Spurgeon himself must be guilty, given that he left his wife for extended periods for his travelling lectures. Here the jury's chairman, G. H.Taylor, called Boniface out for making personal references.

Spurgeon spent some time arguing that celibacy was even bad theology, suggesting that the doctrine of celibacy was based on a false interpretation of scripture and the ideas of a few men. He quoted the biblical command "be fruitful and multiply" and said priests thus live contrary to scripture. Boniface had his own scriptural passages to quote to justify the doctrine. Finally, Spurgeon read from Roman Catholic authors who had condemned clerical immorality through history and referred to eighty councils that legislated against impurity of the priesthood. He noted popes who had mistresses and bastard children, including Pope Paul II who was said to have fourteen concubines. Spurgeon used the fact, and one that Boniface admitted, that the Roman Church had reformatories for clergy who have fallen into sexual sin, as evidence that promiscuity was indeed a problem.

While Spurgeon argued that priests are just like any other men, he proposed that as a group they were somehow more depraved than ordinary men, quoting here a purported ex-priest, anti-Catholic author Jeremiah Crowley, who said "one-third of priests are rotten, one-third are bad, and the other third will stand watching." He read extensively from Crowley's book, *The Pope, Chief of White Slavers, High Priest of Intrigue*, which described priestly misdeeds ranging from sexual sins to the murder of children. Spurgeon used another ex-priest, professional anti-Catholic propagandist Charles Chiniquy, who said that "90 percent of the priests he had known were lewd." Chiniquy, a Canadian priest who left the church and became a Presbyterian minister, provided purported testimony in his books from nuns about the sexual appetites of priests."[36]

Boniface admitted that there were some lecherous priests—there was even one bad apple among the twelve apostles—but he insisted that these examples were the exception rather than the rule. Spurgeon's "logic" was similar, Boniface said, to the assertion that because "a mule is member of the equine family, therefore all horses are jackasses." This comment raised a howl from the audience. Boniface spent much of his time debunking accounts of Chiniquy, Crowley, Seguin, ex-nun Anna M. Lowry, and other anti-Catholic authors Spurgeon had used as authorities. The authors themselves he denounced as liars, frauds, or, in some cases, common criminals. He also read a list of fifty Protestant clergy who had gone wrong, to make the case that they too were as guilty. Boniface proposed that for every bad priest Spurgeon could name, that he would find an equally bad Protestant minister, and he offered his five hundred dollars as a bet. Spurgeon countered that Protestant clergy were not the subject of this debate. Here again chairman Taylor called

Boniface down from straying from the subject at hand. Boniface insisted that to win his bet, Spurgeon would need to prove that all priests are lecherous. Spurgeon answered that admittedly there were some good priests, but that he only needed to demonstrate that the system itself, or the general run of priests, was lecherous to win the debate.

Spurgeon issued a call for the next Arkansas legislature to pass an inspection law, this time with a provision that inspection teams include two physicians to examine nuns, presumably to conduct virginity examinations. Spurgeon indicated that after states pass inspection laws that they will need to enlarge their prisons to make room for the admission of "hundreds of bachelor priests." Boniface decried Spurgeon's call for physicians to examine nuns, and he called for listeners to imagine the insult they would feel if women in Protestant institutions were required to submit to such humiliation. He also noted that when a convent in Little Rock had been demolished in recent years, there were no secret tunnels to the rectory or bones of infants to be found.[37]

One of Spurgeon's central arguments about lecherous priests concerned the alleged abuses of women in the confessional. According to Spurgeon, priests got young women in the confessional to talk about their sexual sins and used the opportunity of these intimate conversations to lure them into sexual relationships. The purpose of the confessional, he said was for priests to break down the modesty of these women and place them under the priest's power. Spurgeon insisted that the priests asked pointed questions about subjects that women could not discuss with their closest family members. Priests deny it, of course, he said, but "it plainly is demonstrated that the more beautiful young ladies are, the longer it seems to take them to make their confessions." Again, Spurgeon relied on the anti-Catholic authors to put together his case, reading from Chiniquy's story of a young wife ruined by the confessional. Spurgeon read from "statistics" to the extent that priests "had ruined and debauched the womenhood of the nation of France," and then he did the same for Spain. Finally, he stated that the Italian government had passed laws regulating the conduct of priests in an effort to protect women there. Part of Spurgeon's presentation involved reading questions, which he claimed came from an official Catholic source, that priests asked of young women in the confessional. The questions covered "almost every form of possible sexual indulgence and exciting of

From Wilbur F. Phelps, *Menace Cartoons.*

the passions"; even the *Menace* said this material was too vulgar to print. Spurgeon turned some particularly explicit printed examples over to the jury to peruse rather than offend the ears of his listeners.[38]

Boniface countered Spurgeon's claims, denying that priests ask lurid questions of women. He explained that priests have very specific training about how to conduct confessions with modesty and discretion. Two married women from the local Catholic parish appeared on the stage and presented a statement they said was signed by a large majority of the women of Sacred Heart Church, swearing that Spurgeon's claims about women in the confessional were false. The *Menace* indicated that the claims of the two local women "created a sensation all over the tent, but the women being well known by most of the audience, it did not have much force." Boniface scolded Spurgeon for polluting people's ears with such lewd language in making his case. And he complimented the men of Morrilton for their restraint in tolerating slanderous falsehoods about what their wives, daughters, and sisters experienced in the confessional. Spurgeon felt Boniface was trying to appeal to southern chivalry to incite a riot, and the *Menace* said extra precautions were taken to protect Spurgeon and other prominent visitors from possible physical violence.[39]

Another key argument Spurgeon used to make his case about lecherous priests concerned the use of female housekeepers in priestly rectories.

He argued that the practice made a mockery of celibacy and practically institutionalized fornication. As he put it, the practice was for the priest "to always have a woman with him in the house—handy." Spurgeon told the audience that the Catholic system actually permitted adultery, for a priest was allowed to seduce a woman once a month or several women a month apart with no consequence from the church. Spurgeon asked, what people would think if an unmarried Protestant clergyman kept a live-in female housekeeper, as Catholic priests do. Celibacy would be from a human standpoint "almost impossible when a woman is always on the scene and always in the home."[40] He said he would believe that the priests are serious about celibacy when they banished women housekeepers from their homes and replaced them with manservants.

As an example of a priest who simply could not control his sexual urges, Spurgeon used Father Hans Schmidt of New York City, who at that very moment was sitting in jail awaiting trial for murdering the rectory's attractive twenty-year-old housekeeper, Anna Aumuller. The two had become lovers, with Father Schmidt himself saying wedding vows for himself and Anna in a private ceremony. After she became pregnant, Schmidt murdered her and the unborn child to hide the evidence of their sexual relationship. He dismembered Anna's body and threw it into the Hudson River. Jury selection for Father Schmidt's trial began on January 19, and lawyers delivered their opening statements on January 21, the last day of the Morrilton debate.[41] Boniface responded that Father Schmidt was mentally ill and should be in an asylum. Spurgeon even had another example to pull out, of a Father Brady, who Spurgeon alleged impregnated his housekeeper. Spurgeon claimed that when she was six months along, Brady shot her in the abdomen but failed to kill either her or the unborn child.

While Father Schmidt paid the ultimate price—he died in the electric chair at New York's Sing Sing prison in 1915, making him the only Roman Catholic priest executed in the United States—Spurgeon went on to argue that most of the time "the church did not punish the dirty priest."[42] In fact, priests were simply moved to another location and their deeds hidden from public view. Even when priests were in danger of civil punishment and sent to the reformatory, they were then turned loose on society again, or even promoted to higher offices in the church.

A parting shot that Spurgeon levied against Catholicism, and Father

Boniface's Benedictine order specifically, concerned a type of liquor that bears the same name. Spurgeon asked his fellow lecturer William Lloyd Clark to come to the stage to present a bottle of liquor labeled "Benedictine." Clark explained he had found the bottle at "a house of ill fame" in Rock Island, Illinois, when he was holding services there, and that the liquor was used "to excite the passions of those who visit these places." The medicinal herbal liqueur was made by monks at a Benedictine abbey in France, according to the label, and had the seal of the Roman Catholic Church. This produced a "veritable sensation" in the crowd, especially when Boniface said he had used the cordial and called it "good stuff." [43] Boniface recommended that every member of the jury take a drink of the Benedictine liquor to see what its effects actually were. There is no evidence that the jury took him up on this suggestion.

As his last appeal, Father Boniface asked the jury not to consider the debate as a religious debate, knowing that as Protestant jurors they would have difficulty siding with Catholicism. He would not grant that Spurgeon's arguments were "Protestant" ones. Instead of a Protestant-Catholic debate, Boniface said it was a *Menace*-Catholic debate. He asserted that the *Menace* had sent Spurgeon to Morrilton and provided means for this "cat fight."[44] Boniface encouraged jurors to focus on Spurgeon's original proposition and whether he had indeed proved it to be true. Spurgeon had the last word of the debate and denied that he was in any way connected to the *Menace* since the previous June. But he asserted that this was indeed a Protestant-Catholic debate, and jurors were right to think of it as a religious event.

The debate ended with the semblance of order as people passed out of the tent quietly. During the entire affair the audience had been remarkably well behaved. Although percolating the sessions with guffaws, gasps, and sideline conversations, the crowd had refrained from showing favoritism to either side until a prolonged applause for Spurgeon at the close of the last session. Boniface did complain about a man snoring loudly near the stage during his presentation on the seventh night and charged that Spurgeon had in fact hired the man to do so just to disrupt his speech. As Spurgeon and his aides were leaving the tent on the seventh night, a woman got in his face, stepped back, and threw a rotten egg, which struck his back, fell to the ground, and broke. She was reaching into her handbag for another when the marshal nearby prevented her. The *Arkansas Echo*, the German-language weekly published in Little Rock, denied that she was a Catholic. She was arrested and charged with assault.

Even Spurgeon and Boniface, other than their harsh rhetoric, generally kept their tempers under control. Each was called out of order by Chairman Taylor once, but otherwise generally abided by the rules of the debate. It is hard to get a sense of the thirty-eight-year-old Spurgeon's personality from the reporting of the debate, but Boniface's passion, energy, and a degree of charisma were apparent. He was reported to have lost eighteen pounds during the ten days of the debate, and the *Menace* described him by the end as hoarse, pallid, and tired.[45] The Catholic press had no use for Spurgeon, with the *Arkansas Echo* referring to him as that "dung beetle" for his concentration on excremental rather than noble products of the Catholic Church. The *Menace*, as much as editors despised the priesthood, nonetheless gave Boniface a few nods, saying he was "above the average Catholic priest. He is of a sunny disposition, quite open and as frank as circumstances compel him to be. He is well versed in priestly lore, but like all priests, his training has stunted not only his intellect, but his human nature as well. If Mr. Boniface could get out of the environment of paganism into the light of Protestant freedom for a while, he would doubtless develop into a useful and enterprising citizen."[46]

The jury convened at the courthouse on Thursday morning, after the debate's final session, to deliberate and declare a verdict. Chairman Taylor announced that nine jurors voted in favor of Spurgeon with three in support of Boniface. Lacking a unanimous verdict and according to the agreed-upon rules, Taylor declared the debate a draw. The *Menace* interpreted it as a victory, declaring: "The Morrilton Protestant-Catholic debate will go down in history as one of the greatest blows Catholicism has suffered in a half century." The *Southern Guardian* claimed that a hung jury constituted a victory for Boniface and a repudiation of Spurgeon. Boniface claimed later that he had won the debate, using as evidence the fact that Spurgeon never asked for the five hundred dollars deposited in the Bank of Morrilton for the proposition that he could prove his statement.[47]

While the debate was a draw, the town of Morrilton may have been the real loser. Obviously, food venders and hoteliers made money from the event, but after the out-of-town guests departed, a more acrimonious

Father Boniface Spanke. *Courtesy of Archives of Subiaco Abbey.*

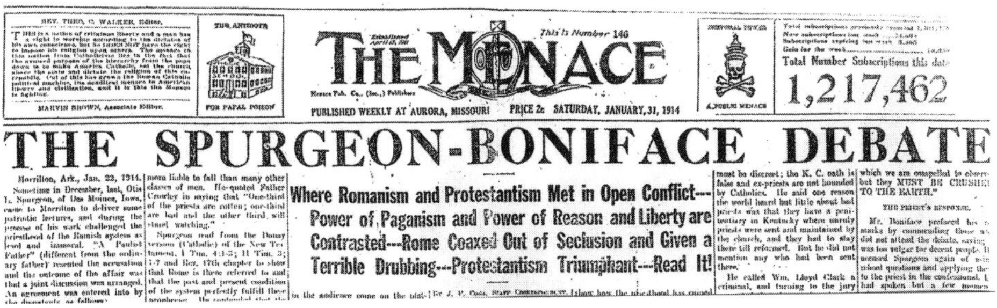

THE MENACE

PUBLISHED WEEKLY AT AURORA, MISSOURI PRICE 2c SATURDAY, JANUARY, 31, 1914

Total Number Subscriptions this date 1,217,462

THE SPURGEON-BONIFACE DEBATE

Where Romanism and Protestantism Met in Open Conflict---Power of Paganism and Power of Reason and Liberty are Contrasted---Rome Coaxed Out of Seclusion and Given a Terrible Drubbing---Protestantism Triumphant---Read It!

The Menace headline of January 31, 1914.

environment remained. The *Menace* praised the fine people of Morrilton for their hospitality but noted that there were a few, including "a preacher or so who have not grasped the importance and gravity of the struggle. . . . [B]ut there is such a healthy sentiment here that they will fall into line." Morrilton's two newspapers apparently took opposite sides, with the *Headlight* printing detailed accounts favoring Spurgeon and the *Democrat* giving less coverage and more even-handed treatment to the Catholic view.[48] The *Arkansas Echo*, Little Rock's German-language weekly, said that in the Morrilton area folks of different religious communities had gotten along well before the debate, but afterward Morrilton had become sadly famous for discord between the faiths. Later in 1914, the local parish priest who had replaced Father Haas in Morrilton, Father Olfen of the Order of the Holy Ghost, described relations between Catholics and Protestants in Morrilton as very tense since the debate. Reporting back to his superior in Pittsburgh, Olfen noted that chapters of the Guardians of Freedom and Knights of Luther had been organized in Morrilton and that anti-Catholic newspapers seemed to be everywhere in evidence. He wished that Boniface had never agreed to debate Spurgeon, and he concluded that it would take some time for Morrilton to recover.[49]

Like Father Olfen, Bishop John Morris in Little Rock held the view that Boniface's debate had damaged relations with Protestant neighbors. Boniface was called back to Subiaco Abbey and his Gospel Wagon missions brought to a halt. The bishop directed the abbot to park the wagon and sell the horses. The Gospel Wagon eventually wound up at St. Joseph's orphanage in North Little Rock, where children played on it in for years to come. Soon after the debate, Boniface was sent to Texarkana for two and a half years, and then on to Wichita Falls, Texas. He disappeared from the pages of the *Southern Guardian*, with the diocesan weekly giving only two short paragraphs at the bottom of the first page to report the results of the debate.[50]

Otis Spurgeon also passed from the Arkansas scene. After leaving Morrilton, he lectured at Russellville, reportedly to a small crowd, and then at a Baptist church in Little Rock, where he apparently called for Protestants to boycott Catholic businesses.[51] Two months later Spurgeon reappeared in the national news in Denver, Colorado. After he had presented his usual lecture against the immorality of the Catholic priesthood, a group of men overpowered a policeman and a personal bodyguard, burst into Spurgeon's room on the third floor of the Pierce Hotel, forced him to a waiting car, and drove him to an isolated spot some twenty miles north of Denver. There the men stripped Spurgeon naked, beat him, and left him on the side of the road. Spurgeon found a ride back to a Denver hospital, where he was treated for a broken nose and other injuries. After this episode, Spurgeon turned to other ventures. He ran unsuccessfully in Iowa for the US Senate in the fall of 1914 as an independent candidate, trailing behind the candidates from the two major parties, garnering less than 6 percent of the vote.[52]

It appears that Bishop Morris was correct, that the likes of Otis Spurgeon and Father Boniface were not the method for bringing understanding or reconciliation between Catholics and their opponents. The temperature only seemed to rise after the Morrilton debate. In April 1914 a conservative Baptist weekly predicted a coming battle between Baptists and Catholics, suggesting more than a war of words: "The war clouds are gathering and the hosts are being marshaled for the struggle, and bloody conflict it will be."[53] In May the Southern Baptist Convention, meeting in Nashville, Tennessee, adopted several anti-Catholic resolutions, including one criticizing the seating of a papal legate in the nation's capital and another protesting "the efforts of the Roman Catholic hierarchy to gain control of our government, and thereby be in a position to fasten either its faith or fallacies upon the consciences of a free and sovereign people."[54] When the Arkansas Baptist Convention met in the following November in Little Rock, it passed an anti-Catholic resolution authored by the Reverend Eugene P. Alldredge, pastor of Immanuel

Otis Spurgeon, from his US Senate campaign poster, 1914. *Courtesy of the State Historical Society of Iowa.*

Baptist Church of Little Rock. The resolution said that because most Protestants had an unblushing ignorance of Roman Catholicism, a news-gathering agency should be established to study and report about "Romanism and other un-American ideas and institutions." The convention concluded with the resolve to encourage lecture bureaus, the circulation of patriotic newspapers, the enactment of legislation, and the election of officials to promote these ideals.[55]

As 1914 wore onward, Baptists and other anti-Catholic forces prepared for the state elections, which sent legislators to the 1915 Arkansas General Assembly who were determined to pass an inspection bill. Herb Lewis announced his candidacy for representative from Benton County. His platform opposed liquor and any attempts to remove the Bible from public schools. In addition, he called for the inspection of nunneries and private schools. The *Menace* heartily endorsed his candidacy. Lewis lost, however, in the Democratic primary, coming in sixth of nine candidates and failing to carry any township but his own.[56] When the general state election was held on September 14, a large number of Democrats broke ranks and voted Republican in the race for superintendent for public schools because the Democratic standard-bearer, W. T. Adams, had earlier in the year participated in the laying of a foundation stone of a Catholic school in Mena and had made some complimentary comments about the quality of Catholic education.[57] Apparently, anti-Catholic forces sent newly elected members of the legislature circulars attacking Arkansas Catholics who held public office or positions of trust, along with a survey asking how they stood on the subject of Catholicism. In December, a public meeting was held at Immanuel Baptist Church in Little Rock to plan for the "needed legislation for convent inspection" that would be proposed at the upcoming legislative session.[58]

Northwest Arkansas was particularly a contentious environment in 1914 for Catholics on a couple of scores. Father J. P. Gillis, a Paulist priest from New York, had given a week of lectures in Fayetteville in January to correct misconceptions about the church, but Herb Lewis suggested that the lectures really aimed to convert non-Catholics. He challenged Father Gillis to debate, but the priest apparently refused.[59] In August an Arkansas-grown anti-Catholic speaker, Basil E. Newton, gave a series of lectures in Gravette. Newton had heard William Lloyd Clark speak at Hope in 1912 and became committed to the anti-Catholic cause. He travelled from Hope to Gravette by way of Aurora, Missouri, where he visited the *Menace* staff, and then lectured for four nights at Gravette's Baptist church.[60]

Besides Herb Lewis, Gravette's other editor, Averal C. Veach, was embroiled in controversy because of his anti-Catholic stance. Veach, a former mayor of Gravette, had expressed such criticism of Catholicism in his two monthly papers, the Masonic *Globe* and the *Sovereign Odd Fellow*, that the head of the International Order of Odd Fellows in 1913, the Grand Sire Christopher Keller, of San Antonio, Texas, asked Veach to desist or change the name of the paper and remove the I.O.O.F. symbol from the masthead. Keller argued that the order made no religious or political affiliations and was forbidden from entering into controversies about these issues. When Veach refused to change his stance, Keller convinced the national grand lodge meeting in the fall of 1913 to order the Odd Fellow lodge in Gravette to expel him or lose its charter. The local lodge of more than one hundred men took no action, saying they would not expel Veach without a trial. This controversy played out locally and among the Odd Fellows nationwide in 1914, with the grand sire urging all Odd Fellows to boycott Veach's paper. Finally, in December, Veach, represented by an attorney, F. O. Butt from Eureka Springs, had an actual trial before his lodge, which unanimously found that he had broken no law or policy and was expressing his constitutional right of free speech. Keller then sued Veach in Federal Court for $5,000 in damages in one more effort to get Veach to change the name of his paper to disassociate it from the Odd Fellows. This suit dragged on until dismissed in 1915 by the federal court in Fort Smith. Veach kept publishing his two monthly papers under the same names. In 1914 he even started a third publication, the *Beacon Light*, which billed itself specifically as a patriotic and anti-Catholic paper. Badly overextended, Veach gave up the *Beacon Light* after a few months, and its subscription list was absorbed by the *Menace* in October of 1914.[61] It boggles the mind to think that for a while in 1914, four anti-Catholic newspapers were published in the small town of Gravette, Arkansas—the *Globe*, *Sovereign Odd Fellow*, *Beacon Light*, and Herb Lewis's *News Herald*.

The Reverend Joseph Scarboro and the *Liberator* also kept the pot stirred from southwestern Arkansas. By the summer of 1914, Scarboro was apparently in bad financial shape and was begging readers of the *Baptist* to buy stock in the *Liberator* or help him get ten thousand new subscribers.[62] In August he asked residents of Mena to put up six thousand dollars for him to move the *Liberator* there. He tried to whip up prejudice in Mena by alleging that the local paper, the *Mena Star*, was controlled by Romanists and biased toward Catholics. As evidence, Scarboro said that the paper had totally ignored anti-Catholic lectures given in Mena by Basil E. Newton and William Lloyd Clark and did not even acknowledge a revival at the Baptist church. The *Star*'s editor responded that Scarboro's allegations were nothing but lies, for no Roman Catholic had a cent invested in the newspaper. By policy, the editor said the *Star* would give no space to cover someone who came to town to abuse a church or another religion.[63] Pastors of some Protestant churches in Mena weighed in to the conflict. They wrote an open letter declaring that the *Mena Star* had been fair to all, Protestant and Catholic.[64]

Thus, since the last meeting of the state legislature in 1913, much had happened in Arkansas to intensify public attitudes of anti-Catholicism.

The new Arkansas General Assembly convened on January 11, 1915, with one hundred representatives and thirty-five senators. Three Republicans sat in the House, none in the Senate. All the rest were Democrats. There were farmers, lawyers, merchants, teachers, insurance agents, physicians, and people of other occupations serving in the House and Senate, and these legislators held various Protestant creeds. Unlike in 1913, no Roman Catholic served in either house.[65] Grant County's representative Robert R. Posey returned to the House, and on Tuesday, January 26, he introduced House Bill 214, a convent inspection bill that was virtually identical to the one he had sponsored two years before. Immediately after the bill was first read on the House floor, Representative Thomas Wilson of Jefferson County moved that it be indefinitely postponed, which would have the effect of killing the bill.[66] The stage was set for a raucous debate both within the Arkansas General Assembly and in the public forum.

Catholics wasted no time in launching their campaign against the bill. Although banished to Texarkana after the debate of 1914 and ignored by the diocesan weekly, the *Southern Guardian*, Father Boniface Spanke jumped right into the battle. On January 27, the day after the Posey bill was introduced in the House, he wrote the *Arkansas Gazette* with the provocative announcement that he wished for the bill to pass and become law. His reasoning was that he wanted to establish the constitutionality of such a law as soon as possible. Boniface believed that a law aiming for inspection only of educational and charitable institutions might pass constitutional muster, but the Arkansas bill calling for inspection of convents and monasteries meant a governmental search of the homes for monks and nuns, thus constituting an unwarranted invasion of privacy. The *Menace* countered in an article entitled "Boniface Bluffing" and blasted Boniface, reminding readers that proper authorities could search a private home when they had reason to believe that "insanitary, immoral or illegal conditions exist" there. "No home however private is exempt from public supervision," the *Menace* concluded. Boniface announced that as soon as an inspection bill became law, he would go "home" to Subiaco Abbey and resist inspection. If arrested, he said, "I shall not for money buy the God-given gift of every American citizen by giving bond, but I will go to Logan County jail till my case is tried to show the cowardly disseminations of religious strife that a Catholic monk is endowed with the same love of liberty as the great orator-patriot who exclaimed: 'Give me liberty, or give me death.'" Boniface vowed to push the case until the Arkansas Supreme Court, or even the Supreme Court of the United States, declared the inspection law unconstitutional.[67]

Prior Augustine Stocker of Subiaco Abbey also seemed to enjoy waging battle in this controversy. As one of the contributing editors of the *Southern Guardian*, he spoke against inspection legislation. Echoing Father Boniface, Prior Augustine argued, "Our monasteries and convents are our homes just as your family hearth is the sacred shrine of your domestic privacy." A law providing for inspection of these locations before there were any specific charges of wrong-doing, he said, constituted a violation of the fourth amendment, guaranteeing the "right of the people to be secure in their persons, houses, papers, and effects, against unreasonable searches and seizures." What was missing here, Augustine argued, was the presentation of evidence that conditions in Arkansas monasteries and convents required such drastic measures. Augustine said that the motivation for the bill came not from any "authentic fact" about Catholic institutions in Arkansas, but from slander and prejudice from individuals and organs imported from outside of the state. Lastly, he argued that the bill was disrespectful to women. He asked the men of Arkansas to consider if they would wish for their mothers or sisters to be subject to inspection and "special police control" as the noble sisters would be under the proposed law.[68] Prior Augustine travelled to Little Rock to meet with other Catholic leaders to prepare a flyer entitled "Four of the Many Reasons Why House Bill 214 Providing for the Inspection of Schools, Convents, Hospitals, etc. Should NOT Be Passed." Augustine's Four Points were these: (1) it is unconstitutional; (2) it is an insult to virtuous women; (3) it is the fruit of religious bigotry; and (4) it is unreasonable. The statement was sent to Arkansas newspapers and printed on a full page in the *Southern Guardian*. Father Ignatius Conrad, the abbot of Subiaco Abbey, wrote a letter to all the Arkansas legislators, asking for them to oppose the inspection bill and inviting them to visit the monastery at any time and see for themselves how it was ordered.[69]

While Prior Augustine and Father Boniface propagandized against the Inspection bill, anti-Catholic forces mobilized support for it. Baptist leaders jumped in with their own politicking. The Reverend Alldredge of

Little Rock wrote a lengthy article about the bill for readers of the *Baptist Advance*, in which he called the bill "one of the best statutes ever placed upon the statute books by an Arkansas legislature." Alldredge denied that the bill was anti-Catholic, saying it put all denominations on equal footing. The very fact that "some denominations" opposed inspection of their institutions provided a reason for the bill to be passed. The state of Arkansas, he said, could not dare allow people to be held against their will in these institutions. As to the argument that inspection would violate the privacy of someone's home, he said that his own home was owned by Immanuel Baptist Church and he could never have the right to hold people in this private home against their will and without due process of law. Alldredge concluded that only such inspections would "allay the growing agitation against cloistered religious institutions in America." The phenomenal growth of the *Menace*, he said, has occurred because the Catholic Church has drawn "the cloak of secrecy about them and the lives of the inmates." The agitation will continue "until the people are allowed to see for themselves."[70] The editor of the *Baptist Advance*, E.J.A. McKinney, was in full agreement. The charges stand, he said, that people were in slavery behind iron bars in convents. The citizens of Arkansas had a right to know if these charges were true, and the state had an obligation to protect its citizens.[71]

The professional anti-Catholic lecturers also stepped into this highly charged atmosphere in Arkansas. In January, two shady lecturers, William Black and Billy Parker, began a speaking tour through Arkansas, spending a couple of weeks in Hot Springs and Little Rock just as the legislators arrived in town. Black, of Bellaire, Ohio, said he had been raised Catholic in a small Virginia town and ordained a priest under Cardinal Gibbons in Baltimore, but he claimed he left the priesthood to launch a career preaching against Rome. The *Arkansas Gazette* described Black as about fifty years old, slight of build, with a sallow complexion and homely face, and "not an eloquent speaker."[72] His partner Billy Parker must have been better with words, for his sobriquet was the "Witty Little Scotchman." He claimed to have spent time fighting in Mexico to overthrow President Porfirio Díaz in 1911, who was closely allied with the Catholic hierarchy. The Catholic press claimed that Parker had formerly been known as a Socialist leader but had been expelled from the party for unknown reasons and prohibited from speaking under the auspices of Socialism. It was at that time that he turned to anti-Catholic lecturing.[73]

Black lectured at the Hot Springs auditorium in mid-January while the manager was out of town, but when the manager returned and learned the nature of the lectures, he denied Black access to the facility. He then finished his series of lectures at a local Protestant church. The *Southern Guardian* charged that the mayor of Hot Springs encouraged the anti-Catholic movement by appointing a guard of several men to protect Black.[74] Meanwhile, in Little Rock, Billy Parker printed a circular advertising a three-night series of illustrated lectures beginning on January 11 at the Grand Lodge Hall of Little Rock's Masonic Temple. The Monday night topic was to be "Rome, the Menace of Civilization," with "Crimes of the Papacy" on Tuesday and concluding with Wednesday's topic, "Is the Oath of the Knights of Columbus True?" The show included a slide show via a stereopticon machine, like Father Boniface had used in the Gospel Wagon. Parker and Black charged an admission of twenty-five cents. However, when Masonic leaders in Little Rock determined the nature of the proposed lecture, they denied them the use of their hall. Parker then found another location, a vacant storeroom in Little Rock's business district. He rented two hundred chairs and printed new circulars, preparing for a seven-night stand. A group of Little Rock Knights of Columbus members visited the proprietor of the storeroom and convinced him also to cancel the lectures. The lecturers refused to give up and arranged to speak in the Moose Hall on January 23, then gave four programs at the First Baptist Church at Twelfth and Louisiana Streets. The Knights of Columbus group even called on the pastor of the church, the Reverend Bowers, protesting his granting of a platform for the men. Governor George W. Hays, a Baptist, even publically expressed his opposition. Some of the church's deacons voted against opening their doors to the lecturers, but the church granted access anyway. The Reverend Bowers explained that his church would never have given the speakers a hearing had not the Knights of Columbus been exerting such undue efforts to stop them from speaking.[75]

The Knights of Columbus members were incensed with the lecturers' claims about their organization, particularly the dissemination by Black and Parker of a fake oath they claimed was used by the Knights. This oath had been the subject of the back-and-forth dispute between the *Southern Guardian* and the *Baptist Advance* two years before. One of the lecturers' prepared programs concerned the oath, and they had the oath printed in its entirety on the backside of their advertisement circulars. The first section of the oath apparently had been composed by anti-Catholics in England in the 1600s and attributed to Jesuits. The oath-taker denounced any allegiance to a Protestant king, prince, or state and promised "to wage relentless war, secretly and openly, against all heretics, Protestants and Masons . . . [and] to extirpate them from the face of the whole earth." According to the oath, the Knights then vowed to "burn, hang, waste, boil, flay, strangle and bury alive these infamous heretics; rip up the stomachs and wombs of the women, and crush their infant's heads against the walls in order to annihilate their execrable race." William Black, Catholic sources said, added three concluding paragraphs to tailor the oath to an American setting. In this section, the supposed oath-taker promised to vote always "for a Knight of Columbus in preference to a Protestant—especially a Mason," even forsaking party loyalties if necessary to do so. In Black's final paragraph, the Knight supposedly pledged: "That I will provide myself with arms and ammunition that I may be in readiness when the word is passed, or I am commanded to defend the Church either as an individual or with the militia of the Pope."[76]

The bogus oath had appeared nationwide during the 1912 election campaigns. In Billy Parker's home state of Pennsylvania, a congressional candidate and fourth-degree Knight of Columbus, Eugene Bonniwell, filed a contest over his defeat in the election, claiming he lost because of the fake oath. The US Congress's Committee on Elections did not overturn the election results, concluding that the winning candidate himself was not responsible. But the congressional committee in early 1913 determined that the oath was indeed false and libelous. Within the next two years, the Knights of Columbus had filed criminal libel suits against persons disseminating the oath in Pennsylvania, Minnesota, California, and Newfoundland, Canada, with the accused found guilty in all four cases. In fact, with the California case, a judge who felt that the vow was anti-Masonic, submitted the oath along with the Knights' authentic ceremonies and rituals to a group of Masonic leaders. They subsequently concluded that the fake oath was "scurrilous, wicked, and libelous" and that they found nothing anti-Masonic, anti-Protestant, or unpatriotic in the Knights' rituals.[77] Black's partner Billy Parker claimed that he got his copy of the oath from the *Congressional Record*, as if that lent authenticity. The *Southern Guardian* explained that the fake oath was in the

Congressional Record only because it had been submitted as evidence of fraud committed by a candidate in a disputed election in 1912.[78]

William Black's reputation was giving anti-Catholicism a bad name in Arkansas. One Protestant clergyman invited Irish-born Monsignor Thomas V. Tobin, the rector of St. Andrews Cathedral, to address the Little Rock ministerial alliance about these local manifestations of the nationwide anti-Catholic movement. Tobin asked the pastors to pressure their Baptist brethren to stop lending their churches for anti-Catholic lectures. As far as he could tell, Tobin said, Black had never been a priest, and he doubted that he was ever a Catholic.[79] Subiaco's prior, Augustine Stocker, attended Black's lecture at the Moose Hall, and he concluded that Black, like many others who earned a living from their claims to be an ex-nun or ex-priest, was a fraud. By his use of certain terminology that Catholics would never use, such as "confessional box," Black inadvertently gave away clues that he had never been a Catholic. When asked specifically for his credentials—where he was ordained, under whom he served—he would give no specifics. Black said that when he heard confessions as a priest, he was forced to "contaminate the minds of pure women by the questions he asked." Prior Augustine called Black's statements pure hogwash. No priest was ever so instructed, Augustine said, and it had never occurred to him to ask suggestive questions in the confessional. Later, the *Southern Guardian* published information from Catholic authorities in Black's home diocese of Wheeling, West Virginia, that found no evidence he had ever been a Catholic, much less a priest. A careful search through lists of all Catholic clergy for the last twenty-five years turned up no priest by the name of William Black. The bishop of Wheeling said Black's claim to have been a priest was a joke in his hometown among Catholics and non-Catholics alike.[80]

While Black was lecturing in Arkansas, he was presented with a golden opportunity to make his lecture program more dramatic and sexy: a seventeen-year-old girl who had run away from a Catholic convent in Hot Springs. Since 1908 Hot Springs had been home to a convent of the House of Good Shepherd (H.O.G.S.), also known as the Sisters of Our Lady of Charity of the Refuge. H.O.G.S. was the order of nuns that anti-Catholics loved to hate, the example singled out when agitators talked of white slavery behind iron bars and convent walls. Founded in France in the 1600s, the order aspired from its beginning

William Black, from the *Daily Texarkanian,* February 6, 1915.

to rescue fallen young women and provide a refuge for them that could provide education and rehabilitation. The order established its first convent in the United States in Buffalo, New York, in 1855. In the early 1900s the convents served as reformatories for girls. Local juvenile and court authorities often committed wayward girls—Protestant, Catholic, or non-religious—to their care. By invitation of Bishop John Morris in 1908, five sisters from Ottawa, Canada, established the House of Good Shepherd in Hot Springs. After a few months in temporary quarters, the sisters purchased a large house on ten acres at 1125 Malvern Avenue. They had room to build a dormitory and a laundry—the order typically earned income by using labor of the sisters and residents—and establish St. Michael's, a boarding school for girls. In 1915 the house contained nuns, Magdalens (penitent women who wanted to live a cloistered life but were ineligible to become nuns), delinquent young women, and girls attending the school run by the sisters.[81]

Sadie Pauline Allison, who worked as an usher in a Little Rock movie theater and who claimed her family were Baptists, had been committed to the House of Good Shepherd in Hot Springs until her nineteenth birthday. Judge Joe Asher of the Pulaski County juvenile court made the committal on July 16, 1914, when her probation officer, Miss Edith Chambers, deemed Sadie as "incorrigible." Sadie's parents, Ben and Lillian Allison of 309 East Third Street in Little Rock, gave their consent, for they were both deaf mutes with a house full of children.[82] Apparently, Sadie ran away from the House of Good Shepherd in November 1914, four months after her committal, and she had been in hiding out in Hot Springs. Sadie heard William Black lecture in January and talked to him afterward at the home of the Reverend Charles N. DeWit, pastor of Park Place Baptist Church, where she asked Black to help her get away from Hot Springs. Sadie accompanied Black on the Little Rock train, and he visited her parents' home. Black traced a kinship connection with Sadie's father, claiming to be a cousin with some relatives in common in Tennessee. Childless, with a wife back in Ohio whom he had married just the previous Christmas, Black told Sadie's parents that he wished to adopt their daughter. Mrs. Allison said he wrote in pencil that he was a man of some wealth and that he would make Sadie his heir. Black indicated that he was a Baptist preacher and made no mention of being an anti-Catholic lecturer. Sadie and her parents agreed to the adoption. On January 29, 1915, the whole group appeared before Judge Asher, the same judge who had remanded her to the House of Good Shepherd six months before. The judge drew up the certificate that made the adoption legal, with Sadie's name being changed to Sadie Pauline Black. The certificate filed in Pulaski County probate court specified that Sadie Black would be entitled to the same inheritance as if she were the natural heir of William Black.[83]

Sadie, described by the *Arkansas Gazette* as "decidedly pretty" with bright auburn hair, accompanied Black on his lecture circuit. They travelled to Morrilton, staying in the Speer Hotel, to Benton (the LaGrange Hotel), and then Hope (the Barlow Hotel), where Black lectured on Monday evening, February 1. Black had added to his standard lectures by producing Sadie on stage as an example of a young girl who had escaped from the convent prison. By this time they were joined by Clarence F. Hall, who worked with Black as a business manager and bodyguard.

Hall was a US Army veteran from Minnesota who had until the previous November worked for the Twin City Streetcar Company before he packed his .38 Colt automatic pistol to travel with Black. On Tuesday morning, February 2, the group departed Arkansas, leaving Billy Parker behind in Hope, for three days of scheduled lectures in Marshall, in northeastern Texas.[84] Here is where the story gets interesting.

William Black lectured Tuesday evening at the Harrison County courthouse in Marshall with a talk entitled "Effects of the Confessional Box." Just before six o'clock the next evening, as Black, Hall, and Sadie returned from a walk, four local Knights of Columbus members arrived at Black's corner room in the Marshall Hotel. The men had attended Black's lecture the night before and were incensed at statements he had made suggesting that their mothers "were open to carnal intercourse with the priest who heard their confessions." They also disputed the bogus oath that Black had printed on the backside of his circulars, as in Little Rock, and on which Black announced a planned lecture.[85]

One of the Catholic men, John Rogers, a building contractor described as a big man wearing a derby hat, approached Black, pointed his finger in Black's face, and told him that he would not be lecturing that night and that the group should leave town. Black responded that he indeed would deliver his lecture that evening, and he reached for the pistol in his hip pocket. Rogers, who was unarmed, caught Black's right arm. Several shots were fired, and the room filled with smoke. When the air cleared, Black was dead and Rogers was mortally wounded, dying there in the room a few minutes later. Rogers had built the very hotel in which he died. Black's bodyguard, Clarence Hall, had shot Rogers twice through the head with his .38 Colt semi-automatic pistol. One of the other Catholic men, John Copeland, a bank teller, shot Black through the heart. Then Hall shot Copeland in the shoulder and abdomen, causing grievous wounds that he managed to survive. Both sides blamed the other for starting the shooting. Sadie, who had been standing right next to Black when he was shot, ran out of the room shouting that they had killed her father and called out for a physician. The bodies were taken to the same undertaker, and Copeland was hauled off to a hospital. Hall and one of the other Catholic men, George Ryan, a lawyer, were arrested and held overnight in the Marshall jail.[86]

Black had reason to be afraid. When Monsignor Tobin had interviewed Black in the Marion Hotel in Little Rock, he noted that Black feared for his life and kept a pistol lying on the desk in his room. Clarence Hall testified that both he and Black customarily travelled armed for self-protection. In fact, in his lecture just the night before his death, Black had claimed that he had been shot at five times and stabbed once and that he expected to die "in the cause." Billy Parker later told the folks in Marshall that he had been shot six times.[87]

Having stayed behind in Hope with the plan of meeting up with Black in Texarkana later in the week, Billy Parker arrived in Marshall on Thursday, along with the mayor of Hope, F. B. Bowden. They tended to Sadie and made plans for the disposition of Black's body, along with the Marshall branch of the anti-Catholic Knights of Luther, who paid the undertaker's bill. William Lloyd Clark, the anti-Catholic lecturer who stirred things up in southwestern Arkansas in 1912, set out for Marshall from his home in Illinois as soon as he heard the news, and on Friday Marvin Brown, editor of the *Menace,* arrived to report from the scene.[88] Meanwhile, Black's body was shipped by train back home to Bellaire, Ohio, and a funeral mass was said for John Rogers.

On Thursday afternoon the examination trial began under Justice of the Peace Frank Young. Every seat was taken in the courtroom, with every person in the crowd first being searched for weapons. There was much questioning of Sadie, especially concerning the details of her adoption, her relationship with Black, and the disposition of their hotel rooms as they were travelling. The actual certificate of adoption was produced, which had been in Black's coat pocket; the document displayed a bullet hole clear through from the same bullet that caused his death. Sadie claimed that one of the other Catholic men shot at her, but that her adoptive father had pushed himself in the way and took the shot, a second shot that struck him in the abdomen. When asked why anyone would be shooting at her, Sadie explained that she was to "sing mass" at the lecture scheduled that night. The grand jury failed to indict Clarence Hall, who killed John Rogers and shot John Copeland, but it indicted all three surviving Catholic men involved in the shooting. The presiding judge, H. T. Lyttleton, scolded the grand jury for its actions, saying that the jurors had allowed "bigotry to run away with it." The trial did not take place until October 1916 in Galveston, Texas, after Judge Lyttleton concluded the men could not get a fair trial in Marshall and ordered a change of venue. Hall returned to Texas to testify. Sadie Black was subpoenaed but could not be required to return to the state. By this time she was a student at Hedding College, a Methodist school in Abingdon, Illinois. She claimed she was suffering from a heart condition that prevented a long trip. The jury deliberated for nearly four days over the case of John Copeland, who admitted to shooting Black, and finally returned an acquittal verdict. The indictments of the two other men were expected to be dropped.[89]

After Black's engagement in Marshall, he and Billy Parker were scheduled to begin a series of six lectures, starting Thursday evening, February 4, at the courthouse on the Arkansas side of Texarkana, a town that straddles the Arkansas-Texas border. But earlier in the day that Black was killed in Marshall, a group of Texarkana Knights of Columbus (surely Father Boniface was involved) secured an injunction from the Miller County judge to close the building to this event, on the grounds that admission was to be charged. Rumors were passing through Texarkana that the Knights were trying to secure a warrant for Black's arrest upon his arrival in Texarkana on the charge of white slavery, presumably for his adoption of Sadie Allison. The mayor on the Texas side of the city, however, allowed the city hall to be used, for Billy Parker spoke there on Friday, February 5, to an overflowing crowd. Parker's subject was the Knights of Columbus. He cataloged a long list of "crimes" committed by the Catholic fraternal organization, culminating in the murder of William Black. He did express some gratification, however, saying, "We got two of their number to their one of ours."[90]

On Saturday, for Parker's second lecture, "The Crimes of the Popes," he had help. William Lloyd Clark, Clarence Hall, and Sadie Allison Black had arrived from Marshall for the lectures, with Hall and Sadie promising to return to Marshall for the convening of the grand jury in the following week. Hall, not usually a speaker at these events, took the stage to "tumultuous applause" and explained what was to happen with young Sadie. She rose to be introduced but did not speak. On Sunday afternoon Clark and Parker lectured to a packed house of men only. But for a larger meeting that evening Sadie was placed on the platform, "weeping and heartbroken," according to the *Menace*. Clark had come up with the plan to sell photographs of Sadie to raise money for her care and education. He pledged to mail the photographs from his home in

Sadie Allison Black, from the *Arkansas Gazette* (Little Rock), October 28, 1916. *Courtesy of the* Arkansas Democrat-Gazette.

Illinois postpaid at ten cents each or three for twenty-five cents.[91]

Sadie's work with anti-Catholicism appears to be short-lived. She had explained that Mrs. William Black had asked her to come live with her in Ohio, but the *Menace* reported that Billy Parker was taking Sadie back to his home in Oil City, Pennsylvania. Sadie's mother told the *Arkansas Gazette* that she wanted to get Sadie back, but it appears she was unsuccessful. After Texarkana, Sadie made an appearance back in Little Rock. The *Gazette* printed an advertisement on February 13 announcing that Billy Parker would be lecturing at Little Rock's Moose Hall on Saturday and Sunday, February 13 and 14. Parker promised to have Clarence Hall and Sadie Allison Black in tow and to explain how William Black met his death. Before leaving Arkansas the anti-Catholic professionals announced their plan for a grand automobile tour for the spring and summer starting from Milan, Illinois as soon as weather would permit, with the whole group participating—Clark, Parker, Hall, and Sadie. By 1916 Sadie was attending college in Illinois, perhaps on the income generated by her association with William Black, and by 1920 she worked as a nurse in a hospital in Chicago.[92]

While all the drama unfolded with Sadie's adoption and Black's death, the Arkansas legislators were presumably reading the newspapers as they debated the Convent Inspection Bill. In fact, it was the very next day after the shooting in Marshall that the House voted on the bill. Representative Thomas A. Wilson of Jefferson County spoke against the bill on the House floor, calling it anti-Catholic and intolerant. James R. Yerger of Chicot County deemed the bill unconstitutional. Also speaking against the bill were Thomas H. Rogers of Logan County, Phillip L. Burrow of Perry County, Robert B. Wallace [or Wollace] of Pope County, and Louis Joseph from Texarkana, the House's only Jewish member. Robert Posey, J. E. Hawkins of Columbia County, Usco A. Gentry of Hempstead County, and others championed the bill. The final vote was sixty in favor with thirty-four opposed. The diocesan newspaper suggested that support for the inspection bill was greatest among representatives from rural districts where "Catholics are few and bigotry abundant," while those opposing the bill were legislators from "the best cities and towns in the State," including Little Rock, Fort Smith, Hot Springs, Pine Bluff, Jonesboro, Texarkana, Helena, Paris, Batesville, Danville, Booneville, Stuttgart, and Morrilton. The *Guardian* noted that representatives who hailed from locations that had convents and Catholic institutions to a man, voted against the bill.[93]

After it passed the House, the bill prompted even more public discussion throughout Arkansas. The newspapers chimed in, with the *Sheridan Headlight* and *Gravette News Herald*, as expected, championing the bill, but with a number of other papers opposing it as religious bigotry, including the *Arkansas Gazette*, *Helena World*, *Fort Smith Times Record*, and the *Pine Bluff Daily Graphic*. The *Jonesboro Evening Sun* called the bill a disgrace to the state and suggested such legislation emanated from ignorance of the Catholic Church and the good accomplished by its institutions. "It's an even bet," the paper said, "that no member who has ever been sick in a Catholic hospital voted for the bill. . . . Jonesboro and Craighead County boast of its Catholic hospital, its convent and organization of Benedictine Sisters, its kind-hearted priest, who is a product of this county and a man respected and loved by both Catholic and non-Catholic." The Reverend Hay Watson Smith, pastor of Second Presbyterian Church at Fourth and State Streets in Little Rock, from the pulpit urged his congregation not to believe the falsehoods spread by anti-Catholics. The Reverend Doctor Adolphe H. Poppe of Little Rock's German Lutheran Congregation specifically repudiated the so-called Knights of Luther as having no connection to his church body.[94] As the House bill went to the Senate for consideration, a group of thirteen prominent Protestants in Pine Bluff, including a circuit judge, the county judge, and a physician, sent a written petition to their senator Thomas White, asking him to vote against this "vicious un-American measure." They argued that the Sisters of Charity convent in Pine Bluff was beyond reproach and such a bill resulted from ignorance rather than any real need. The *Menace* responded that if nuns of Pine Bluff were as virtuous as said, then they had nothing to fear from inspection. The paper concluded, "Thirteen apologists of Pine Bluff are baying at the moon."[95]

On Tuesday, March 2, the Senate took up the Convent Inspection Bill, allotting an hour for debate, thirty minutes for each side, before the vote. Senator George F. Jones of Little Rock first called for a postponement for an amendment to exempt Pulaski County from the bill, a motion that was quickly voted down. Jones launched into an assault on the bill, calling it vicious, malicious, drastic, and unconstitutional. Senator Clyde Going from the Twenty-ninth District (Poinsett, Jackson, and Mississippi Counties) spoke the remainder of the allotted time, arguing a constitutional point that the bill interfered with personal and religious freedoms. Speaking for the bill, Senator J.O.A. Bush, of Hempstead and Nevada Counties, and Senator B. H. Greathouse, of Washington County, argued that the bill was the best way to quell suspicion against Catholic institutions by allowing them to demonstrate their innocence. When the vote was taken, supporters of the bill won twenty-two to eight. Despite the *Southern Guardian*'s suggestion that Governor Hays veto the legislation, he signed it on March 11. It became Arkansas Act 130.[96] Arkansas was the first state in the United States to enact a convent inspection law. The Georgia legislature passed a similar bill a few weeks after Arkansas. Convent inspection bills failed in 1915 in Minnesota, Missouri, Texas, North Dakota, Iowa, Colorado, and Oregon.[97]

In early May, the first convent inspection took place under the new law. In the western Arkansas town of Mena, a small congregation of the Sisters of Mercy had operated a school, the St. Joseph Academy, for a couple of decades. Edward J. Doyle, an anti-Catholic editor of Mena's *Dixie Press* and reported to be a member of the Knights of Luther, was the first name of twenty on a petition calling for the convent's inspection. Polk County sheriff H. W. Finger dutifully conducted an official inspection, accompanied by Dr. G. P. Dunman, the county health officer. The sheriff indicated that it was his first time ever to set foot in a convent, and he arrived with apologies to the sisters. After touring every nook and cranny of the facility, he reported that all was in order. In fact, he was effusive in complementing the nuns, especially Sisters Catherine and Loretta, for their cordial cooperation. He even stated his intention to return on a social call accompanied by his wife. The *Southern Guardian*, as one might expect, crowed that the inspection provided a full vindication. Even the *Dixie Press* conceded that the sheriff found nothing amiss and trotted out the argument that inspection served a positive good because it removed suspicion. The *Menace* was less generous, saying that the inspection would not go far in allaying suspicion, for "Papal preserves in Arkansas have had time to clean up." The *Baptist Advance* decried the inspection, saying Sheriff Finger gave the convent too much advance notice: "Too much time, brother, too much time." He had received his petition on a Saturday and waited until Tuesday afternoon to inspect. [98] The *Menace* noted that Subiaco Abbey had not yet been inspected, and the paper expressed hope that Father Boniface would have his hand called in his threat to defy inspection. Later in 1915, in November, Abbot Ignatius of Subiaco wrote J. B. Cook, sheriff of Logan County, inviting him to make his inspection under the "unjust and unconstitutional Posey Act." He recognized it was his duty to permit the inspection, the abbot said, but he did so under protest. Sheriff Cook made his inspection on December 5, looking through the monks' rooms, the kitchen, the cellar, the student section, and every corner of the building. He found nothing of concern.[99]

Anti-Catholicism monopolized public attention and bore legislative fruit in Arkansas through a combination of ignorance, sexual paranoia, sincere piety, and con-artistry. The fervor of prejudice against Catholics in Arkansas and nationwide probably peaked in 1915, as fears of the sexuality of priests and nuns combined with the triumph of statewide prohibition and the association of Catholics with liquor. The editors of Little Rock's *Baptist Advance* combined the two themes in their criticism of the first inspection at Mena. Sheriff Finger, they argued, had given the Sisters of Mercy enough time to hide their liquor before he inspected. After convent inspection became law and did not produce any cases of sexual slavery, the energy in anti-Catholicism shifted to the next ogre to slay: alcohol.

CHAPTER 3

Liquor and War, 1915–1919

WHILE IMAGES OF sexually depraved priests abusing nuns and Catholic laywomen energized anti-Catholic prejudice in Arkansas, the legislative victory of 1915 and the resulting inspection took some of the wind out of the sails of the movement. In general, anti-Catholic sentiments lessoned in the United States in the latter part of the decade. In Arkansas, prejudice against Catholics surfaced again in the campaign to ban alcohol and through anti-German paranoia when the United States went to war in 1917. As Catholics tried hard to demonstrate their loyalty by providing chaplaincy and other services to troops, the local training base, Camp Pike in North Little Rock, became an arena of competition between Baptists and the Roman Catholic Church.

Anti-Catholicism was at its height in Arkansas, and perhaps in American history, in the spring of 1915. The *Menace*'s subscriptions peaked in April at just over one and a half million. To put this number in some perspective, the *New York Times* had just more than a quarter of a million subscribers in 1915.[1] The *Menace* was clearly a phenomenon. Depending on one's perspective, the newspaper was the darling or the great Satan of the anti-Catholic movement. The other anti-Catholic papers were imitators of the *Menace* and took much of their content from the larger weekly. The *Menace* by 1915 was the largest employer in Aurora, Missouri, with a staff of 135. The sheer quantity of paper coming in and newsprint shipping out required special trains for delivery. The US Post Office had a substation in the *Menace* plant. The *Menace* published a list of inexpensive books in addition to the newspaper, and the office arranged schedules for anti-Catholic lecturers.[2] The paper was a huge commercial enterprise. Catholics charged that the owners, Wilbur F.

Phelps and Earl McClure, made $300,000 and $100,000, respectively, off the newspaper, and managing editor Marvin Brown scored $50,000.[3]

At the vortex of the anti-Catholic movement in the 1910s, the newspaper was constantly battling the Catholic Church, and in turn the *Menace* was on the receiving end of counterattacks by the Catholic press and in the legal system by the Knights of Columbus. The postmaster general of Canada banned the *Menace* from the mails of that country in April 1914. Catholics made similar efforts unsuccessfully to get the paper banned in the United States. These efforts just gave the *Menace* and its followers cause to complain that Catholics were trying to suppress freedom of speech and the press and provided extra publicity for the paper. Recognizing that the US Constitution protected the right to bigotry, Catholics instead used as the rationale for suppression of the *Menace* and other such papers that they printed obscene, indecent matter, which should have no protection as free speech. Rather than rule on the issue, the US postmaster general passed on the complaints about the *Menace* to the Department of Justice for prosecution, according to a section of the Penal Code that prohibited the circulation of obscene material through the mail. In February 1915, as the Convent Inspection Bill was being discussed in the Arkansas legislature, four officers of the *Menace* were indicted in federal court in Joplin, Missouri, on several counts of sending "obscene, lewd, lascivious, filthy indecent matter" through the mail. The newspaper was no stranger to the courtroom; its publishers were in and out of court for some case almost every year. In 1914 a priest from Wheeling, West Virginia, Father F. P. Rossman, brought charges against the *Menace* for libel because of an article that falsely accused him of licentious behavior. A jury in a federal court sided with the plaintiff, requiring that the *Menace* pay him $1,500. Another case involved a candidate for county sheriff in Missouri who sued the *Menace,* claiming that its slander had cost him the election. This case was settled out of court.[4]

The obscenity case finally came before the federal court in Joplin in January 1916. The evidence presented largely consisted of newsprint and book publications collected by the Knights of Columbus. Ultimately, the jury sided with the *Menace*, accepting the argument that the material in question was already circulated by mail in many sources. Moreover, suppressing this information, however objectionable it might be, threatened First Amendment rights. As one might expect, the *Menace* editors crowed about the vindication, passing it off as a victory for the US Constitution as well as the truth.[5] Besides litigation, a couple of US representatives from New York and Boston, respectively, brothers Fitzgerald and James A. Gallivan introduced two bills in the House that would exclude from the mail publications devoted to maligning of religious organizations and societies. The bills never got out of committee.[6]

Catholics fought back in other ways. At its national convention in August 1914, the Knights of Columbus created the Commission on Religious Prejudices, which had its first meeting in January 1915. The commission planned an agenda that would involve an investigation of the cause and state of anti-Catholic prejudice, a propaganda campaign to correct the misinformation, and support for governmental efforts to prosecute or ban "bigoted publications" from the mails.[7] When the commission produced it first report in August 1915, it provided a list of some three dozen anti-Catholic newspapers, including J. A. Scarboro's *Liberator* and A. C. Veach's *Globe*. The commission suggested that the anti-Catholic agitators could be divided in three groups: those who failed to understand other beliefs than their own or who failed to appreciate constitutional rights of religious freedom; those who wanted to destroy not only Catholicism but all religions and government too; and those who professed principled motives but were really out to make money off of prejudice. In other words, the commission said there are bigots, anarchists, and shysters. The report described the anti-Catholic societies, such as the Guardians of Liberty and Knights of Luther, noting that Lutherans had repeatedly disclaimed any connection with the later organization and condemned its aims and methods. The report recommended a program of lectures, press activity, and patriotic endeavors to educate the American people about the true nature and aims of the Catholic Church. One tool in this campaign that the commission gave special mention was the weekly paper, *Our Sunday Visitor*.[8]

Our Sunday Visitor, the most popular publication in American Catholicism, was specifically founded to combat anti-Catholicism by an enterprising priest in Huntingdon, Indiana, Father John Francis Noll. Noll had purchased a state-of-the-art print shop. In 1912, he reprinted a few pages from the *Menace* to send to priests asking if they would support a national paper to counter this sort of anti-Catholic propaganda. The first issue of *Our Sunday Visitor* rolled off the press on May 5. The paper from its beginning aimed to provide simple, wholesome reading material that would arm the faithful to refute the anti-Catholic charges. The paper was distributed to parishes weekly for families to take home after Sunday mass. Father Noll envisioned that Catholics would share the *Our Sunday Visitor* with their non-Catholic friends and neighbors. He boasted in 1914 that the paper reached fifty thousand readers of the *Menace* and other bigots. Father Noll battled the anti-Catholics in other ways. He wrote a letter to bishops in the United States recommending that they send a representative to the lecture of any professed ex-priest or ex-nun who would stand up and ask where the priest was ordained and to what religious order he or she belonged, the kind of questions that Prior Augustine Stocker asked of William Black in Little Rock in January 1915. Noll gathered information about more than a hundred anti-Catholic agitators and published it in a booklet entitled *Defamers of the Church: Their Character*. He also distributed a poster listing the stock claims of anti-Catholic lecturers, offering a thousand-dollar reward to anyone who could prove any of the charges true. He was never required to pay. Father Noll became nationally known through his work. In 1925 he was appointed as bishop of Fort Wayne, Indiana.[9]

Perhaps the counter efforts were successful, for it appears the intensity of anti-Catholic activity began to decline in 1915. Subscriptions to the *Menace* provide a good barometer of the levels of anti-Catholic feeling nationwide, and they dropped after April 1915. Once the pattern of decline began, the paper stopped publishing the subscription numbers on the front page.[10] The *Menace* claimed that at 4:00 a.m. one morning in early August 1916 someone tried to blow up the press room, but the three explosions and a fire failed to stop even that week's issue. The damages totaled around a thousand dollars.[11] Like the *Menace*, the *Liberator* had troubles in 1915. Out of money, Joseph Scarboro stopped publishing the paper some time that year and moved back to his native Georgia. He later said he lost every dollar he had "fighting Romanism."[12] Moving past the convent inspection issue in 1915, the anti-Catholic movement attached itself to other issues. One of these issues was the demon rum.

The same Arkansas General Assembly that passed the Convent Inspection Act also voted in statewide prohibition. The liquor issue in Arkansas and nationally had been brewing for years and had many sources besides antipathy to Roman Catholicism. In fact, the enacting of a prohibition law in 1915 was almost anti-climactic in the sense that most of the state was already dry. Since an 1879 law had mandated local option on the sale of alcohol, each township and incorporated town had voted every two years to determine whether the locality would be dry or wet. By 1906, fifty-four of Arkansas's seventy-five counties had gone completely dry, a higher proportion than the nation as a whole, which was just over half of the counties. In February of that year prohibition activist Carry Nation had come to Arkansas and declared Governor Jeff Davis the worst governor in the Union. Davis had been expelled from Little Rock's Second Baptist Church in May 1902 on the charges of public drunkenness and gambling. Ms. Nation was arrested in Hot Springs when she entered a bar on Central Avenue and lectured the customers. She evidently liked the state, for two years later she retired to a farm just outside Eureka Springs, where she died in 1911.[13]

Arkansas's Methodist and Baptist churches exercised leadership on the liquor issue, and it was one of the few issues on which Southern and Missionary Baptists marched to the same tune. The cause was making great progress, with seven additional counties going dry in 1910 and only twelve left wet.[14] The Southern Baptists organized actions against newspapers, businesses, and political candidates in Arkansas who failed to oppose saloons. Local congregations exercised discipline against members known to use intoxicating beverages or frequent saloons. Between a thousand and fifteen hundred Southern Baptists were excommunicated in Arkansas congregations in the 1910s for offenses such as drinking, smoking, dancing, or gambling. The Arkansas Baptist Convention had a standing Temperance Committee. In 1912 the convention sent one of its members, the Reverend E.J.A. McKinney, editor of the *Baptist Advance*, to Washington, D.C., to lobby Congress for the Sheppard-Kenyon bill, a measure that aimed to restrict shipment of liquor into areas that had been voted dry.[15] The Missionary Baptist State Association had a standing Prohibition Committee since the first association in 1902. Throughout the first decade of the century Missionary Baptists were preaching and editorializing for prohibition in Arkansas. For Ben Bogard it was pretty simple: "The man who lines up with the whisky side is on the side of the devil and should be dealt with as an enemy of righteousness." In March 1912, Bogard went on a lecture tour of northern Arkansas speaking for prohibition in Mountain Home, Cotter, Yellville, Melbourne, Harrison, and Berryville.[16]

By 1912, the anti-liquor forces in Arkansas were turning their efforts away from local option to statewide prohibition. In the March Democratic primary, the dry forces aligned behind incumbent governor George Donaghey, who favored statewide prohibition, over his challenger US representative Joe T. Robinson, who supported keeping the local option. When Robinson won the primary, the anti-liquor activists then used a newly approved local initiative process to gather signatures and get a prohibition measure on the ballot for the fall 1912 election. Also on the ballot was a disfranchisement measure that proposed a grandfather clause for the state constitution, which would effectively disfranchise remaining African American voters while leaving illiterate white voters alone. The grandfather clause initiative may have motivated a larger-than-normal turnout by African American voters, and in the September election both measures were soundly defeated in counties with large black populations. The measures failed overall as well.[17]

The prohibitionists then turned their attention to the state legislature, which convened in January 1913. Senator L. Clyde Going of Poinsett County introduced a bill, drafted for him by the Arkansas chapter of the Anti-Saloon League, that would require a majority of adult white residents in any locality to sign a petition in order for a liquor license to be granted there. When passed, the Going law added women to the petition process, showing a recognition that many women opposed drink. It forbade black Arkansans from signing the petition, showing the perception that African Americans favored alcohol. Immediately the liquor forces claimed that the law was unconstitutional and began to collect signatures for a referendum. Southern Baptists cheered later in 1913 when they said the state attorney general, William Moose, gave an opinion about the constitutionality of the law and ruled that "Italians and others than the white race are not eligible to sign petitions for saloons any more than are negroes." This understanding appears to be Baptist wishful thinking that Italians would not be classified as white, rather than Moose's actual opinion about the law. Nonetheless, under the Going law several additional Arkansas counties became dry in 1914.[18] Thus when the Arkansas General Assembly of 1915 convened, it was more of a small step than a major leap to enact statewide prohibition, as the large majority of representatives and senators hailed from dry counties.

In the debate that took place between 1911 and 1915, there was some identification of Catholicism with liquor. The *Southern Guardian*, which spoke for the diocese, took a stand against the prohibition initiative in 1912. An editorial by Subiaco's Prior Augustine advocated curbing the abuse of alcohol, rather than banning its use. Another by Father J. M. Lucey of Pine Bluff contended that use of alcohol should be a private matter, while he admitted that he personally was a teetotaler and planned to vote for the initiative.[19] During the legislative debates in 1913 and 1915, the Catholic paper had much to say about the convent inspection bills but generally kept silent about the Going bill and the prohibition bills. On the other hand, anti-Catholics linked the liquor issue with Roman Catholicism. As one might expect, the Baptists led the charge against drink. The Reverend Allen Hill Autry had asserted that Catholics lined up with the liquor interests in all the Baptist battles against the saloons. He asserted that two-thirds of the retail liquor dealers in the United States were Catholics and that much of the liquor profit supported the Roman Catholic Church. Catholics exceeded other religious groups in inebriation, Autry said, and Catholic intemperance led to swearing, gambling, adultery, and other forms of vice.[20] The *Baptist Advance* ran an article by E. P. Alldredge, pastor of Little Rock's Immanuel Baptist Church, on February 5, 1914, entitled "The Catholic Church and Whisky." Alldredge suggested that if one looked at the names on the petitions signed to allow saloons in the Little Rock area under the Going law, one would find a large number of communicants in the Catholic churches. The paper expressed its pride that a Baptist governor, George W. Hays, signed the prohibition bill into law in 1915.[21] Similarly, the Missionary Baptist paper editorialized in November 1914 that one could not fight rum without fighting Rome.[22] Herb Lewis was less restrained in his language in a December 1913 editorial: "Rum and Romanism always go hand in hand. With the Protestant churches and the moral elements fighting to rid this country of the curse of liquor, we find Rome allied with the booze gang, against prohibition." Lewis also asserted that the Roman Catholic Church controlled much of the liquor traffic in the United States. He expressed dismay that in his own northwestern Arkansas in the summer of 1912, evidently Tontitown, a bunch of Catholics held a picnic "where dancing and all sorts of sports filled the program . . . and in all probability the 'beer garden' was wide open, too." Likewise, the *Liberator* linked liquor with Catholicism, saying that "even Arkansas is contaminated with Romanism, Rum, and Rottenness."[23]

There was indeed some correlation, if not a conclusive relationship, between anti-Catholic and anti-liquor legislation in the 1915 Arkansas General Assembly. A majority of the representatives who voted against prohibition, fifteen of twenty-three, also voted against the Convent Inspection Bill. These fifteen were primarily from the more urban counties (Pulaski, Jefferson, Garland, Sebastian, Miller) and Arkansas River Valley counties (Logan, Franklin), which had the greatest Catholic population.[24]

The battle was not entirely over. After the Prohibition Act went into effect on January 1, 1916, and the remaining saloons closed their doors, the "wets" immediately began a campaign for an initiated act to overturn prohibition and return to the local option. This measure got on the ballot for the November 7, 1916, general election. The Baptist press lobbied against the proposed act throughout the fall but seemed more concerned that votes of African Americans, rather than Catholics, would tilt the balance to the wet side. The paper rejoiced when the act was voted down in November by fifty thousand votes, a two-to-one margin, noting that even African American voters were against it. Herb Lewis railed against an unnamed staff member of the *Guardian* who was working on behalf of the initiated act, proving that "Rum and Rome are inseparable."[25]

The general assembly that convened in January 1917 would make prohibition ironclad in Arkansas. On January 8, the US Supreme Court upheld the constitutionality of the Webb-Kenyon Act of 1913, the federal law making it a crime to transport alcohol into an area that had been voted dry. Catholics feared that the Webb-Kenyon Act might stop the shipment of wine into Arkansas for sacramental use. Once the general assembly convened, legislators immediately began debate on a proposed "bone-dry" bill to outlaw the transportation of alcohol into Arkansas. On the evening of January 24, Southern Baptist governor Charles H. Brough signed the bone-dry bill into law at a banquet at the Marion Hotel in Little Rock, where he was addressing the state chamber of commerce. The businessmen responded by singing "How Dry I Am." The law did make two exceptions, allowing the shipment of communion wine to clergy and alcohol to physicians and druggists for medicinal use.[26] One legislator, whom the *Guardian* called "a notorious bigot," tried to get the exception for communion wine removed but failed to get a hearing. The editor of the *Baptist Advance* said he had no desire to ban wine used in church rites, although he did want to go after "the beer gardens and wine-fests of Catholics." Herb Lewis was less generous. He seemed to have no objection to the medicinal exception, but he groused about the exception to allow priests to receive shipments of wine, for "hundreds of Romanist bachelor 'fathers' have been drunker than boiled owls—and it may be absolutely necessary for these special-privileged keepers of Roman dens and dungeons to have a large supply of booze on hand for doing hocus-pocus and holy-water acts." Lewis thought that if Protestants could use grape juice in their communion rites, Catholics could do so as well. The bone-dry law, Lewis said, was a missed opportunity.[27] Later in 1917 in neighboring Oklahoma, the state attorney general issued an opinion that Oklahoma's bone-dry law made the use of wine even for sacramental purposes unlawful. A group of Roman Catholic priests challenged the opinion and won in an Oklahoma court. From Gravette, about ten miles east of the Oklahoma line, Herb Lewis opined his disgust at the decision, saying, "Boozers, whether bachelor priests or Roman bartenders, who insist on violating our laws in the name of 'religion' should be sent to prison—or back to the Pope to stay."[28]

The last step for the anti-liquor forces was the enactment of nationwide prohibition. While the Roman Catholic Church on a national level took a stance against prohibition, Catholics in Arkansas seem to have acquiesced to the reality by 1919. The Arkansas General Assembly ratified the Eighteenth Amendment on January 15, 1919, with very little fuss. The diocese's weekly paper, after mid-1915 simply titled the *Guardian*, made no mention of prohibition in the issue before or after the ratification of the amendment. The success of prohibition, like the enactment of convent inspection legislation, took away some of the fuel from the anti-Catholic movement. As the battle between wet and dry forces was raging in the 1910s, Protestants had manned the barricades on the one side and Roman Catholics generally on the other. But after the state and nation became dry, the focus turned in the 1920s to enforcement. Bootleggers and moonshiners became the target, and alcohol became less associated with Catholicism.

As the liquor issue wound down as the decade wore on, the Great War was escalating as the dominating public concern. Here too there were religious implications. When war broke out in Europe in August 1914, President Woodrow Wilson's administration staked out a position of neutrality for the United States. Wilson himself and many of his southern and Protestant supporters had sympathetic leanings toward Great Britain. Besides sharing a common Anglo-Saxon political and cultural worldview, the United States had closer economic ties with Britain and the Allies than with Germany and the Central Powers. The British Navy prevented transatlantic trade with Germany while American companies freely sold arms and munitions to the Allies. Britain and France borrowed heavily from American banks, which only further eroded the spirit of neutrality. Some Americans, led by former president Theodore Roosevelt, went further and advocated "preparedness," fully expecting that the United States would eventually enter the war on the side of the Allies and should prepare by enlarging and better training the country's military forces.

On the other side were many Roman Catholics in 1914. People of German and Irish descent dominated the Catholic hierarchy in the United States. Many Catholics from German backgrounds were openly pro-Germany, while Irish Americans were definitely anti-British, if not always pro-German. Of all immigrant communities in the United States, Germans were probably the most successful and established. More than eight million Americans at the 1910 census had been born in Germany or had at least one parent born there. German Americans had several strong organizations to promote their interests, including the German-American Alliance and a specifically Catholic organization called the Central Verein (Union). Both of these organizations openly supported Germany during the early years of the war.[29]

Catholics in Arkansas mirrored the positions staked out nationally regarding the war. In the fall of 1914 an editorial in the *Southern Guardian* called for an embargo of arms to all belligerents, meaning, of course, to the Allies. The diocesan paper would repeat this call for "true" neutrality and arms embargoes in later issues.[30] The paper printed a defense of the German position on the beginning of the war written by Roger Weems, a Conway college student who had spent the summer of 1914 in Germany as diplomatic failures nudged Europe step by step into war. Weems charged that American newspapers were prejudiced against the Germans and had presented a propagandistic account of the war's origins to the American public.[31] Similarly, the Arkansas Deutsche-Römisch-Katholischen Staatsverband (German Roman Catholic State

Association) held its annual meeting a few weeks after the beginning of the war at Subiaco and urged members to enter a united protest against the anti-German bias of the American press. The delegates passed a resolution calling for a generous offering to be collected to reflect the affection for their land of birth and to be used to mitigate distress brought about by the war. In 1915 the Staatsverband meeting at the Church of St. Boniface in Perry County called for the government to protest British attacks on US-German trade and for an embargo of trade with Britain if these threats on legal commerce continued. The Staatsverband, meeting in 1916 on Columbus Day at St. Edward's Catholic Church in Little Rock, in conjunction with the state Knights of Columbus, repeated this call and specifically advocated an embargo on arms and munitions to Great Britain.[32]

Some Arkansans viewed this posturing by Catholics as disloyal. Herb Lewis blasted the "Romanist Nits of Columbo, and German Catholic hyphenates of Arkansas" (notice his use of "Nits," the common term meaning "lice") for meeting on Columbus Day to direct the government in its foreign policy. For Lewis, the "holiday" for Columbus, a man who was no more than a pirate and who did not discover America, was simply a "Romish event which Rome tries to palm off as an 'American' day." Lewis argued that the Staatsverband had overstepped its bounds to meet "as a bunch of Germans, foreigners under the thumb of the pope, and venture to pass resolutions, dictating to this American Government what it should do. The English, French, or Russians in America have not attempted any such underhanded dictation." Lewis told the German Catholics of Arkansas that if they claimed to be citizens of America, they should act the part.[33]

Lewis and other Protestants in Arkansas criticized papal efforts to mediate between the warring sides in Europe. Pope Pius X had died on August 20, 1914, just two weeks after German troops had crossed into Belgium. His successor, Pope Benedict XV, from the beginning of his papacy tried to influence war and peace. The *Baptist Advance* had editorialized in December 1914 against the pope's failed attempt to broker a Christmas truce, saying, "Who has been more responsible for wars than the pope or popes of Rome?" Herb Lewis was characteristically less restrained in his condemnation of the pope's meddling in political affairs, referring to Pope Benedict XV, who was born Giacomo Paolo

The 1915 meeting of the Deutsche-Römisch-Katholischen Staatsverband, at St. Boniface Church, New Dixie. *Courtesy of Timothy G. Nutt.*

Giovanni Battista della Chiesa, as Pope Cheese, Daddy Chiese on the Tiber, Janitor Chieze of the Vatican, or Dago Benedict, among other names. He was only slightly less respectful than he had been in referring to Pope Pius X as "the 'howly father' Pope Pius, Joe Sarto, dago imposter."[34]

The American entry in the war on the side of the Allies in 1917 had a complex impact on anti-Catholicism in Arkansas and the nation. Diplomatic relations between the United States and Germany fell apart in 1917 when Germany resumed unrestricted submarine warfare and news broke about the interception of the Zimmermann telegram. In this famous diplomatic note, the German foreign minister, Arthur Zimmermann, proposed that if the United States entered the war against Germany, Mexico should attack across the Rio Grande to retake its lost territories of Texas, New Mexico, and Arizona. For anti-Catholics, especially Herb Lewis, Mexico embodied all the evils of a Catholic country controlled by Rome, whose clergy kept the people in poverty and ignorance. Lewis said Mexico's plight was "400 years of slavery to the Howley Father."[35] Now the intrigues of this decadent Roman Catholic government, Lewis believed, threatened to pull the United States into the larger conflict. President Wilson took his call for war to Congress, and on April 6, 1917, the United States officially entered the Great War on the side of the Allied Powers.

The German-Catholic position promoting neutrality and embargo

of arms to the Allies ended immediately with the US entry into war. Bishop John Morris preached about patriotism and loyalty to civil authorities in his Easter sermon, the Sunday following entry into the war. The *Guardian* was replete with patriotic material in the weeks following. By May an American flag was posted on the editorial page weekly.[36] The diocese sold land around St. Joseph's Orphanage in North Little Rock to the federal government for the creation of Camp Pike, where troops were trained for the war. Bishop Morris encouraged Catholics to buy Liberty Bonds. He allowed priests to serve as "Four Minute Men," whereby speakers would give four-minute addresses in public venues urging individuals to buy liberty bonds.[37] The bishop presided over a "military mass" at St. Andrews Cathedral featuring a soldiers' choir, followed by a parade with mounted police, an infantry band, and Knights of Columbus flag bearers, to a fund-raising banquet with more than five hundred guests. The Knights of Columbus erected a building at Camp Pike for spiritual and recreational activities for the troops, including mass on Sunday mornings at 8:00 and 9:30.[38] The students of Subiaco Academy formed a khaki-clad cadet corps to drill, complete with a band whose favorite marching tune was "Over There." On at least one occasion the German-speaking Subiaco cadets elicited panic when they marched past a local farmer who was sure that the Germans had arrived in Arkansas.[39]

There is some evidence that the common war effort muted

Subiaco cadets. *Courtesy of Archives of Subiaco Abbey.*

anti-Catholic feelings as all Americans were called on to serve their country. The Knights of Columbus Commission disbanded in 1917, indicating that the war had ended the sharp prejudice against Catholics so evident before entry into the war. In Mena, formerly a hotbed of anti-Catholicism, the first war death was a Roman Catholic lad, Frank Fried. During his funeral, every store in Mena closed, and the whole community reportedly turned out to pay tribute to the first local boy to die in service to his country. City and county officials were honorary pallbearers at the funeral mass presided over by Father A. P. Gallagher.[40]

Yet in other ways the war brought new prejudices against Catholics, particularly those whose native language was German. A wave of anti-German hysteria swept the country by the summer of 1917. Rumors flourished about spying and sabotage by German Americans. Wilson's attorney general, Thomas Gregory, pushed the Espionage Act through Congress to suppress dissent and antiwar activities. He supported the creation of an organization, the American Protective League, to serve as a network of amateur volunteer detectives to investigate individuals suspected of disloyalty. Anyone born in Germany or who spoke German was a natural candidate for their scrutiny. Kraut was renamed liberty cabbage, hamburger became liberty steak, and frankfurters permanently transformed into hot dogs. Richard Wagner and Johann Sebastian Bach dropped off musical programs. The use of the German language in Lutheran and Catholic parochial schools and church services came under attack. Some states actually outlawed the teaching of German.[41]

Similarly, in Arkansas there was a generalized anti-German sentiment. Little Rock's German National Bank renamed itself the American National Bank, and Meyer's Bakery became temporarily the American Bakery. The German-American Bank and Trust of Paris, Arkansas, dropped the "German" from its name. The small community of Germania, in Saline County southwest of Little Rock, was renamed Vimy Ridge, for the battle that took place in northern France the week after the United States entered the war. Little Rock's second German-language weekly newspaper, the *Arkansas Staatszeitung*, which aimed at a German-Lutheran audience as opposed to the *Arkansas Echo*'s mainly German-Catholic readership, went out of business in August 1917. Its editor, Curtis Ackermann, an unnaturalized German, was arrested for disloyalty and disrupting enlistments. Ackermann was alleged to have offered a "powder" to a friend that would make him seem sick when appearing before the exemption board. It was said that his newspaper had been printing anti-Belgian and pro-German editorials. Ackermann was nicknamed "the Kaiser" while in the Pulaski County jail and then was shipped to Fort McPherson, Georgia, to be interned for the duration of the war.[42]

On April 13, in the week following the US entry into the war, the abbot of Subiaco received the order to dismantle the abbey's wireless apparatus. Apparently, rumors were circulating that the monks were receiving communications from the Imperial German Government. The sheriff of Logan County arrived to dismantle the set. Apparently knowing little about radio, he asked the monks: "If I were to chop it up with my axe, would that be dismantling it?" Rumors also abounded that the abbey had six or seven levels underground where monks were storing arms and ammunition in large quantities. Prior Augustine tried to remind Arkansans that he and many of the German-speaking monks at Subiaco were actually Swiss German in origin, and that the abbey itself was an offspring of St. Meinrad Abbey in Indiana, which was a daughter abbey of Einsiedeln Abbey in neutral Switzerland. Apparently, there were sufficient complaints to Washington, D.C., that the postmaster general there ordered the postmaster of Memphis, Tennessee, to investigate Subiaco. He forwarded the order to the postmaster of Fort Smith who dutifully inspected every corner of the abbey in early April 1918. He liked what he saw enough that he later sent his son to the boarding school, Subiaco Academy.[43]

Individual German Americans became victims of prejudice, especially in 1918. Father Weibel, who had served parishes in Arkansas since his arrival in 1879, was arrested in Pocahontas by a plainclothes policeman merely for speaking German. In Fort Smith two German Americans were speaking German when an officer stopped them, asked if they were speaking German, and said they must speak English. One of the men said no, they were speaking French. The officer said French was acceptable, so the two men resumed their conversation in German.[44] Elsewhere the attention was not so benign. On the night of March 27, 1918, in Hartford, a small community in Sebastian County south of Fort Smith, a group of local citizens went on a rampage against several German Americans accused of disloyalty. First, they attacked Charles Jarzak, said to be a bootlegger and a former German mounted policeman, for uttering support for Germany "in vigorous terms." They whipped Jarzak and several other German American men, forced them to get on their knees, apologize, and kiss the American flag. The officers took the men to Fort Smith to be tried for violating the espionage act.[45] The next day, Frank Oberle, another German American in Jamestown, just south of Clarksville in Johnson County, refused to fly Old Glory from his storefront and would not buy war savings stamps. A group of twenty-five to thirty men severely beat Oberle. The mob threw him and his possessions in the street, ordering him to leave the town. He escaped to Clarksville, where a physician treated a five-inch gash on his head and other wounds. It is not surprising that a few weeks later that the Catholic Board of Education for Johnson County banned the teaching of German in Catholic schools and preaching in German in Catholic churches in the county.[46] The next day the pastor of Fort Smith's Evangelical Lutheran Church announced that the German language would no longer be used in the parochial school or in church services there. A Lutheran pastor in Johnson County, William Roerig, was also driven from his home in 1918 by armed men.[47]

This sort of German American prejudice mirrored developments in the country as a whole, with violent attacks reaching a climax in April 1918. The most infamous incident took place in the early morning hours of April 5 when a mob of more than two hundred men in Collinsville, Illinois, accused a German alien, Robert Prager, of spying for the German Reich. They staged a drunken ceremony in which Prager was forced to kiss the American flag and sing "The Star-Spangled Banner." Prager was then hanged.[48]

Anti-German sentiments may have in fact replaced anti-Catholic prejudice to some degree during the war. But yet some Arkansans still combined their prejudice against Catholics with this anti-German hysteria. Herb Lewis continued to rail against Pope Benedict's attempts to broker peace or curb atrocities during the war. He would "rather have a peace plan from the head of Mormons, it would be American, at least," he said. While it seems a monumental effort to conflate the interests of a Catholic pope with that of a Protestant German Kaiser, Lewis somehow managed to present the two leaders as the evil twins of anti-democratic autocracy. He repeatedly renounced the "duplicity of Kaiserism and Romanism" and "German-Papal intrigue and skullduggery," which he said were in a combined effort to "uphold autocracy and the rule of Tyrants, Monarchs, and False Gods."[49] Lewis complained that "Old Daddy Chiese condemned the bombing of German and Austrian cities but said nothing when the Kaiser's men bombed London."[50]

A particular pet peeve for Herb Lewis was an alleged favorable position for Roman Catholics in US military camps and facilities. He complained that nuns serving in the Red Cross were allowed to wear their habits and thereby "advertise popery by wearing their special sectarian superstitious garb." Lewis had a vested interest, for his oldest son, Wyric, was called into service with other boys from Benton County. They served in an Arkansas guard unit that became Company B of the 142nd Field Artillery, assembled at Fort Roots in North Little Rock in the summer of 1917 before being sent for training at Fort Beauregard, Louisiana. It galled Herb Lewis when the Protestant chaplain was replaced by a Catholic priest who spoke English with a French accent, for a unit of two thousand men of which only fifteen were Roman Catholic. In Lewis's view, this was just another attempt to proselytize Protestant boys by the "Howley Roman Humbug."[51] Wyric's unit arrived in France just a couple of months before the fight ended. His father's only wish when the war ended and armistice terms were drawn up was that "Old Pope Ben" would "keep his beak out and attend to private affairs."[52]

Similarly, Baptist leaders in central Arkansas were unhappy about the Catholic role at Camp Pike, the US army installation developed in northern Pulaski County to train troops for the war. Renamed in 1937 Camp Joseph T. Robinson for the late senator from Arkansas, the camp was built quickly in the summer and fall of 1917. Over the course of the war, Camp Pike trained more than twenty-two thousand troops bound for Europe. While the war raged in Europe, Baptists and Catholics warred with each other over spiritual access to the men at Camp Pike. With its national organizational system, the Roman Catholic Church could quickly and significantly get involved in the war effort. Even before Camp Pike was completed and receiving recruits, the *Baptist Advance* complained about the over-representation of Catholic priests among the chaplaincy in the US Army, saying that a third of army chaplains were priests when Catholics composed only a sixth of the county's population.[53] Missionary Baptist leader Ben Bogard also complained that 53 of the Army's 144 chaplains were Roman Catholic priests, when Baptists claimed only 16; Methodists, 24; and Presbyterians, 8. He believed the very practice of military chaplains, paid by the government, was a dangerous union of church and state.[54] In previous wars, chaplains served individual regiments, but in the Great War military authorities centrally planned and made policy governing chaplaincy. The Department of War dictated that only two religious organizations erect buildings on bases, the Young Man's Christian Organization (YMCA), through which Protestant organizations and even Jewish bodies would minister to soldiers, and the Knights of Columbus, which would work on behalf of Roman Catholics. Camp Pike received its first soldiers in September 1917, and by November a YMCA and a Knights of Columbus Hall had quickly been built. The Knights of Columbus Hall was dedicated on Sunday, November 4, 1917, with a crowd of four thousand people, mostly Catholics brought in by a special train from Little Rock. Governor Brough; the camp commander, Major General Samuel D. Sturgis; Bishop Morris; two Catholic chaplains; and other dignitaries gave speeches. The event ended with a rousing singing of "America." Masses were said in a chapel within the Knights of Columbus Hall on Sundays at 8:00 and 9:30.[55]

Southern Baptists jumped into service quickly as well. The Arkansas Baptist Convention paid the salary of the Reverend J. O. Johnston, who began working on October 15 as the Baptist pastor for Camp Pike. By the end of the month Johnston was working out of the YMCA Hall and already claimed 421 conversions since he began preaching. By the end of January 1918, his conversion tally had risen to more than 1,900. Johnston bragged that he had even preached to the "Negro soldier boys" on two occasions. In April he preached to an integrated crowd of 300 black and 200 white men. By the summer of 1918 he was preaching in the open air to crowds of 1,500 to 2,000.[56]

While the Southern Baptists concentrated on preaching along with passing out religious tracts, New Testaments, snacks, and magazines, Roman Catholics organized a wide array of activities for soldiers at Camp Pike. Father Louis Phaneuf, a post chaplain who arrived from New Jersey, taught a French class. The Knights of Columbus Hall sponsored boxing and wrestling events, musical sing-alongs, amateur hour contests, concerts, motion picture shows, comedians, and a Baptist preacher's worst dream—dances. Wives of the Little Rock Knights of Columbus sponsored the dances on Monday nights at the hall at Camp Pike, bringing in fifty girls from Little Rock. On other occasions the Knights brought the boys off post for dances at St. Edward's Parish Hall and the Knights of Columbus Hall on Scott Street in Little Rock. In all these cases, the Catholic wives chaperoned, and girls could only attend if they had a card of invitation.[57] By May 1918 the Knights of Columbus had expanded to a second building and had ordered a third, a prefabricated structure erected on site, which was dedicated in late September.[58]

Baptists complained about the favored position of Catholics at Camp Pike. It rankled Southern Baptists that Catholics had their own building and could work in the camp as a denomination while Baptists were required to work through the YMCA. Clearly envy was part of this equation. The editor of the *Baptist Advance* had toured the Knights of Columbus facilities at Camp Pike and pronounced them as well built and furnished and superior to those of the YMCA. The Knights halls each had rolling partitions that, when moved, revealed a functioning altar, so that the editor exclaimed that they were "practically Roman Catholic churches." Moreover, in August 1918 the Baptist camp pastor received notice that only chaplains actually employed by the military establishment would receive access to the troops. After ten months of service at Camp Pike, the Reverend Johnston, along with his secretary/song leader S. E. Kirby, became unemployed. The *Baptist Advance* encouraged readers to write their congressmen and the president to complain about this policy change. Representatives of the Northern and Southern Baptist Conventions pleaded with the third assistant secretary of war, Dr. Dean Keppel, in Washington, D.C. But Keppel stood by the position of the Department of War, which he said intended to deemphasize denominational distinctions in the camps. Editor McKinney asked if indeed denominationalism was to be stamped out, then "why give the lighted candles and priestly paraphernalia of Romanism preeminence in our camps?"[59]

At the suggestion of President Wilson and the secretaries of war and the navy, an appeal went out in the fall of 1918 for the United War Work Campaign, a bid to raise $170,500,000 for the moral welfare of soldiers, with $100 million to go to the YMCA, $30 million to the Knights of Columbus, and the rest to other groups. The goal's total amounted to roughly $1.75 for every man, woman, and child in the United States. The public was asked to give money to the common fund from which it would be divided out to the various groups. Editor McKinney of the *Baptist Advance* objected to the plan, for he said it would have Arkansans contributing $170,000 that would go to the Knights of Columbus. He said he would not give a penny to the fund if part of his donation would end up in the hand of Catholics, "with their camp dances and Catholic camp mass." Catholic leaders, on the other hand, were happy with the plan and recognized that it was coming under fire from some Protestants. The *Guardian* urged Arkansas Catholics to give generously so that Catholic donations would exceed the $30 million the Catholic War Council would receive, and thus Protestants would not be able to say their money supported Catholic work.[60]

The Missionary Baptists also complained of Catholic privileges in the camps, with Ben Bogard saying, "Why don't they use the Y.M.C.A. like the other denominations?" Bogard too opposed the common fund drive, saying Catholics only wanted "union" when money was raised. While Bogard supported the purchase of Liberty Bonds and War Thrift Stamps, he advised Missionary Baptists to avoid giving to YMCA, YWCA, Red Cross, or any of such efforts, but to save their donations for specifically Missionary Baptist missions.[61] In general, the Missionary

Baptists had nothing to do with the ministry at Camp Pike, apparently refusing to work through the YMCA in conjunction with other denominations. While the *Baptist Advance* had weekly updates of the work at Camp Pike, the Missionary Baptist newspaper, the *Baptist and Commoner*, made no mention of the camp until May 1918 when Bogard complained that nobody could preach at Camp Pike without the consent of the YMCA man. The YMCA had cooperated so nicely with the Knights of Columbus, Bogard added, that "Baptists should steer clear of the whole business."[62]

While both groups of Baptists sparred with Catholics over some of these practical matters of funding and access to troops, the Missionary Baptists took one further step and incorporated the Great War into their anti-Catholic theology. The Reverend J. A. Scarboro had used Revelation 17 as the central Bible passage linking Catholicism to the Whore of Babylon that was corrupting the Christian church. From the cotton fields of Georgia, and with four sons wearing army uniforms in 1918, Scarboro had time to ponder the meaning of events of the war and its relationship to biblical prophecy. In April 1918 he sent an article back to Arkansas for the *Baptist and Commoner*, "The Eighth Beast," that explained that Revelation 17 and 18 predicted the destruction of Catholicism in a great world war. Chapter 17 prophesized that a despotic eighth beast would arise that would rule with ten kings, and that they would "hate the whore," eat her flesh, and burn her with fire. After the destruction of Babylon, the beast and his satraps would then turn against the Lamb, Christ. But they would lose the battle, and authentic biblical Christianity would prevail. Scarboro believed that the course of the war showed that the German Kaiser was such an eighth beast bent on absolute world domination. The fiery destruction of French cathedrals by German artillery was evidence of the beast's war on the Harlot Rome. Another proof was the degree to which belligerents on all sides had totally ignored the pope's efforts to mediate the war and how Catholic citizens had yielded their first loyalty to the state, rather than to the pope. Joined with the "unspeakable Turks and Mohammedans," the German despot would slay Babylon and then be slain by Christ himself and cast into perdition. Good riddance for the Germans, Scarboro suggested.[63]

Even though the intensity of anti-Catholicism seems to have waned somewhat after 1915, the prejudice found other ways to be expressed.

Anti-Catholicism shifted from a preoccupation with priestly sexual perversions to the crusade against alcohol and paranoia in wartime about German-speakers, who in Arkansas were primarily Roman Catholics. Ironically, in 1917 and 1918 Baptist leaders in Arkansas were complaining that Catholics had too great a role in the war effort, especially with the Arkansas boys at Camp Pike. After all this service by the Catholic Church in the Great War, anti-Catholics led by the Ku Klux Klan in the 1920s would assert that Roman Catholics were not even truly Americans.

CHAPTER 4

Catholics and the Ku Klux Klan, 1921–1925

ON JULY 4, 1924, Little Rock witnessed one of the grandest parades and assemblies in its history, the Independence Day "Kommemoration" of the Ku Klux Klan. As many as thirty thousand Klansmen, Women of the Ku Klux Klan, and adolescent boys in the Junior Klan gathered for a day-long program of events. Special trains brought Klan folk from Memphis, Hot Springs, and El Dorado, and regularly scheduled trains added extra coaches to bring people from other Arkansas towns, with the railroads giving a special Klan rate. The Little Rock police closed streets and directed traffic. Many businesses put banners in store windows proclaiming "Welcome Ku Klux." The day culminated with a parade led by mounted police followed by color bearers, then Klan dignitaries in cars, mounted Klansmen on robed horses, Women of the Ku Klux Klan waving from floats and cars, a marching band, the Junior Klan marching in procession, and finally the Little Rock Klan on foot bringing up the rear. The parade began on the grounds of North Little Rock High School, went south to the Arkansas River, crossing into Little Rock on the Main Street Bridge, and then continued south on Main to Twenty-Sixth Street. There, on a forty-acre plot by the light of an enormous fiery cross, the crowd listened to speeches and watched as Klan officials "naturalized" a group of new members. The evening ended with a fireworks show.[1] It sounds like a slice of Americana, except that one had to be white, Protestant, and native born to participate. The keynote address by a national Klan lecturer from Indiana was on the subject "America for Americans."

While public expressions of anti-Catholicism had declined after

America's entry into the Great War, the Klan's rapid growth and presence in most every Arkansas town in the early 1920s brought an institutional mechanism for prejudice against Roman Catholics. Some of the same people who had been speaking out against Rome in the 1910s—Baptist preachers, fake former priests and nuns on the anti-Catholic lecture circuit—in the early 1920s were doing so on behalf of the Ku Klux Klan. The renewed anti-Catholicism of the Klan focused on the theme "One Hundred Percent Americanism," arguing that Catholics were not authentic, loyal Americans.

The new Klan had been founded in 1915 on Stone Mountain, near Atlanta, Georgia, when a former Methodist clergyman and insurance salesman, William Simmons, and a group of friends raised a burning cross in a ceremony inaugurating the Invisible Empire of the Ku Klux Klan. Their costumes and symbolism clearly hearkened back to the Reconstruction-era Ku Klux Klan. But Simmons's Klan was not purely historical. It gained inspiration from D. W. Griffiths's film about the Reconstruction Klan, *Birth of a Nation*, which had premiered earlier in the year. The film was based on Thomas Dixon's novel, *The Clansman*, which had added some whimsical touches such as the burning of a cross. Although it built upon a romanticized image of the historical Klan, the new Klan was more of a nativist organization, opening membership to Protestant native-born white males eighteen years and older. The order grew slowly until 1920, when Simmons hired two professional marketing agents, Elizabeth Tyler and Edward Young Clarke, who used a recruitment strategy reminiscent of a pyramid scheme. Professional recruiters, called Grand Goblins, worked as regional representatives who developed a network of state recruiters under them, called King Kleagles, who each had a group of Kleagles working beneath them recruiting locally. Of the $10.00 fee a new Klansman would pay at initiation, $4.00 stayed in the pocket of the local Kleagle, while $1.00 went to the King Kleagle, fifty cents to the Grand Goblin, and $2.50 to Tyler and Clarke, with the remaining $2.00 going to the Klan central treasury. Kleagles began recruiting within lodges of existing fraternal orders, and they borrowed many of the features of these organizations, such as elaborate rituals and secret handshakes. They also targeted men's groups in local Protestant churches. Membership skyrocketed in southern and mid-western states in 1920 and early 1921. Founder Simmons, along with promotional geniuses Clarke and Tyler, became wealthy almost instantly.[2]

By 1921 the Klan was well established in Texas, Oklahoma, and Louisiana, and in the summer recruiters arrived in Arkansas. A. E. Brown, a King Kleagle, and his brother L. J. Brown worked out of a room in the Marion Hotel in Little Rock and by the fall had organized Arkansas's first Klan, the Little Rock Klan No. 1. Chapters in each state would be numbered consecutively by the order of the founding. An attorney and former Republican and Bull Moose Party activist, James A. Comer, led the Little Rock chapter as Exalted Cyclops. He became the Grand Dragon of the Realm of Arkansas until his death in 1934. The Klan spread quickly in Arkansas. By December a Klan presence was evident in Prescott, Gurdon, Hot Springs, Malvern, and Russellville.[3] By mid-January 1922 the Klan had travelled up the Arkansas River Valley, with chapters in Fort Smith, Ozark, Clarksville, Morrilton, and Conway.[4]

The first big Klan rally in Arkansas took place in February 1922, just off US Highway 65 south of Little Rock, where hooded men from Little Rock, assisted by Klansmen from other chapters in central Arkansas, "naturalized" about 650 "aliens," men in street clothing ready to take their vows to enter the society. At about eight o'clock on this clear night, the men knelt before a flaming cross, kissed the American flag and the Bible, and swore their allegiance to the Klan. In April of the following year, another huge rally, preceded by a barbecue dinner, took place east of Little Rock at Galloway. An estimated ten thousand men attended to initiate a thousand new members and hear Hiram W. Evans give the keynote address. Evans was a prominent Texas Klansman who in late 1922 had wrested control from Simmons and would rule the Klan as Imperial Wizard until 1939.[5] Charles Alexander, the historian of the Klan in Arkansas, has estimated there were twenty-five thousand Klansmen in the state by the spring of 1922, although estimates are really guesses when dealing with a society that kept the names and numbers of its membership a closely guarded secret.[6] Harry Knowles, a Klan lecturer and Disciples of Christ pastor in Little Rock, estimated seventy-five thousand members in the state by mid-1922.[7] By August 1923 there were at least 135 Klan chapters in the state. Thus basically every Arkansas town, large and small, had a Klan.[8] Nationally, there were probably four million Klansmen at its peak, along with a half million women who joined the Women of the Ku Klux Klan, which opened its national headquarters in Little Rock in 1923.[9]

In understanding the 1920s Klan, one must guard against the

tendency to confuse it with the original Klan of the Reconstruction era or the Klan of the modern civil rights movement and recent years. The Reconstruction Klan had been a paramilitary political organization led by prominent ex-Confederates who tried to terrorize former slaves to keep them from leaving their plantations or registering to vote. The Klan of recent times, the 1950s and thereafter, consists of various groups in southern states that resisted the enfranchisement of African Americans and other civil rights measures such as integration of schools and public facilities. The modern Klan has used the robes, rituals, and cross-burning of the 1920s Klan but has been much less organized, with a more working-class flavor. Hollywood has introduced the public to this Klan, known for its racism and violence. In today's era of relative tolerance the modern Klan has increasingly become perceived as a hate-group on the radical fringe. The 1920s Klan, in contrast, was a highly organized national movement with chapters in all forty-eight states. Its membership was largely middle class, and local leaders were often the most prominent men in the community. Throughout the South and Midwest, the 1920s Klan was very much a mainstream movement.

While the Klan made a point to keep its membership rolls and officers secret, one can peek under their robes and masks. By a stroke of luck, an officer of the Monticello, Arkansas, Klan No. 108 failed to destroy that chapter's membership lists and minutes. These records form one of the only surviving bodies of evidence for a local Klan in the 1920s South. Monticello's Klan included the town's leading citizens. The mayor and half the city council joined the Klan, as did the county sheriff, treasurer, coroner, and assessor. The president of the agricultural college, now the University of Arkansas–Monticello, and his son were members, as were ten other male faculty and seven students. Many members were white-collar business and professional men, including thirteen ministers of the Gospel, eight physicians, five realtors, three teachers, and twenty-three merchants, while the largest occupational group was farmers, many of whom lived outside of town. The Exalted Cyclops was the pastor of Monticello's Methodist Church. There is no reason to think Monticello's membership was exceptional.[10] A Jonesboro newspaper in the summer of 1922 noted that the membership of that city's Klan No. 72 included heads of the city government and utilities, the post office, and Chamber of Commerce as well as bank presidents, department store

Hendrix College Student Klan Chapter, 1923 yearbook, *The Troubadour. Courtesy of Hendrix College Archives.*

owners, pastors of local churches, physicians, and some farmers from the surrounding countryside.[11] Hendrix College, a Methodist institution in Conway, which was perhaps the state's leading liberal arts college, had a student chapter of the Klan in 1923.

While the Reconstruction and the modern Klan movements were all about denying fundamental rights to African Americans, the 1920s Klan had a much more diverse and comprehensive agenda. It too was a racist organization, declaring white supremacy as a fundamental principle in its charter and oath. The 1920s Klan occasionally acted against African Americans who violated racial taboos or challenged the status quo. But white supremacy was firmly entrenched in the South in 1922. Other enemies appeared the greater threat: Catholics, Jews, immigrants, bootleggers, moonshiners, labor organizers, criminals, moral reprobates, and even modernists who embraced liberal theology or supported the idea of evolution.

For the most part, the Arkansas Klan espoused a nonviolent, and in some cases charitable, agenda. Part of the attraction of the Klan was surely the entertainment value to relieve the boredom of small-town life: the pageantry, opportunity to dress in costume, the camaraderie, the secret night-time meetings in the open air, the public parades and marches. The Klan's interactions with the public were largely in the pose as a benevolent institution. Throughout Arkansas in 1922 and 1923 it was common for a group of white-clad Klansmen to interrupt a Sunday church service or revival meeting, solemnly processing forward to present a Protestant pastor or evangelist with a cash donation and letter commending him for his work. The Conway, Hot Springs, and Coal Hill Klans raised money to keep the public schools running when district coffers ran dry. The Jonesboro Klan donated a hundred dollars to a family whose home was blown away in a storm.[12] Klans in Little Rock, Hot Springs, Malvern, Russellville, and Gurdon presented gifts of money to the poor at Christmas.[13] The El Dorado Klan raised money and broke ground for a Klan hospital that was never built.[14] The Klan purchased an 846-acre tract of land in Lincoln (Washington County), which it promoted as a Klan park for the public. The Fort Smith Klan donated a hundred dollars to buy free milk for poor children of the city.[15]

In addition to this philanthropic activity, the Arkansas Klans posed as adjuncts of local authorities in efforts to preserve law and order. They frequently issued rewards for criminals and bootleggers. Occasionally, local Klans resorted to vigilante violence with the assent or acquiescence of law officials. For example, an oil strike in southern Arkansas in 1920 had made boomtowns of El Dorado, Norphlet, and Smackover. The congregation of transient men in these towns brought a bevy of speak-easies, whorehouses, and gambling dens. In February 1922 the El Dorado Klan gave notice to "bootleggers, gamblers, wild women, and other undesirables" to leave town. The Klan even told property owners who rented to these lawbreakers that they were being watched and "would be taken care of."[16] Later that year in November an organized band of men, many wearing their Klan robes and hoods, attacked the dens of iniquity around Smackover. At one point the melee became a shoot-out when twenty-five of the targeted vice operators responded with gunfire. One saloon keeper was shot dead, and about a dozen individuals were whipped, then tarred and feathered. The county sheriff arrived conveniently after the fighting was over and estimated that two thousand "undesirables" had been driven away.[17] In Garland County

Little Rock Klan Plays Santa Klaus, Breaking all Records of City

The above picture shows a few of the two hundred baskets which were given the poor and needy in Little Rock on the Sunday before Christmas. The Women and the Knights of the Ku Klux Klan co-operated in making this event the greatest donation to charity ever made upon Christmas day by any fraternal organization in the history of the city.

The benevolent Little Rock Klan, from *Imperial Night Hawk* (Atlanta, GA), January 9, 1924.

near Hot Springs, moonshiners ambushed Klansmen as they were leaving a late-night meeting, killing one Klansman and wounding another.[18]

There were other assorted cases of extra-legal violence in Arkansas. In the Cooter neighborhood southeast of Crossett, two hundred Klansmen in robes blew up a dozen dipping vats to protest a recent law requiring cattle to be dipped as a protection against external parasites.[19] Klansmen in the Arkansas Ozarks responded to the strike of workers on the Missouri and North Arkansas Railroad, which began in 1921 and lasted into 1923. The Klan lynched a striker in Harrison in January 1923 and flogged two other men accused of sympathy with radical labor.[20] Most common was violence against moral offenders: moonshiners in the Ozarks whose stills they destroyed, white men who consorted with African American women, or the downright immoral.[21]

While the Klan's list of adversaries was long, some historians have suggested that anti-Catholicism was the strongest and most nationally consistent rallying point. This was especially the case after Hiram Wesley Evans became Grand Imperial Wizard in 1922. One scholar, Thomas Pegram, has suggested that antipathy toward target groups was greatest where their numbers were the smallest. The Indiana Klan, for example, was more anti-black than anti-Catholic, while the Atlanta Klan was more anti-Catholic. Large Roman Catholic populations in southern Louisiana and El Paso, for example, curbed anti-Catholicism among Klansmen there.[22]

The emerging Arkansas Klan was much influenced by Hiram Wesley Evans, a dentist from Dallas, Texas, who led the Klan there and in 1922 determined to take over the reins of power nationally. Around the time Evans spoke at the huge rally near Sweet Home, Arkansas, in April 1922, he was transferring to the Atlanta office to take the role of "Imperial Kligrapp" or national secretary over the day-to-day affairs of the Klan. Evans would use this position later in the year to nudge the Klan's founder, William Simmons, upstairs to a largely ceremonial and powerless position of "Emperor" as Evans became Imperial Wizard. Simmons was known to drink liquor, enjoy pornography, and frequent prostitutes. And a New York newspaper had just exposed the moral failings of his assistants, Mr. Clarke and Miss Tyler, by digging out the story that in 1919 Clarke, a married man, had been arrested for disorderly conduct—drunk, partially clad, and in Miss Tyler's presence. Clarke's wife sued him for divorce with the charge of desertion.[23] Evans was a man of sterner moral stuff. Arkansas's Grand Dragon, James Comer, was among a small group of Klan leaders who had gathered at Atlanta's Piedmont Hotel on the eve of the national Klonvokation in November 1922 and plotted the coup that removed Simmons and promoted Evans. Comer would be rewarded with a seat on the Klan's Imperial Koncilium, and he would become one of Evan's closest allies. Simmons recognized that Evans had staged a successful coup, and in 1923 began organizing a women's Klan organization he called the "Kamelia" as a way to reassert his role in the Klan movement. The women's organization forced a final showdown with Evans, who was planning a women's organization of his own. A statewide Klan meeting in May led by Grand Dragon James Comer endorsed Evans and denounced Simmons. Evans's organization for women, the Women of the Ku Klux Klan, was chartered in Little Rock on June 10, 1923. In January 1924 Evans made the break with Simmons official by banishing him permanently from the Klan along with his protégé Edward Clarke. Evans's version of the Klan had the greatest influence on Arkansas, and he emphasized political activity on the local and national levels.[24]

Evans was more anti-Catholic than Simmons, for he authored an entire book on the threat of Catholicism, entitled *The Rising Storm*, published by the Klan press in Atlanta.[25] His agenda included immigration restriction legislation, strict enforcement of prohibition laws and other moral legislation, opposition to federal aid to parochial education, restrictions on Catholic schools and teachers, and campaigns against any Roman Catholic political candidates.[26] In the inaugural issue of the Klan's national weekly magazine, the *Imperial Night Hawk*, Evans authored the lead article, "The Attitude of the Knights of the Ku Klux Klan Toward the Roman Catholic Hierarchy."[27]

As Evans rose to dominate the Klan, Arkansas was one of the first states to see Klan politicking in elections. Soon after the Klan was organized in Little Rock, it tried to influence the city's elections. In April 1922 Klansmen tried to oust a Roman Catholic alderman, Edward L. Younger, from office. Younger had defeated a challenger, Charles M. Snodgrass, in the Democratic primary in December 1921, before the Klan was well organized. When the city election was held on April 4, 1922, Klan voters had resolved to scratch the Catholic man's name and write in the name of Snodgrass, who was a Klansman. Snodgrass won the election, with 1,040 votes to 462 for Younger. With this success in removing a Roman Catholic incumbent in April, the Little Rock Klan prepared over the summer to dominate the Democratic primary for county offices coming up in August. Under Comer's leadership, the Klan in effect held its own primary and then run-off election to choose candidates to unite behind in the upcoming August 8 official Democratic primary. The Klan published its list of approved candidates for county, district, and state offices. Klansmen provided automobiles to carry voters to the polls and positioned five workers at each polling place on primary day. All the Klan-backed county and district candidates won the Democratic nomination, which in one-party Arkansas meant certain victory in November. By scratching their names from the ballot, the Klan also refused to vote for four unopposed candidates—three Jews and one Catholic—for the county Democratic committees.[28]

In the same primary election in northeastern Arkansas's Mississippi County, an incumbent city treasurer of Blytheville, a Roman Catholic man named Curtis J. Little, lost the election to a Klansman. He later filed suit against the city clerk, a justice of the peace, and another man for distributing a circular printing the bogus Knights of Columbus oath and claiming that Little had taken the oath when he became a member. In his suit, Little denied that he had ever taken such an oath and accused the three men of slander. He paid for an ad in the *Blytheville Courier* in which he asserted that he was not defeated because of failing at his job, "but because the Ku Klux Klan organization with paid lecturers and soured defeated office seekers, made many of you, who have always been my friends, believe that I was not a good American because my mother raised me a Catholic."[29]

The Klan targeted Catholic businesses as well as politicians. One of the first activities of the newly formed Jonesboro Klan in the summer of 1922 was to boycott Catholic and Jewish businesses in the city. The Jonesboro newspaper, which took an anti-Klan position, asked readers to imagine what would happen if the city lost a bank, a basket factory, a handle mill, three or four large lumber mills, four department stores, and a dozen other businesses owned by Catholics and Jews on Main Street.[30] Around the same time, signs went up in the windows of some Little Rock businesses—a drug store uptown, a shoe store and a barber shop on lower Main Street, and a couple of cafes on Louisiana Street—advertising "100 per cent American" or "Strictly American." Little Rock's Catholic weekly, the *Guardian*, suggested a counter-boycott of these businesses.[31] Klansman Ben Bogard responded that the "patriotic" Little Rock businesses were so busy they had to turn customers away. If the Catholics call a boycott, he said, "Let us patronize our own. . . . Just give our trade to real Americans." Bogard charged that Catholics' loyalties lay "across the sea, and the religion they profess is a foreign religion, the quicker we invite them to go back to the other side of the big pond the better it will be for us."[32]

More than actions, the Klan movement inspired a verbal assault against Catholicism. Several Arkansas Klansmen left behind a written record that displays the varied dimensions of anti-Catholicism in the early 1920s. Some of these were the same personalities who had been spokesmen for anti-Catholic prejudice in the 1910s while others emerged as new leaders. One dominant personality was the Reverend Benjamin Marcus Bogard. The leading figure within the Missionary Baptist Church, Bogard had led the walkout from the Southern Baptist Convention in 1902, when he was pastor of a Baptist church in Searcy. Bogard left Arkansas in 1912 to serve various churches in Texas until returning in 1920 to pastor Antioch Baptist Church in Little Rock. Thus he was in Texas during the years that the Arkansas General Assembly debated the anti-Catholic legislation of 1913 and 1915, when his friend Joseph Scarboro led the religious opposition to Catholicism. Bogard arrived back in Arkansas in 1920 at the age of fifty-two and would serve as pastor of Antioch Baptist Church for the next twenty-seven years. In addition he was the business manager of the Baptist Publishing Company and editor of the Missionary Baptist weekly, the *Baptist and Commoner*. He was a prolific writer, debater, and preacher, who in the last year of his ministry, in 1947, was featured in the Ripley's "Believe It or Not" column for preaching continuously for sixty-one years, without missing a single Sunday.[33] Bogard claimed to have been a member of the Klan since its earliest days in Arkansas. In fact, as the Klan was getting organized in Little Rock in the fall of 1921, Bogard led a tent-meeting revival in which he preached seventy days straight to crowds as large as a thousand people. The *Guardian* charged that Bogard was camouflaging a Ku Klux Klan gathering as a revival meeting, preaching "100 per cent Americanism but less than one half of no per cent Christianity."[34] By the spring of 1922, Bogard served as a Klan lecturer, presenting a stock speech, "The Ku Klux Klan Exposed," in which he "exposed" the principles for which the secret order stood. The speech was published as a booklet and sold for ten cents a copy from Bogard's home address at 1712 Rice Street in Little Rock.[35] His Baptist Publishing Company also distributed the pamphlet, along with a full range of anti-Catholic books for around a dollar a piece with titles such as *The Devil's Prayer Book (for Men Only)*, *Behind Convent Bars*, *Popery Unmasked*, and *Rum, Rags, and Religion*, and a list of forty-five smaller pamphlets selling for ten cents each.[36] As his Missionary Baptist colleague and friend the

Reverend Joseph Scarboro had led the anti-Catholic crusade in the 1910s, Bogard would tirelessly oppose Catholicism through the Klan, his pulpit, and the Missionary Baptist weekly paper in the 1920s.

The Reverend Benjamin Marcus Bogard. *Courtesy of the Arkansas History Commission.*

Another Klansman whose words form a record of anti-Catholicism was Basil Edwin Newton of Hope. Newton had been won over to the anti-Catholic cause by hearing William Lloyd Clark in 1912, and he then went on the lecture circuit himself. Sometime after 1920 he moved from Hope to Little Rock and became a Klan lecturer. It was Newton who ignited a firestorm of controversy nationally in September 1923 when at a Klan lecture in Charleston, West Virginia, he boasted that the organization had 227 members in the US House of Representatives and 27 in the Senate. Moreover, he said the Klan had held an initiation ceremony in the dining room of the White House. Members of President Warren Harding's administration quickly denied this assertion, and it has since been much discussed by historians.[37] One can assume that opposition to Rome was a chief element in Newton's Klan lectures, given his earlier work as an anti-Catholic lecturer. At some point in the 1920s he published a forty-three-page booklet entitled *The K.K.K. vs. Enemies*, which declared in its first sentence: "This little book is designed to show to the world the Klan's chief enemy—Romanism."[38]

Also contributing to the discussion were the Reverend Harry G.

Knowles and the Reverend John H. Moore. Knowles was the pastor of Little Rock's First Christian Church (Disciples of Christ), the home congregation of Grand Dragon James Comer. Knowles became a state Klan lecturer and is known to have spoken at Klan gatherings and to public audiences throughout Arkansas. While the exact content of his Arkansas speeches is unknown, it is likely that they included the sort of anti-Catholic positions he articulated in a speech to Klan women in Chicago in 1924, published later that year as *Eight C's for Klanswomen.* Another Arkansas Klan lecturer was the Reverend John H. Moore, a Baptist preacher in Pine Bluff. Moore gave a talk at a public Klan meeting at the Booneville courthouse in late October 1923. The state Klan newspaper, the *Arkansas Traveller*, reported that after the singing of "Nearer My God to Thee" and "America," he spoke against efforts of Catholics to do away with public schools and take control of political offices in the United States.[39]

And lastly, representing a more secular Klan perspective of anti-Catholicism, was Herb Lewis, still publishing the *Gravette News Herald* until he sold the paper in 1925. While Lewis never admitted membership in the Klan, his paper served as a mouthpiece for Klan news and views, especially after Gravette had its own Klan, Chapter No. 85, which had a membership of around two hundred. Lewis was more than a mouthpiece; he was a cheerleader who proudly promoted the Klan agenda, excerpted pieces from Klan publications, and printed notices of Klan meetings and events. By the end of 1924 he began a series of boxed advertisements with the heading "Reasons Why You Should Become a Klansmen," with the fourteenth and last reason published in June 1925, shortly before he sold the newspaper. In his last issue of June 26 he editorialized: "Let us hope that our citizens will ever find a way, have access, to keep in touch with this great Klan movement which means so much to this country." The *Arkansas Traveller* printed material sent from Lewis. It reported on November 5, 1923, that somebody in Gravette had accused Lewis of being a "Kluxer." He did not seem to mind the accusation, the paper concluded, "in fact, he all but admits it much to the disgust of a Papal few." Clearly, Lewis's *Gravette News Herald* reflected a Klan perspective. And for Lewis the chief issue, as in the 1910s, was opposition to the Roman Catholic Church.[40]

Professional anti-Catholic lecturers also worked with Klan leaders to get out the message against Rome. Just as the *Menace* served as a

Herb Lewis promoted Klan activities in his paper, the *Gravette News Herald*, July 6, 1923.

speakers' bureau in the 1910s, booking anti-Catholic lecturers for locations that wanted them, in the 1920s the Klan organized the tour schedule of anti-Catholic speakers.[41] Some of the lecturers and much of their material were simply recycled from before, but a few new personalities appeared on the circuit in the 1920s. The Reverend Joseph Scarboro returned to Arkansas from Georgia in the spring of 1922 to give his standard anti-Catholic lectures in Benton County.[42] Ben Bogard later in the spring sponsored a supposed ex-nun from Chicago who claimed to have escaped from the House of Good Shepherd. The *Guardian* charged that he was appearing with this unnamed speaker in the Little Rock Klan hall (at Fourth and Main Street) and was directing her lecture tour through the state.[43] The country's most notorious anti-Catholic lecturers, Helen Jackson and L. J. King, visited the state in 1923. Helen Jackson, like Bogard's speaker the year before, billed herself as an escaped nun who had fled both a House of Good Shepherd in Kentucky and a convent in Detroit, Michigan. Her presentations titillated audiences with stories of sexual abuse and infanticide of the Maria Monk variety. She published her story as *Convent Cruelties, or My Life in a Convent*, and the book went through seven editions between 1919 and 1924. Jackson often lectured wearing the garb of a nun and travelled with King, a Klansman who claimed also to have been formerly a Roman Catholic. King had been on the lecture circuit in the 1910s, and to Klan audiences in the 1920s he repeated the same worn stories about priests and girls in the confessional, sexual tortures, and other perversions that resulted from clerical celibacy.[44]

Helen Jackson arrived in Little Rock in February 1923 and began looking for a location to speak. In late May, King began a week-long lecture series in Gravette and, according to Herb Lewis, spoke to immense, appreciative crowds. An advertisement in Lewis's paper claimed that for twenty-five cents one could see King wearing the robes of a bishop and also six nuns who would recite ordination vows, sing the high mass, chant the Latin litany for the dead, and sound the convent gong. While he was at it, King endorsed the Klan as the "salvation of Americanism" against Catholic threats to American government, institutions, and ideals.[45]

A man going by the name of Charles Walker, claiming to be an ex-priest, began a series of anti-Catholic lectures in Dardanelle and at the courthouse in Russellville in early 1924. After one of his talks, a Russellville man, James R. Wilson, confronted the speaker, announcing that "Walker" was actually an ex-convict named Roy Crane, who had served six years at Fort Leavenworth for draft evasion and anarchy during the Great War. Wilson signed a deposition before a justice of the peace asserting that in 1917 he had helped a sheriff arrest Crane in Ardmore, Oklahoma. Crane—alias Walker—said he was leaving for Oklahoma to get evidence of his identity and innocence, but he never returned. Meanwhile, the sheriff of Pope County received photographs of Roy Crane as a prisoner and documents about his conviction and sentence.[46]

Some homegrown Arkansas speakers cashed in on the renewed wave of prejudice. Gerald Sheehan surfaced in Conway in 1921 and lectured in various locations in Arkansas in the early 1920s, claiming to have been a priest for eighteen years. Sheehan said he had entered the priesthood to please his mother, but then after her death gave up his collar and became a Baptist minister. Catholics countered that no Gerald Sheehan was ever ordained as a priest in the United States.[47]

And then there is the enigmatic case of Christian Henry Reeb, an anti-Catholic speaker and author who lived in Little Rock and Texarkana in the early 1920s. When he gave a series of anti-Catholic lectures at the courthouse in DeQueen, his handbills claimed that he was a former altar boy and active Catholic for twenty-one years. By 1923, when he was lecturing in Meridian, Texas, he was described as a converted Catholic priest.[48] It appears he did come from a Catholic background, born in New Orleans in 1879 to a German father and a mother who was half Italian and half Irish. By 1910 Reeb was married with three young children, boarding with the family of his wife's aunt in Little Rock. Reeb held various jobs, as a laborer, then deputy constable, and by 1914 was a janitor at the Immanuel Baptist Church, whose pastor, Eugene P. Alldredge, took a very public anti-Catholic stand. In 1919 or early 1920, Reeb was separated from his wife, Fanny. He made his way, along with his sons, aged ten and twelve, to the Florida coast, where he abandoned the two boys on the beach. The younger son remembered it well because he was badly sunburned while waiting for a father who never returned. Somehow the boys returned to Arkansas, for they show up in the 1920 census living with their mother's aunt in Little Rock, as in the 1910 census. C. H. Reeb, at the 1920 census, was living in East Macon, Georgia, with a new wife, Carrie, and serving as a preacher of the Gospel. By 1923 Reeb was back in Arkansas and had married a third time to a woman named Helen and was working as an itinerant preacher and anti-Catholic lecturer.[49] His eleven-page pamphlet, *The Roman Catholic Church: An Idolatrous Institution*, was published in Little Rock, and a hundred-page booklet, *The Counterfeit Church,* came out as well. Later in 1923 Reeb moved to Fort Worth, Texas, to attend the Baptist Theological Seminary. Reeb had another family with his third wife and lived with them in Oklahoma, Tennessee, and Florida, where he died in 1934.[50] Reeb's family record calls his credibility as an anti-Catholic lecturer and minister of the Gospel both into question.

While the anti-Catholic lecturers and some of the Ku Klux Klan rhetoric simply rehashed much of the same material as in the 1910s, the Klan concentrated on a perceived Catholic threat to national institutions and the government itself. This theme was not exactly new, for the *Menace* and anti-Catholic lecturers had made this point before. But for a Klan movement that touted "One Hundred Percent Americanism," the chief criticism of Roman Catholics became their suspected disloyalty to the United States of America. Irony abounds in that a movement with its center of gravity in the former Confederate states would tout its patriotism. The early 1920s were a time when Confederate reunions became public events and Lost Causers erected monuments to fallen Rebel soldiers on courthouse lawns all around the South. But southern Klansmen did not appear to regard their memorializing of secession from, and war against, the United States as inconsistent with their ultra-patriotism and their portrayal of Catholics as inauthentic Americans. Arkansas Klansmen expressed their nationalistic opposition to Roman Catholicism through their support for restrictive immigration laws, campaigns against Catholic intrusion into politics, and concern that parochial schools subverted the role of public education.

This study argued earlier that the Dillingham Commission's exposé in 1911 of the magnitude of immigration from southern and eastern Europe served as a trigger for the new wave of anti-Catholic prejudice that rose in the 1910s. However, with Europe in turmoil after 1914, immigration to the United States declined during the years of the Great War. By 1920 immigration figures began to spike upward again. The public perception arose that vast hordes of impoverished Europeans were again ready to descend on the gates of America. In the US House of Representatives, Albert Johnson, a Republican from southwestern Washington who was chair of the House Committee on Immigration, introduced a bill to suspend all immigration temporarily. William Dillingham still reigned in the Senate as the expert on immigration. He proposed a rival bill that established quotas for European immigration based on 5 percent of the foreign-born population in the United States from each country according to the 1910 census. Dillingham had first proposed such a quota system in 1913, but it went nowhere with the advent of World War I. When this bill went back to the House, Johnson and Republicans abandoned their suspension bill in favor of the quota bill, negotiating the 5 percent down to 3 percent, with a maximum of 355,000 European immigrants in a year. President Woodrow Wilson used a pocket veto to kill the bill, simply ignoring it until he left office. Republicans reintroduced it after President Warren G. Harding was sworn in. Harding signed the bill in May 1921. Although the law was temporary, to last just one year, the act signified the beginning of a national quota system for US immigration policy. When the year was up, in May 1922, Congress extended the law for two more years while its committees drafted more permanent legislation.[51]

While the US Congress was debating immigration restrictions, the Klan was building its membership in Arkansas. Klansmen in the state lobbied for restriction and painted the Roman Catholic Church as the number one enemy on the immigration front. Herb Lewis in January 1922 urged his readers to demand that their congressmen support the Johnson bill. Later in the year he said America needed a "Fiery Cross to illuminate the skulls of congressmen who are tardy in stopping the inflow of foreigners who have no knowledge or respect for the Civil laws and Institutions of America."[52] Ben Bogard explained in his *Ku Klux Klan Exposed* that limiting foreign immigration was a foundational principle of the Klan. There was a time, he said, when the United States needed immigrants, but that time had passed. Moreover, the character of immigrants had "materially changed," Bogard said. While formerly settlers came to till the soil, get absorbed into the population, and adopt American customs, now they kept to themselves in colonies, he said, retaining their foreign customs and languages. "Since they prefer to live in the foreign style," he said, "and be dominated by a foreign religion we prefer that they stay on the other side of the big pond where they belong."[53] Similarly, Harry Knowles said the Klan challenged "the foreign hordes that will not adopt American ideas and standards of living."[54] Basil Newton made it clear that Klansmen were "working to eliminate the undesirable, and welcome the desirable from across the sea." The undesirable elements, he said, "have proven themselves unfit for association with the people who own this nation." For Newton, the contributions of aliens to America included high rates of crime, mental illness, financial fraud, white slavery, and venereal disease. He made it clear that the degenerate immigrants were disproportionately Catholic. The Roman priesthood, he said, cried out against immigration restriction and supported an open-door policy.[55] Herb Lewis agreed that

Roman Catholic priests were deliberately trying to bring immigrants in an attempt to make America Catholic. The Catholic hierarchy, Lewis said, opposed immigration restriction for it counted "every crook, ignoramus and diseased, decrepit and intellectually deficient creature from Catholic countries as more membership and voting power."[56]

In their diatribes against Catholic immigrants, Arkansas Klansmen saved their most harsh language for Italians. Herb Lewis said 70 percent of the "scum of Southern Europe who are here are incapable, having less sense than a ten-year-old child."[57] In a pamphlet written for young girls, the Women of the KKK instructed girls on the topic of race, explaining that the recent immigrants to the United States were entirely different in temperament and blood than earlier immigrants:

> The Southern Europeans come to America, go to work for a great corporation at less than one-half of what an American can work for. He can do this because his racial training and his way of living back home make it possible. He can live on garlic and a little cheap meat. He was never used to more than that, so why does he want it here? His wife—if he is married—will keep a dingy hut for him, and they will raise from three to five times the number of babies the Anglo-Saxon mothers will raise. They do not know anything about Mather or Brewster or the Pilgrim Fathers. Their religion is invariably Roman Catholic. . . . America must be kept Protestant if she wants to be kept American.[58]

This sort of disdain for newcomers was reserved specifically for Roman Catholic immigrants. In 1923 Little Rock became the international headquarters for a new Klan auxiliary, the American Krusaders, which welcomed Protestant immigrants who were denied membership in the Klan because of their foreign birth. On August 27, the American Krusaders was incorporated in Pulaski County Circuit Court, with James Comer along with Herschel C. McCall and Fred J. Gifford, the Grand Dragons of Texas and Oregon, respectively, and Martin W. Rose of Seattle as trustees. Rose, a naturalized citizen originally from Canada, had earlier founded a similar organization, the Royal Riders of the Red Robe, whose members wore scarlet gowns instead of the Klan's white ones, but Rose's organization had never been incorporated. With relatively few foreign-born Protestant residents, Arkansas seems an unlikely location to charter such an organization. There is no evidence that the Krusaders ever had a chapter in the state. The choice of Little Rock as the headquarters more reflects Comer's close alliance with Hiram Evans. The Krusaders organization provided additional income opportunity for Comer, given that the charter gave the trustees control over the regalia, jewelry, ritual, and other belongings, even though Comer, McCall, and Gifford, as native-born Americans, were ineligible to join the organization.[59] By the end of 1924 the Krusaders claimed to have chapters in forty states. In Newago County, Michigan, the Krusaders chapter included seven members from Canada, three from Germany, two each from England, Scotland, Sweden, and Finland, and one each from Holland, Austria, and France. The majority were nationalized citizens with the remainder immigrants who had begun the process to become citizens. The Little Rock Supreme Headquarters processed the applications, which included a lengthy questionnaire asking such questions as whether the applicant could read and write the English language and if one would denounce all obligations to a former government. Comer probably received a share of the ten-dollar initiation fee of each new member.[60]

The organization of the American Krusaders, a Klan for Protestant immigrants, indicates that the Klan anti-immigration position was primarily an expression of anti-Catholicism. When the US Congress finally developed a permanent immigration policy, the Johnson-Reed Act of 1924, it put the Klan's position into law. The new act lowered the national quotas from 3 percent to 2 percent and set a maximum number of immigrants through the quotas at 155,000. And the quota calculation used as its baseline the 1890 census, not the 1910 census or the 1920 census, which had just come available. Use of the 1890 census, of course, meant smaller quotas for southern and eastern European nations whose Catholic populations had dominated the immigration after that time. The 1890-based quotas were temporary anyway, for under Senator David A. Reed's leadership, the final version of the bill called for permanent quotas to take effect in 1927 that would reflect the national origins of the present-day population. A quota committee was created to estimate the national origins of the one hundred million Americans, many whose ancestors had come to the New World long before census records showed national origins. Thus, the committee had the onerous task of estimating national origins for millions of Americans based on the perceived ethnicity of their surnames, an imprecise task at best. When this system finally took effect in 1929—twice postponed by Congress—the quotas from Catholic countries such as Italy, Poland, and Ireland were further reduced, as well as the quota for Germany, while the quota for Great Britain was further enlarged. National origins of African Americans, Indians, and those with backgrounds elsewhere in the Americas or Asia were completely disregarded. The Johnson-Reed Act, also known as the National Origins Act, would prove extremely effective. There would be fewer immigrants arriving in the following forty years, from 1931 to 1971, than had come in the decade 1901–1910, even though the population of the United States in 1970 was twice what it was in 1910.[61] All seven of Arkansas's representatives and both senators voted for the National Origins Act of 1924.[62]

Besides immigration restriction, another Klan focus was public education, and here too the Klan position had an anti-Catholic component. In fact, restricting immigration and promoting free public schools were the dual strategies to minimize the threat of Catholic aliens on American culture. The Klan's promotion of public schools was the flip side of the coin to its opposition to parochial education. In 1920s Arkansas, religious schools claimed a tiny fraction of the whole. If the Klan's own information is to be believed, the monthly magazine *Kourier* claimed in 1924 that 455,362 children in Arkansas were educated in public schools as compared to 1,900 in parochial schools. The vast majority of these parochial schools were Roman Catholic.[63]

Arkansas Klansmen argued that Catholic schools kept immigrants from learning the essential components of American culture and citizenship. Parochial schools, Klansmen said, were a tool of the papacy designed to perpetuate an authoritarian culture as opposed to a democratic American one. Basil Newton said that Catholic schools taught students to be "Catholics first and Americans maybe." Herb Lewis argued that religious schools allowed students to evade the requirement of compulsory school attendance, and he demanded that teachers in Catholic schools in Arkansas have a state teaching license.[64] Lewis cheered the state of Oregon for passing a law with Klan support in 1923 making public school education mandatory, attempting in effect to shut down Catholic education. A federal court overturned the law in the next year.[65]

The Arkansas General Assembly did not entertain such a bill but instead passed a law, Act 614 of 1923, which required that all public and private schools display the American flag and teach American history in every primary grade plus one full year in high school. The law stated that this history instruction aimed for patriotic goals, to instill in the hearts of students love of country and devotion to the principles of American government. Herb Lewis said, "This law will worry the Romanists, but it should serve to help Americanize pupils who attend their schools."[66]

Klansmen saw protection and strengthening of the public school system as the way to defeat the influence of Catholicism. Arkansas Klans gave money to support their local public school systems. In Conway in 1922 an envelope with $116.20 mysteriously appeared on the desk of Conway's director of schools, the Reverend C. M. Reves. In a letter to the *Conway Weekly News*, the Klan announced that besides this cash gift, it had pledges of $6,648.50 toward the school fund. In another small Arkansas community, the Klan purchased a park adjacent to a school and donated the land to the local school board.[67] But especially under the leadership of Hiram Evans in 1923, the Klan actively promoted educational reform at the highest levels, in the US Congress. A series of bills were working their way through Congress in the early 1920s to create a national department of education at the cabinet level. This department would centralize curriculum and provide federal financial support to public schools. In 1922 and 1923 the incarnation of these goals was the Towner-Sterling bill. The bill also included specific funding to Americanize immigrants by teaching newcomers English and the basics of American government. The Klan directed its members to work for the passage of Towner-Sterling. Herb Lewis instructed his readers to demand of their congressmen that they vote for the bill.[68] The Towner-Sterling bill and later versions of it all failed; a cabinet-level department of education would not exist until 1980. But in the early 1920s the Klan struck an unusual alliance with progressive interest groups, such as the National Education Association and the Arkansas Education Association, in promoting a centralized program of education. The Roman Catholic Church consistently opposed the Towner-Sterling bill and the other bills, which further generated the wrath of the Klan.

Klansmen in Arkansas and elsewhere feared that Catholics were trying to infiltrate the public education system by getting Catholic teachers and administrators into the schools. Grand Dragon Comer made this charge in an article in the *Arkansas Traveller.* He reported that a Catholic teacher in Little Rock had her students debate this question: "Resolved, That the Knights of Ku Klux Klan Should Be Abolished." Comer complained, however, that the teacher chose only Catholic students to debate both sides of the issue and that she made clear that she agreed with the affirmative argument.[69] Ben Bogard wrote about a Catholic school in Iowa that had been made the community's public school and thus supported with taxation. All the teachers were nuns, he said, except for one "sweet little Protestant." Bogard feared that if Catholics gained political power, the Iowa model would be followed all over the country. "Free public schools," he said, "are the biggest enemy of Catholicism."[70] Arkansas's diocesan paper, the *Guardian,* noted that a Little Rock Baptist preacher, perhaps Bogard, had been railing from the pulpit against Catholic teachers in the Little Rock schools. The paper responded that there were just a few Catholic teachers in the district, and they were licensed just like anyone else.[71] Klan lecturer Basil Newton also charged that the Catholic hierarchy strove to get its communicants installed as teachers in the public school and that it directed followers to vote against bonds that would fund public schools. He said, "Rome hates the American public school as well as advanced Protestant civilization." Newton believed the public schools were, in fact, "purely a Protestant institution." Newton said no Protestants were ever employed in Catholic schools, but Catholics wished to be employed in "Protestant public schools." The Catholic plan, Newton said, was to "destroy Americanism and erect the empire of Romanism."[72]

Besides a conspiracy over personnel, Klansmen imagined a Catholic plot to influence the curriculum of schools, particularly with the subject of history. School textbooks were awash with anti-American material that must be refuted, said Basil Newton. J. H. Moore, state Klan lecturer from Pine Bluff, declared in an address at Gravette that "alien and papal propaganda now spread upon the pages of school books shall be eliminated."[73] Herb Lewis editorialized for the cause of free textbooks in Arkansas schools and state control over the choice of books as a way to keep "sinister powers" from using school books to foster anti-American ideals. He noted, as an example, history textbooks used in Michigan and Indiana which "eulogize for the papal system," showing pictures of political leaders "bowing before the pope and the coronation of Mary." He wanted to see legislation in the Arkansas General Assembly to correct this problem.[74]

While it is more challenging to teach a Catholic version of algebra or chemistry, the subject of history, according to these Klansmen, was at the focus of Catholic propaganda. The Klan was responding in part to an initiative by the Knights of Columbus in 1921 to "rescue" American history and cultural heritage from the myth of exclusively Anglo-Saxon origins. Edward McSweeney, a Knight from Boston who had formerly been an immigration officer for many years at Ellis Island, recommended that the Knights form a historical commission to combat the increasingly popular Anglo-Saxon interpretation, by writing new histories that would correct errors of fact and omission. The Knights at their Supreme Council gathering in San Francisco in September 1921 announced the commission and appointed leading Catholic historians, political scientists, and other academics, with McSweeney as chair. The commission produced some of its own pamphlets but also offered prizes for new historical monographs by academic historians and for school materials prepared by educational professionals.[75] While the Knights of Columbus created their Historical Commission in response to the "One Hundred Percent American" rhetoric of the revived Ku Klux Klan, the very existence of the commission gave the Klan "evidence" of a Catholic attempt to re-write American history. Herb Lewis said such a commission necessitated "an American organization to counteract such a program of internal enemies." By December 1921, Lewis had read of some of the commission's first published pamphlets describing plans for a new school history of the United States. He called the proposed text "a book of fiction, deceit, and gall" and insisted that this Jesuit scheme to "hoodwink sleepy Americans" was "deceptive, uninvited, undesired, and as poison as a snake in the grass." He warned every state and county school official and anyone with influence over the publication of school books to defeat the plan of the "Papal Nites" to boost popery in public schools. Newton argued that the textbook commission was evidence of Rome's conspiracy to keep the world in ignorance and teach falsehoods.[76] With the Knights of Columbus remodeling of American history, Lewis said, "George Washington is likely to be replaced by St. Patrick, and Lincoln by the Boss of Tammany and St. Anna's shinbone may become

Cartoon from the *Rail Splitter,* from Michael Williams, *The Shadow of the Pope.*

the national emblem."[77] In reality, the commission financially supported the publication of several academic monographs on specific subjects in American history, but it never produced a Catholic version of a school history textbook before the Knights of Columbus disbanded the commission in 1925.[78]

While anti-Catholic movements in Arkansas in the 1910s had

considered the Knights of Columbus as the personification of Catholic conspiracy, the Klan took up this position anew, especially with the efforts of the Historical Commission. The Klan continued to disseminate the bogus Knights of Columbus oath, and Knights in Arkansas and other states initiated lawsuits against publishers and those who circulated the false oath. The Knights offered a reward to any person who could provide proof that this oath was in any way authentic.[79] Copies of the bogus oath had appeared by August 1922 in the Helena area and in April 1923 in Fort Smith. Local Knights of Columbus in these communities communicated with the national office for advice on how to stop the dissemination of the oath. Luke Hart, the Supreme Advocate of the national organization, advised the Arkansas Knights that if they could ascertain the identity of the persons who either printed or disseminated the oath, they should lodge a formal complaint with the local prosecuting attorney under charges of libel and slander.[80] Later in August 1923, L. B. Barry Jr., a Fort Smith Knight, complained to Hart that an evangelist had been holding meetings in a town in western Arkansas in which he slammed the Knights and read from the bogus oath, in addition to performing faith cures. One performance was in a special service for the Ku Klux Klan. Hart offered to send five thousand dollars to Arkansas for the Knights to use in a publicity campaign as a reward for anyone who could prove the authenticity of the oath. By September, the evangelist had moved on to preach in Colorado.[81]

The national and state officers of the Knights of Columbus considered filing libel charges against the Arkansas Klan weekly newspaper, the *Arkansas Traveller*, when the paper printed the bogus oath in issues of October and November 1923. Luke Hart wrote the state secretary of the Arkansas Knights, Joseph C. Carroll Jr. of Little Rock, asking what prospects there would be from a judge and jury. Carroll explained that all of the Little Rock and Pulaski County officials with the exception of two aldermen and one circuit judge were active Klan members and had been endorsed and elected by the Klan. The sheriff and the entire force of the prosecuting attorney's office, Carroll said, were active Klansmen. Under such conditions, Carroll concluded that it would be useless to attempt any action against the *Arkansas Traveller*.[82] The bogus oath surfaced again in 1924 in Harrison in the form of handbills printed by the local newspaper and disseminated by an unknown party.[83]

Ben Bogard and Herb Lewis continually reminded their readers that Knights had kidnapped and beaten Otis Spurgeon in 1914 and accused the "Romanist Nites of Popery" of the murder of William Black in 1915.[84] Lewis charged that Knights were the military arm of Catholicism, a virtual army for Rome that was secreting arms and munitions. He noted that the Knights wore a sword as part of their regalia. An unnamed Arkansas Klansman writing for the *Imperial Night Hawk* in 1924 agreed, saying that the militant Knights of Columbus were preparing to "do battle with American Protestantism." The Knights, he charged, were the most powerful organization in the United States, and they took their orders directly from Rome.[85] There is some irony that the Catholic institution the Klan most detested was a fraternal organization that professed a blend of patriotism and religious devotion, with a secret ritual and elaborate regalia, that occasionally committed vigilante violence to attain its goals. In other words, the Klan's imagined Knights of Columbus looked much like a mirror image of the KKK itself.

What these Klansmen feared most were Catholic attempts to exert control in the political arena. Ben Bogard charged in his *Ku Klux Klan Exposed* that the pope wanted to control the whole world, while Basil Newton announced that Romanists wanted to destroy the US government and replace it with rule by the pope.[86] Catholics had for years, Bogard said, been placing their own people in positions of influence in government and culture. He said Catholics held a majority of public offices while they were a minority of the population. Herb Lewis was more specific, claiming that 70 percent of public office holders in the United States were Catholics, when they composed less than 20 percent of the population.[87] Catholics had a deliberate plan to get their members into high public offices, Bogard said, asking readers to note how many Catholics received presidential appointments. If Catholics ever took over the government, he continued, loyal Protestants "would be tortured and put to death."[88] Harry Knowles called for every Anglo-Saxon Protestant to unite with the Klan in voting for officials and laws that would keep the United States free from the grasp of Rome. While Bogard decried the Catholic officials for directing followers to vote only for members of their own faith, he told his readers to refuse to vote for a Catholic candidate no matter which party ticket the candidate represented.[89]

The worst fears of these Klansmen were realized when Al Smith, the

Catholic governor of New York, made a bid for the Democratic nomination for the presidency in 1924. Alfred Emanuel Smith was everything the Klan disliked. Born in a tenement on Manhattan's Lower East Side, he hailed from Irish, Italian, and German immigrant stock. He served as an altar boy at his local Catholic Church and as an adult joined the Knights of Columbus. In the early 1900s he ran for state assembly as the candidate of Tammany Hall, the notorious political machine that controlled the city of New York. After service in Albany and in various positions in New York City, he was elected as the Tammany candidate for governor in 1918. When he appeared on the national political stage in the early 1920s, Smith epitomized the city slicker from the biggest and baddest of cities, complete with his East Side accent, his fedora hat, and cigar. A heavy drinker, he made no secret of his opposition to prohibition.[90]

Smith entered no primaries in 1924 and only began to act like a candidate in the months before the Democratic National Convention was to convene in late June. Herb Lewis immediately began his verbal assault against "Al(cohol) Smith . . . and his gang of Roman politicians, supported by the papal red-caps, alien crooks, German brewers and Irish saloonkeepers" who, Lewis said, were preparing to stack the deck for Smith's nomination for president or, failing that, vice president. Moreover, Lewis charged that Smith's men were trying to make the Klan an issue for the upcoming convention, for "if they can keep the American Democrats' eyes on the Ku Klux Klan, they figure they can slip in their Booze candidates and Roman intriguers and get by with it."[91]

Lewis correctly anticipated that the Klan itself would be a chief issue for the 1924 Democratic convention and that Al Smith would be a polarizing figure there. Even before delegates assembled at New York's Madison Square Garden on June 24, it was clear that the first contentious issue would be a platform plank condemning the Ku Klux Klan, proposed by the northeastern/urban wing of the party. A group of Klan leaders, including Virgil C. Pettie, the secretary of the Arkansas Democratic Party organization and delegate-at-large, assembled in New York in advance of the convention to strategize efforts to oppose the anti-Klan plank. Imperial Wizard Hiram Evans and his inner circle of advisors, including Arkansas's Grand Dragon James Comer, set up their headquarters in the McAlpin Hotel. The Klan planned to press delegates to oppose the anti-Klan plank and disseminated a stream of letters and publications touting Smith's Catholicism, his "wet" position, and his Tammany Hall background. Before the meeting began, the Klan claimed to control 85 percent of the Georgia delegation and 80 percent of the delegations from Arkansas, Texas, and Kansas.[92] Meanwhile, the rest of the Arkansas delegation took a special train from Arkansas to New York—five Pullman cars, a diner, a club car, and baggage car—stopping over for four hours of sightseeing at Niagara Falls.[93] After an opening prayer by the cardinal archbishop of New York, which surely provoked the ire of the anti-Catholics, the longest national party convention in American history began.

Most of the work of preparing a party platform took place by committee prior to the national convention. But on the evening of June 28, on the convention floor delegates fought over the anti-Klan plank. William Jennings Bryan had crafted language calling for obedience to the orderly process of law and deploring any religious or racial prejudice, but not specifically naming the KKK. Others, including Al Smith, insisted that the platform should condemn the Klan by name. A round of speeches alternately condemned and defended the Klan to the accompaniment of raucous cheers, jeers, whistles, boos, and hisses. When the vote was finally taken at 11:35 p.m., the anti-Klan plank failed by one vote out of more than a thousand cast. The Klan would not be named in the platform. All eighteen of the Arkansas delegates voted against the anti-Klan plank.[94]

The other divisive issue of the convention was the stalemate that emerged between Al Smith and William Gibbs McAdoo, the candidate supported by most of the Klan. Born in Georgia and raised in Tennessee, McAdoo moved to New York City as a young man, where over the next twenty years he rose to prominence through his work to build tunnels under the Hudson River. He became part of President Wilson's cabinet as secretary of the treasury and then married Wilson's youngest daughter, Eleanor. In 1922 he and his family moved to California. So when he began his campaign for the Democratic presidential nomination, he could claim to be more of a national candidate than Al Smith, with support particularly from the West, South, and Midwest. McAdoo took a strong "dry" to Smith's "wet" stand, but he refused to be pulled into the Klan controversy after Smith pushed for the anti-Klan plank. With the Klan siding with McAdoo, Smith's supporters dug in their heels. Given that convention rules required a candidate to get two-thirds of the votes, a standoff was practically guaranteed.[95]

Besides the blocks supporting McAdoo and Smith, the other

nominating votes went to an assortment of local sons, including Senator Joe T. Robinson of Arkansas. The central committee of Arkansas's Democratic Party in April had decided to cast its eighteen votes for Robinson after the state's general assembly had the month before gone on the record as endorsing him for president. But the bigger question for the Arkansas delegation, and other states with favorite sons, was when and to whom the votes would go after the first ballot.[96] On the first day of the convention, former Arkansas governor Charles H. Brough gave the speech nominating Robinson. Speaking in a practically inaudible tone, Brough gave one of the shortest and dullest nomination speeches, which, according to some observers, took Robinson out of contention on the first day.[97] Nonetheless, the Arkansas delegation held fast to Robinson in subsequent ballots as it became more and more clear that neither Smith nor McAdoo could muster enough votes to gain the necessary two-thirds majority. The deadlock buoyed the optimism of the Arkansas delegates, who held out Robinson as a compromise candidate. After McAdoo and Smith mutually agreed to bow out after two weeks, the Arkansas delegates were almost giddy, for rumor had it that Robinson was the second choice of the largest number of delegates. The shift to Robinson never materialized. John W. Davis, a West Virginia lawyer and relative unknown, became the convention's choice, with Charles Bryan, brother of William Jennings Bryan, as Davis's vice presidential running mate. The eighteen Arkansas delegates persisted in voting for Robinson through all 103 ballots.[98]

Imperial Wizard Hiram Evans and Arkansas's leading Klansmen James Comer and Virgil Pettie could leave New York boasting about saving America from rum and Romanism by defeating Al Smith's candidacy. But the Democratic Party was so bruised by the factionalism displayed at the convention that it failed to recover. John Davis apparently lost most of the Klan vote after he denounced the Klan in a speech in New Jersey in August. Davis invited the Republican nominee, Calvin Coolidge, to declare his position on the Klan, an invitation Coolidge simply ignored. After defeating Al Smith at the Democratic Convention, Klansmen were left without a candidate to support. Ben Bogard noted before the election that William Jennings Bryan was not campaigning for Davis even though his own brother was Davis's running mate. The reason why, Bogard explained, was because Davis had sided with the

Catholics and denounced the Klan as soon as he received the nomination. Bogard said: "To vote for Davis is to vote with the Catholics and the liquor crowd for he has openly allied with them. . . . Some of us are either going a fishing this next election day or we shall vote for Coolidge."[99] The Republican candidate Calvin Coolidge trounced Davis in the November election, winning 54.0 percent of the popular vote, to Davis's 29.0 percent, with a third-party candidate, Robert La Follette, taking 16.5 percent.[100]

By the time of the Democratic National Convention in June and July of 1924, however, the Ku Klux Klan had begun to lose its hold in Arkansas. The Klan's attempts to "manage" state elections in 1924, rather than its involvement in national politics, brought the decline of the Klan in Arkansas. After Grand Dragon Comer had such success in the city of Little Rock and in the Pulaski County elections in 1922, he set his sights on Klan domination of the Democratic nomination process for state offices. The problem in 1924 was which Klansmen to support among the many who aspired for public offices. Comer's solution was to hold a Klan primary on May 28 to choose the candidates that Klansmen would support on August 12 for the Democratic Party primary. Comer's preferred candidate for governor was Lee Cazort, a thirty-six-year-old former state legislator from Johnson County. Also wanting Klan support was Jim G. Ferguson, the state commissioner of mines and a member of Little Rock's Klan No. 1. On the evening of May 28, as a heavy rain fell across nearly the entire state, Klansmen met to vote their preferences for governor and other state offices. Cazort won over Ferguson by a four-to-one margin. In Pulaski County, the Klan also held a mail-in primary to choose a full slate of candidates to stand for county and district races in the August primary. Thereafter, Cazort openly campaigned for the nomination as the Klan candidate. The problem was that Ferguson failed to step down as had been agreed, but instead continued to run. He increasingly turned his campaign against Comer, a former Republican and Bull Moose supporter, accusing him of manipulating both the Klan and the Democratic Party. By July two other candidates had stepped up in an attempt to get Klan votes, Jacob R. Wilson, a state senator from El Dorado, and Thomas J. Terral, a former secretary of state. The Little Rock Klan voted to suspend Ferguson's membership and announced that Terral had been rejected for membership in Klan

No. 1. Terral had managed to get initiated into a Klavern in Louisiana. Wilson had been removed from the Little Rock Klan after a delegation from El Dorado petitioned for his expulsion. Thus, instead of uniting the Klan under one candidate, four Klansmen were still seeking the Klan vote. Two additional candidates were running, Hamp Williams, an attorney from western Arkansas, and John Martineau, a chancery judge in Little Rock. Of the lot, only Martineau took an anti-Klan position in his campaign. Cazort's opponents ran against Comer more than Cazort, accusing the Grand Dragon of trying to "Republicanize" the Democratic Party. When the returns were counted in August, Terral won the nomination, defeating Cazort, Martineau, Ferguson, Williams, and Wilson, in that order. Terral easily defeated his Republican opponent in the November election and became Arkansas's twenty-seventh governor. Most of the Klan-supported candidates for other state offices won the nomination, and the Klan kept its grip on offices in Pulaski County. But the bickering over the gubernatorial nomination had done its damage to the Klan in Arkansas. The state convention of the Democratic Party in September passed a resolution barring any candidate from receiving the party's nomination if the candidate had been chosen by a pre-primary sponsored by any organization. The keynote speaker, former US Senator Walter F. Kirby, announced, "There is no room in the Democratic party for an invisible empire."[101]

Besides the Klan's meddling in the state Democratic primary, Grand Dragon Comer schemed with some state Republican leaders to swing the Klan vote to the GOP in the November presidential race. Soon after the Democratic nominee John Davis had spoken against the Klan, Comer approached Harmon C. Remmel, the state Republican committee chairman, about getting a meeting with a representative of the Coolidge candidacy to discuss Klan support for the Republican ticket. The meeting never materialized, and it is questionable to what extent any Klan votes defected from the Democratic to Republican ticket. But Comer's politicking would erode his influence greatly.[102]

James Comer remained the Grand Dragon of the Arkansas Klan, but opposition to him only increased once he tangled with the Democratic Party establishment. Adding to Comer's problems in the summer and fall of 1924 were his associations with the Women of the Ku Klux Klan (WKKK). Hiram Evans had sanctioned the chartering of this organization in Little Rock the year before, surely out of his close association with Arkansas's Grand Dragon. Comer put eight thousand dollars of his own money into the organization to get it started. In return, the WKKK hired him as the attorney, which provided him with income and influence over the organization. The first Imperial Commander of the WKKK was Mrs. Lula Markwell of Little Rock, a former court stenographer and schoolteacher who had been president and treasurer of the Women's Christian Temperance Union (WCTU) in Arkansas for twenty years. In February of 1924, after serving less than a year, she resigned abruptly. Miss Robbie Gill of Little Rock, the Imperial Secretary, replaced Markwell as Imperial Commander, instead of the Imperial Vice-Commander, Alice Cloud, of Dallas, Texas.[103] Robbie Gill had been a secretary and stenographer in Comer's law office for ten years. She moved the national headquarters of the WKKK from the second floor of the Ancient Order of United Workman building to a Little Rock mansion that was quickly dubbed the "Imperial Palace." When Robbie Gill married James Comer the following June, the other Klanswomen had had enough. Alice Cloud and a couple of other Klanswomen filed suit in Little Rock against Robbie Gill Comer and James Comer, charging them with extravagance and misappropriation of WKKK funds for their personal benefit. In addition, Miss Cloud charged that Robbie Comer had illegally taken control of the organization. Specific charges mentioned $18,000 that Comer was alleged to have received as legal fees, the purchase of a luxury automobile for his use, and Mrs. Comer's $750 crown as Imperial Commander. The Comers promptly suspended the three women from membership in the WKKK. Imperial Wizard Evans sent a message of full support for Mr. and Mrs. Comer from Klan headquarters in Atlanta. The suit failed when a chancery judge, John Martineau, ironically the only Democratic candidate for governor in the previous year who had taken an anti-Klan position, declared that he lacked jurisdiction. But he did rule that the plaintiffs had the right to examine the books of the WKKK. The accounts indicated that the WKKK had taken in nearly a third of a million dollars in 1925, but had spent all but $18,000. Much of that money went to the Comers, the plaintiffs said, who had become wealthy from the sale of WKKK robes and regalia. James Comer had sold a factory that made WKKK robes, which was valued at $23,000, to the WKKK for a whopping $72,000. The three Dallas women documented, in addition,

left: James Comer, from the *Kourier* (Atlanta, GA), January 1931. *Courtesy of the Butler Center for Arkansas Studies.*
right: Imperial Commander Robbie Gill Comer. *Courtesy of Corbis Images.*

how the Comers had wasted WKKK funds equipping the Klan mansion with goldfish, songbirds, police dogs, and a piano.[104] In addition, nine Little Rock Klansmen filed suit against James Comer charging that he had enriched himself to the tune of $200,000 of the Klan's money, and they demanded an audit of the organization's funds.[105]

The negative publicity for the Comers, the Klan, and the WKKK took its toll. On the evening of November 5, 1925, a gathering of three thousand Little Rock Klansmen passed a no-confidence resolution concerning James Comer. They announced they were seceding to form a new organization. A few days later the men filed for and received a charter for their "Independent Klan." Shortly thereafter most of the women of Little Rock's WKKK seceded to form a women's auxiliary of the new Klan organization. More litigation followed over ownership of property. The Klan filed a suit to prevent the seceding group from using the name "Klan," and thereafter the splinter group became the "Mystic Knights of Arkansas." James Comer remained the Grand Dragon of the Arkansas realm of the KKK with Robbie Gill Comer as commander of the WKKK, but the organizations by the end of 1925 were mere shadows of their former selves. By early 1926, according to Charles Alexander, fewer than ten thousand Klansmen remained active in the state. The

Mystic Knights never had the organizational energy of the former Klan and soon disappeared from the record.[106]

Meanwhile, on the national level, events of 1925 conspired to deflate the KKK from its peak. The trouble began in Indiana, the state with the largest Klan membership in the entire country. David C. Stephenson, the former Grand Dragon of Indiana and the Klan leader with the highest profile outside of Hiram Evans, was accused and convicted of the abduction, rape, and murder of a young woman, a schoolteacher he had been seeing romantically. On one evening in March 1925, Stephenson and three other men forced her to drink whiskey until she was intoxicated and then took her to Stephenson's private railway car. On the journey from Indianapolis to Chicago, he raped and abused her repeatedly. The young woman died a few weeks later of staph infection, from the numerous deep bites he had inflicted on her body, and from the effects of some pills that she had taken in an attempt at suicide.[107] With widespread media coverage in 1925 of the Stephenson trial and his conviction in November 1925, the damage to the Klan, an organization that presented itself as the defender of prohibition and the honor of women, was incalculable. Klan membership plummeted nationwide.

The Klan declined in Arkansas and most of the nation about as fast as it had arisen. But between 1921 and 1925 it provided an institutional mechanism to promote anti-Catholic views, along with a posture of anti-Semitism and white supremacy. The Klan's opposition to Catholicism centered on the belief that Catholics were simply not authentic Americans whose devotion to country trumped their loyalties to their church hierarchy. To oppose Catholicism, the Klan fought for immigration restriction and was successful in charting the course of American immigration policy for the next thirty years. Klansmen and women championed the public schools as opposed to parochial education. They promoted a curriculum that would teach students a white Protestant patriotic version of American history. Finally, the Klan worked to keep Roman Catholics from achieving public offices, all the way from local positions to the presidency of the United States. The next presidential election in 1928, when a Roman Catholic, Al Smith, actually succeeded in getting the Democratic nomination, would pull together what was left of the Klan and the anti-Catholic movement into one more blowout before it began to subside in the 1930s.

CHAPTER 5

Al Smith, Joe T. Robinson, and the 1928 Election

GOVERNOR AL SMITH'S bid for the presidency in 1928, the first time in American history that a Roman Catholic received the nomination from a major political party, marked a climax of the anti-Catholic movement of the early twentieth century. But it was also a bookend, for his defeat calmed the fears of Catholic opponents and for others brought Catholicism more into the center of the country's political life. The 1928 election particularly stirred Arkansans, for Governor Smith chose a Methodist senator from Arkansas, Joe T. Robinson, as his vice presidential nominee. Robinson was the first Arkansan, and the first southerner since the Civil War, to secure a place on a presidential ticket.

Smith's aspirations for the presidency had come a long way from the fractured, acrimonious standoff that was the 1924 Democratic National Convention. He was anything but a sore loser. Smith and his supporters left Madison Square Garden to prepare the transition of his candidacy from a northern, urban, Catholic, wet candidate to one with more national appeal. Given how firmly his Democratic opponents had dug in their heels in 1924, his consolidation of support from within the party in 1928 appears all the more remarkable. He had received national exposure in 1924—both positive and negative. But things changed as the Klan spiraled into decline in 1925. Smith's Democratic rivals more or less faded away, leaving him the front-runner for 1928. William McAdoo, badly bruised by the 1924 convention, had no public office from which to keep himself in the public eye. By 1927 he realized he was no longer a viable candidate and announced in September he would not seek the nomination. Pro-Smith leaders meanwhile worked quietly behind the scenes to woo southern and western Democrats to moderate their views of Smith. His advisors worked with Smith to tone down his loud Lower-East-Side New-York-City persona, an act he simply could not turn off. One advisor suggested he refrain from being photographed with a cigar or showing his gold teeth.[1] By 1927 it was clear that Al Smith—flashy suits, New York accent, and all—was the man to beat for the Democratic nomination.

A national discussion of Smith's religion and what it meant for a presidential campaign began in the spring of 1927. In April, the *Atlantic Monthly* published "An Open Letter to Governor Smith," written by Charles C. Marshall, an Episcopal layman and retired lawyer. Marshall asked Smith to respond to a couple of simple propositions about his Catholicism as it related to holding high political office. Marshall's first premise was that the Roman Catholic Church by definition was intolerant by claiming to be the one true church. Secondly, he asserted that the official teaching of the church since Pope Boniface VIII's bull *Unam Sanctum* in the fourteenth century had placed the church as sovereign over the state. Marshall asked Smith if he could be a loyal Roman Catholic and still uphold the Constitution of the United States. The Ku Klux Klan and other anti-Catholics had been arguing throughout the 1920s that a Roman Catholic political official could not.

In the following month, Smith responded, hoping to air the issue of his Catholic faith and put the matter to rest. While he admitted he wrote as a Catholic layman and not a theologian, he denied that the propositions asserted by Marshall were held by any American Catholic. To Marshall's first point about theological intolerance, Smith said this teaching was relevant only for Catholics. No other dogma but the official Roman Catholic one was tolerated for Catholics, Smith said, but this intolerance did not apply to non-Catholics. To the second point, he said he had never experienced a conflict between his Catholic faith and his official duties, and such a conflict had never been claimed either by the people of New York or Roman Catholic authorities. Smith ended his response with a summation of his creed as an American Catholic, which affirmed the freedom of conscience of all people and religious sects, absolute separation of church and state, and support for the public schools and the right of parents to choose whether their child is educated in a public or religious school. He specifically recognized no power of his church institutions to interfere with the operations of the Constitution of the United States.[2] Smith's response was simple and articulate, and he was widely perceived as having won the debate with Marshall.[3]

The serious discussion about the possibility of a Catholic president began among Arkansas Protestant evangelicals as the Marshall-Smith debate was taking place. An article in the *Baptist Advance* in May painted a word-picture of the visit of papal legate Cardinal Giovanni Bonzano to New York in 1926, where in "breathless silence Governor Alfred Smith and the mayor bowed their knees to him and humbly kissed the papal ring." The article report noted that the Knights of Columbus had asked President Calvin Coolidge to intervene on behalf of the Roman Catholic Church in Mexico and asked readers to imagine how Al Smith would handle such a request if he were president.[4] Ben Bogard began his assault on the prospect of a Smith presidency in his September 1, 1927, issue of the *Baptist and Commoner*. Bogard said he respected any man's right to choose his religion: "If he wants to be a Catholic or a Mormon or a Mohammedan it is his business." But it is unsafe, Bogard continued, to put into office a man who belongs to a worldwide organization "that openly declares its intention to rule the world." While Smith claimed that he would not favor the Catholic Church if elected, Bogard reminded readers that Smith still bowed down and kissed the ring of the pope's representative. He concluded his attack on Smith and Catholicism by reprinting a series of false assertions of the sort disseminated by the Klan about the monopoly of Catholics in public offices: that 61 percent of the State Department officers, 70 percent of the Treasury Department, 73 percent of the Department of Justice, and 60 percent of the Bureau of Education were Roman Catholics. The Roman Catholic Church, Bogard wrote later in September, "is a political-religious machine" and it must be opposed.[5]

The revival of discussion of Catholicism brought to mind the broader threats of Catholicism to Arkansans. The *Baptist Advance* in September published an editorial about the rapid growth of Catholicism in Arkansas over the previous twenty years, taking its information from a recent article in the *Guardian*. The Baptist paper noted with alarm that the number of parishes had increased from 73 to 107, the number of priests from 26 to 60, and the number of nuns from 250 to 675. Twenty years before, the church had 29 schools and 1 college educating 3,000 students, the paper noted, while by 1927 Arkansas Catholics had 46 schools, 7 academies, 2 colleges, and a seminary educating in all approximately 7,000 students. The article concluded that "the Catholic religion is deadly; in its true essence it is only baptized (?) paganism." The paper challenged Baptist readers to act with zeal to prevent friends, neighbors, and children from getting drawn into the Catholic fold.[6] In their annual state convention in November in Jonesboro, Southern Baptists went on record as opposing any candidate for the presidency of the United States who opposed a strict enforcement of the Eighteenth Amendment, singling out specifically Al Smith, Maryland governor Albert C. Ritchie, and Missouri senator Jim Reed.[7]

Another sign that anti-Catholicism revived in 1927 was a piece of legislation introduced in the state's general assembly that targeted the Knights of Columbus. In February, Representative Joseph J. Bevill of Nevada County filed House bill number 269, which would make it a felony offense to hold membership in any secret or oath-bound association affiliated with an organization whose "seat of government is in a foreign country or whose executive officer is not a citizen of the United States." The felony conviction would call for at least a year of hard labor or a minimum fine of one thousand dollars, or both. Representative Bevill denied that the bill was specifically aimed at the Knights of Columbus, although it appears otherwise. The bill was referred to the Judiciary Committee, but apparently did not make it to the House floor.[8]

While it had substantially declined, the Ku Klux Klan kept its anti-Catholic campaign going. The Klan had barely a public presence in Arkansas by 1927, in comparison to the profile between 1922 and 1924. However, Robbie Gill Comer, who continued on as Imperial Commander of the Women of the Ku Klux Klan, still had the chance for her ideas to see print. She devoted the majority of her address in August 1927 at the quadrennial convention of the WKKK to a wide-sweeping denunciation of Catholicism. Her aim, she said, was not to discuss the Roman church as a religion, but to consider its political ambitions and reach. "The Church of Rome," she said, "claims a God-given right to control all secular governments." She branded the denials of this "fact" by American Catholics as simply falsehoods. The Catholic strategy, Mrs. Comer said, was to lay low until the church had more than an even chance of success: "And now, they aim at the highest possible mark—the presidency of the United States." Al Smith should never be president, she said, for if there was ever a conflict between church and state, he would be obligated as a Catholic to obey the pope. "Our leaders," she concluded, "must look for their guidance to America, and not to Rome."[9]

In her address, Robbie Comer drew liberally from a forty-page pamphlet published in 1927 by the WKKK entitled *Out of Their Own Mouths Shall They Be Condemned*. The pamphlet used supposed Catholic sources to answer the questions posed by Klanswomen, such as: "Is it true that Roman Catholic authorities are endeavoring to make America Catholic? . . . that the Roman Catholic Church denounces Democracy? . . . that it claims the right to set aside the laws of the State? . . . that it opposes the public school system of America?" and, finally, "Why should no Roman Catholic be elected President of the U.S.?"[10] Clearly the possibility of a Smith candidacy focused Klan rhetoric on the perceived threat by Catholicism.

The issue of Catholicism and Al Smith's aspirations for the presidency became especially relevant to Arkansans in January 1928 when the state's senior senator, Joe T. Robinson, denounced intolerance against Catholics in a well-publicized debate on the US Senate floor. Robinson countered Senator Thomas Heflin, a Democrat from Alabama, who on the morning of January 18, 1928, delivered a well-worn speech opposing Catholicism and Al Smith's expected candidacy for the presidency. Robinson's stand against religious bigotry garnered national attention, won him both praise and condemnation from Arkansas constituents, and would lead Robinson to be chosen as Smith's running mate later in 1928.

Joseph Taylor Robinson might appear an unlikely champion of a Catholic New York governor. He was born in 1872 in Lonoke County, Arkansas, the son of a local farmer and physician. Soon after he passed the bar and became a small-town lawyer, he ran for representative to the Arkansas House of Representatives, becoming the youngest member of the legislature at the age of twenty-two. Eight years later he took on a seasoned Democratic opponent for Congress, defeated him, and cruised to victory over the Republican candidate in November. He entered the US House of Representatives in 1903 at the age of thirty. In five terms in the House, he made a name for himself introducing legislation to regulate railroads. He supported a host of bills in a progressive vein, such as a pure food and drug bill and a graduated income tax measure. Robinson ran for governor in 1912, defeating incumbent governor George Donaghey in the Democratic primary. He gave up his seat in the US House and took the oath as governor of Arkansas on January 16, 1913. Shortly before his inauguration, Arkansas senator Jeff Davis died in Washington, D.C. Robinson declared he could better serve the state in the Senate than the governor's office. On January 28, the Arkansas General Assembly voted for Robinson as the replacement for Davis, and he resigned the governor's position. He had the distinction of having served as a congressman, governor, and senator, all in the space of two weeks.[11]

Thus, Joe T. Robinson's tenure began as US Senator in 1913, a career that would last until his death in 1937 in Washington, D.C. Robinson was a loyal Wilson man, supporting American entry in the Great War, the League of Nations, and the Versailles Treaty. By 1920 he had a high enough profile within his party to be named the chairman of the Democratic National Convention in San Francisco. At the end of 1923 he became the minority leader in the Senate. By summer of 1924 he even had presidential aspirations, with the Democratic National Convention in New York City, which has been described above.[12]

It is difficult to establish Senator Robinson's religious opinions before his speech in January 1928 defending Catholicism. A life-long Methodist, Robinson attended church when in Arkansas, but rarely while in Washington. When running for governor in 1912, Robinson favored local option rather than incumbent governor Donaghey's position of total prohibition. Later as senator he supported the dry position, although he was known to enjoy a drink of whiskey in private company in Washington or on trips abroad.[13] The Catholic state newspaper, the *Southern Guardian*, had taken Robinson to task in the short period in 1913 when he was governor for so-called bigoted anti-Catholic comments in a speech given to Arkansas teachers. He had praised Martin Luther "for proclaiming religious freedom and general education as the right of all mankind" at a time when "Europe and all the world were steeped in ignorance and superstition; when priest and King combined the powers of church and nation to keep the devoted and subject ignorant." Robinson responded to the criticism that he was not reflecting on any church or its members, but merely using expressions he himself had learned in school. Afterward, the diocesan paper seemed to hold Robinson in favor, reporting in 1920 that he was touring New York state with Governor Smith as his "campaign pal" and noting that it made no difference to "Old Joe" that Smith was a good and staunch Catholic. In 1925 at the sixth annual banquet of Mount St. Mary Academy in Little Rock, Robinson gave the sisters an address commending their work and sacrifice, and he was followed on the platform by Bishop John Morris.[14] Yet it came as something of a surprise in January 1928 when Robinson came out on a national stage denouncing anti-Catholic bigotry.

Robinson's adversary, Senator Thomas Heflin, who later admitted his membership in the Ku Klux Klan, had emerged in 1927 as the vocal spokesman for anti-Catholic views in the US Congress. He had a stock speech against Catholicism and Al Smith's aspirations to the presidency that he had given multiple times both on and off Capitol Hill. His presentation became even more strident in January 1928 after the Hearst newspapers reported that the Mexican government was bribing four US senators, including Heflin, to oppose Catholicism. The Senate ordered

Senator Joseph Taylor Robinson. *Courtesy of Special Collections, University of Arkansas Libraries, Fayetteville.*

an investigation, with Joe T. Robinson serving on the investigating committee. The documents suggesting bribery were later found to be forged. But the charges worked Heflin into a lather. Wearing a long coat and cream-colored vest covering his considerable girth, Heflin stood at the Senate rostrum for two and a half hours refuting the allegations of bribery and suggesting a Catholic conspiracy behind the charges. He went on to denounce politicking by the Knights of Columbus and the papacy, the Al Smith candidacy, Tammany Hall, and Catholic attempts to takeover public education and purchase elections.[15]

Finally, Joe T. Robinson, red-faced and pointing a finger at the senator from Alabama, took the floor to respond. Robinson, a man well known for his temper, clearly had lost patience with Heflin.[16] While he acknowledged that Heflin and the other senators were the victims of false allegations and he criticized William Randolph Hearst for publishing them, none of this justified Heflin's claim that the Catholic Church was behind the forged documents. Robinson said he had heard the senator from Alabama give his anti-Catholic speech too many times before: "I have heard him denounce the Catholic Church and the Pope of Rome and the cardinal and the bishop and the priest and the nun until I am sick and tired of it, as a Democrat." Heflin dared Robinson to make that speech in Arkansas. Robinson responded: "I will make the speech in Arkansas, and I will make it in Alabama too." Heflin shot back, "If you do, they will tar and feather you." Robinson said, "He says that if I say here or in Arkansas or in Alabama that I am tired of hearing him abuse and denounce the Catholic Church, and the agencies of the Catholic Church, they will tar and feather me. That is illustrative, my friends, of how a good man can go wrong, and how far wrong he can go, and what a fool he can make of himself after he has gone wrong." The whole tenor of Heflin's speech, Robinson said, was "unwholesome and harmful." Robinson continued that Heflin had said that Al Smith could not be nominated for president by the Democratic Party because he is a Catholic. But Robinson said, "I believe, Mr. President, that one who is a Catholic has just as much right to apply for the favor of his party associates as one who is a Methodist or a Baptist, and I believe that when you deny that right you deny a fundamental principle of this Government."[17]

The exchange had become bitter, acrimonious, and personal. Heflin said that if Robinson were going to "fight the Roman Catholics' battle," then he should not remain the Democratic leader within the Senate. He went on to ask that Robinson be removed from the special investigative committee dealing with the Mexican bribery allegations. On the following day, Senator Robinson called for a Democratic caucus to vote on his continued leadership of the party. With Heflin and a few others absent, the Democratic senators affirmed their support for Robinson, with one dissenting vote, and he kept his post as minority leader and his place on the special committee.[18]

The Heflin-Robinson exchange made front-page news across the United States. As Robinson emerged as a national spokesperson for religious toleration, his office was deluged with mail from Arkansas and across the nation reacting to his speech. He received speaking invitations from around the country, including Heflin's home state, Alabama. Newspaper editorials for the most part lauded as heroic Robinson's defense of religious liberty, Catholicism, and Al Smith. His stature in the Democratic Party rose. Commentators mentioned his name as a compromise candidate should the coming presidential convention prove to become deadlocked as in 1924. Word of his defense of Catholicism apparently even reached Rome. According to Robinson family lore, some years later when he visited the Holy See and had an audience with the pope, Robinson received a cane in appreciation for his well-known defense against anti-Catholic bigotry. He gave the cane to the bishop of Little Rock.[19]

The reception of Senator Robinson's speech provides a gauge of attitudes in Arkansas toward religious intolerance and Catholicism. In the days following January 18, Robinson received sixty-six letters from all parts of the state either praising or criticizing him for his comments. The positive letters outweighed the negative by more than a three-to-one margin (fifty-one to fifteen). The complimentary letters came disproportionately from larger towns, particularly Little Rock, Fort Smith, and Pine Bluff, and from political officials, attorneys, and businessmen. One letter from Marion was written by an attorney but endorsed with signatures of the Crittenden County sheriff, judge, and circuit clerk, the sheriff of Poinsett County, and the circuit clerk of Cross County. The bishop of Little Rock, John Morris, thanked Robinson, saying he was proud that the assault against anti-Catholicism was made by a senator from Arkansas. A few other Catholic laymen and individuals representing

Knights of Columbus chapters in Arkansas praised Robinson. On the other hand, a larger portion of the critical letters was from small-town and rural parts of the state and from Protestant clergy. The pastors of First Christian Church of Mammoth Springs and First Baptist Church of Pine Bluff opposed Robinson's position.[20] Several constituents reflected the sentiments of an angry strawberry farmer in Judsonia, who told Robinson that the voters of Arkansas would "clean your plow" in the next election if he supported "the Catholic whiskey bunch."[21]

Newspapers in Arkansas responded similarly to the speech. Most small-town weeklies ignored the Heflin-Robinson squabble. A smaller number printed reports from news services, and an even smaller number took an editorial position. But the breakdown between positive and negative reporting mirrored that of the letters. Of the sample of Arkansas newspapers reviewed, eight (in Little Rock, Fayetteville, Malvern, Hot Springs, Springdale, Newark, and Texarkana) editorialized in favor of Robinson's speech while two, the *Benton Courier* and the *Dardanelle Post Dispatch*, criticized his remarks.[22] Both the state dailies, the *Arkansas Gazette* and the *Arkansas Democrat*, took a strong position favoring Robinson's position. The *Democrat* called it a struggle, "Decency vs. Demagoguery, " with Robinson administering a needed spanking to Heflin, "like a schoolmaster of old." The *Gazette* said that Robinson had done many a good day's work in the Senate, "but rarely or never a better one than when he placed himself squarely across the path along which Senator Helflin [*sic*] of Alabama was raging anew in the fury of intolerance and abuse." The Malvern paper declared that Heflin was "either below the scale in intelligence, or else he is a player of low politics." The *Springdale News* called Heflin's speech "the bray of an ass . . . a vicious and uncalled-for attack on all Catholics in general and Governor Smith in particular." The small-town Newark newspaper editorialized that "Senator Robinson has performed a public duty" in chastising Heflin, who spoke for bigots, not Democrats. The *Dardanelle Post-Dispatch*, on the other hand, declared that "this is a Protestant country" and that the South would never stand for a Roman Catholic and liquor man such as Al Smith.[23]

The national attention and the generally positive response to his attack on religious intolerance may have convinced Joe T. Robinson that he might become Smith's choice for vice president, should Smith get the nomination in June. By the end of January Robinson made clear that he did not intend to run for the presidential nomination.[24] On March 17 he gave a speech to a Catholic audience, the Friendly Sons of St. Patrick in Philadelphia, in which he denounced "intolerance and all its loathsome brood, ignorance, falsehood and oppression." He called for remembrance of the guarantee of religious freedom as laid out by the founding fathers.[25] Shortly after Robinson's Philadelphia speech, the Arkansas Democratic Committee convened on March 23 at Little Rock's Marion Hotel to select delegates to the upcoming national convention in Houston. The common assumption before the meeting was that the delegation would cast its votes for Robinson, as it had done in 1924. But Robinson sent the chair, J. S. Utley, a letter that was read at the meeting declaring that he was not a candidate. The senator recommended that delegates go to Houston "uninstructed," that is, that they be left free to cast ballots in accordance with their own judgment.[26]

Given that delegates would not be lining up behind a favorite-son Robinson candidacy, the key question for the Little Rock meeting concerned whom they would then support. Battle lines were readied to oppose any candidate who might dismantle prohibition, meaning, specifically, Al Smith. Dr. A. C. Millar, the editor of the *Arkansas Methodist* and the state leader of the Anti-Saloon League, asked for the floor to address the assembly. In what was probably a tactical move, Millar had just the day before announced his candidacy for the party's nomination for lieutenant governor. He reminded listeners that southern Democrats favored prohibition and that the state had voted for prohibition twelve years before by a two-to-one margin. Millar then introduced a resolution that would bind the state committee to oppose the presidential nomination of anyone opposed to the Eighteenth Amendment. The pastor of Pine Bluff's First Baptist Church, Dr. Selsus Estol Tull, submitted his own more specifically anti-Catholic resolution to the committee. Tull proposed the following language: "We regard that any man who is bound in religious conscience or affiliation by an allegiance to any ecclesiastical power which claims and seeks directly or indirectly political rights and recognition in the government of nations is thereby presumed disqualified to impartially administer political office under our constitution." In other words, any Roman Catholic was to be categorically opposed. The state committee voted down Millar's resolution and failed to take any action on Tull's. The group did, however, approve a resolution offered by the state Women's Christian Temperance Union, which advocated the vigorous upholding of the Constitution and enforcement of the law. This passage brought an angry response by W. H. Abington of Beebe, the speaker of the state House of Representatives, who declared the committee needed no such resolution to force it to observe the law. The meeting concluded with the election of the delegates to the Houston convention.[27]

The public perceived that this meeting prepared the way for Arkansas delegates to support Al Smith. The *Arkansas Gazette* reported that 90 percent of the delegation favored Smith. The party's secretary, H. L. Lambert, denied that the committee had deliberately selected pro-Smith delegates, but there was no way of knowing, given that the delegation's caucus would not take place until after they arrived in Houston. Privately, the chairman of the state Democratic Committee said he had heard no more than five of the twenty-two delegates and twenty-two alternates say that they intended to vote for Smith.[28] Nonetheless, the state Democratic Committee meeting marked the beginning of the organized opposition to a Smith presidential candidacy in Arkansas, with or without the inclusion of Robinson on the party's ticket.

Drs. Millar and Tull quickly emerged, with Ben Bogard and Grand Dragon James Comer, as the leaders of the anti-Smith campaign in Arkansas. Alexander Copeland Millar appears as the unlikely figure to lead an anti-Catholic movement, but his life-long advocacy of prohibition would make him an opponent of Al Smith. He had come to Arkansas in 1887 at the young age of twenty-five to become the second president of Central Collegiate Institution in Altus, which became Hendrix College and moved to Conway in 1890. He was president of Hendrix until 1902 and then again from 1910 to 1913. Thereafter, he was the editor of the *Arkansas Methodist* until his death in 1940. He was elected president of the executive committee of the Anti-Saloon League of Arkansas in 1924 and served on the national board of this organization.[29]

Tull's opposition to Al Smith focused less on the alcohol issue and more generally attacked Smith's religion. Born in Louisiana, Tull came to Arkansas around 1909 to pastor Pine Bluff's First Baptist Church, a congregation of the Southern Baptist Convention. He moved on to Kentucky in 1919 and then Texas before returning to the Pine Bluff

Dr. Alexander Copeland Millar. *Courtesy of Cathy Millar Woods.*

church in 1923.[30] Tull had introduced an anti-evolution resolution passed by the National Baptist Convention in Houston in 1927 and supported the Arkansas Baptist Convention's resolution passed at its meeting in Jonesboro that year pledging members to oppose any presidential candidate against prohibition.[31] He had written an "open letter" to Senator Robinson just before his famous debate with Heflin, asking him to do what he could do to block a Smith nomination, telling him that he knew scores of Baptist and Methodist preachers who would "take the stump" against him if Robinson advocated Smith's election. Tull's open letter was printed in the *Baptist Advance* and the Klan's *Kourier Magazine*.[32] After Robinson took his stand in the Senate, Tull wrote again castigating the senator, proclaiming to Robinson that Catholicism "is not religion in the sense that Methodists and Baptist beliefs are religions. Catholicism is a vast, intriguing murderous POLITICAL power." Tull closed his letter to Robinson by advocating that Catholics be driven out of both the Democratic and Republican Parties.[33]

Tull made his thoughts public by penning a long article for the *Baptist Advance* entitled "Should Al Smith Be President?" He subsequently published it as a pamphlet and sold it for twenty-five cents. Tull first tackled Smith's record of opposing prohibition, considering it treason to attempt to annul one of the "sacred stipulations of the Constitution of the United States." Then Tull explained that, the whiskey question aside, "Smith should never be president of the United States because he is an orthodox, endorsed and representative Catholic." While Robinson and others had quoted founding fathers in arguing that religion should never be a test for the selection of political authorities, Tull argued that Catholicism was more than a religion:

> CATHOLICISM IS A VAST, DANGEROUS, INTRIGUEING, BLOODY, POLITICAL SYSTEM, AND HAS ALWAYS BEEN. . . . THE DANK OF THE DUNGEON, THE TORTURE MACHINE, THE ASHES OF A MILLION MARTYR FIRES, THE CRY OF STARVING WOMEN AND INNOCENT BABIES, THE BLOOD AND DEATH OF TEN THOUSAND BATTLE FIELDS, ARE THE WITNESSES TO THE ROMAN CATHOLIC CHURCH IN POLITICS.

Lowering his volume, Tull continued: "It is impossible for Catholicism to synchronize with American ideals. Every Catholic owes his first allegiance to the pope. He therefore can not become a true American." Before closing, Tull made swipes at Tammany Hall, the papacy, the Knights of Columbus, the Catholic Daughters of America, Jesuits, Catholic schools, and, finally, Joe T. Robinson for betraying his Protestant constituency and labeling those who oppose Catholics holding public office as "intolerant."[34] Tull was not merely venting; he aimed to influence the Democratic political machine in Arkansas. Shortly before the state Democratic Committee meeting in March, he wrote an open letter to the chairman, J. S. Utley, asking why the Democratic Party had become the Catholic Party and the Whiskey Party. He requested the committee to instruct the Arkansas delegation against the nomination of either a wet or Catholic candidate for the presidency or vice presidency.[35]

After Millar and Tull failed to influence the Democratic meeting, they, along with Klansmen Ben Bogard and James Comer, worked to sway Democratic delegates and mobilize public opinion in Arkansas to head off a Smith nomination at Houston in late June. In April, Tull prepared a certificate for voters to sign attesting their opposition to the nomination of Smith or "any other Catholic or wet candidate." The certificate further declared that should a wet or Catholic candidate be nominated, then these voters would refuse to vote the Democratic ticket. Tull's plan was to circulate copies of the certificate in churches, Sunday school classes, clubs, fraternal orders, or anywhere that ten voters or more might be likely to express themselves. The results would be shared with party leaders before the Houston convention.[36]

A. C. Millar similarly concentrated on efforts to influence Arkansas's delegates to the upcoming convention. On behalf of the Anti-Saloon League, he sent questionnaires to the delegates, asking them to explain their positions regarding the Volstead Act and the Eighteenth Amendment. One of the delegates, W. H. Abington, who had responded testily to the resolution passed at the meeting on March 23, 1928, challenged the right of the Anti-Saloon League to use strong-arm tactics to influence delegates. Millar also began to distribute material throughout Arkansas about Smith's prohibition record.[37] In early June, Millar wrote to Senator Robinson, who would be chairman of the state's delegation a few weeks later in Houston. He warned Robinson that a majority of Arkansas voters would go Republican or refuse to vote if Smith received the nomination. Moreover, the Democratic Party would be defeated in the South and discredited nationally. Robinson responded politely that the Democratic Party was neither a prohibitionist nor anti-prohibitionist party. Should the party endorse a wet candidate, Robinson said, it would not justify bolting from the party.[38] Just before the convention assembled in Houston, Millar was instrumental in gathering eighty-one prohibition leaders for a meeting on Mount Sequoyah in Fayetteville, sponsored by the Methodist Church, the Women's Christian Temperance Union (WCTU), and the Anti-Saloon League. The national president of the Anti-Saloon League, Dr. Eugene Crawford, was there from Washington, D.C., and others attended from Oklahoma, Tennessee, and Texas, as well as Arkansas. For several days the group caucused about strategies to oppose a Smith candidacy. Millar combined the trip to Fayetteville with some campaigning for his candidacy for lieutenant governor.[39]

In addition to these efforts of Millar and Tull, the Ku Klux Klan in

Arkansas prepared for the Democratic Convention. Although membership in the Klan had declined after 1924, James Comer remained Grand Dragon of the Realm of Arkansas and evidently saw the Smith candidacy as an opportunity to get the Klan back in the public eye. Imperial Wizard Hiram Evans had visited Arkansas in early March to promote a new Klan group "degree," the Knights of the Great Forest, whose preamble was "Down with Al Smith."[40] After the Democratic meeting on March 23, Comer quickly jumped in to register his alarm that the state's delegation would cast its support for Smith. On March 29, the Little Rock Klan prepared a mass mailing, apparently sent out to more than fifteen hundred men, probably former Klan members, in the Little Rock area, declaring that the nation's welfare was in peril with the risk of losing the Volstead Act. The letter announced a meeting for April 2 to develop a plan to avert this calamity.[41] The Grand Dragon also wrote a letter to the Arkansas delegates to the Houston convention urging them to oppose Smith because of his Catholic faith. One of the delegates, Charles Evans of Booneville, sent the letter to Al Smith. In Smith's speech in Oklahoma City in September, when he addressed head-on his Catholicism, he pointed out that the Grand Dragon of the Arkansas Klan was sending letters around the state telling people to oppose Smith on account of his religion.[42]

Comer simultaneously went on a campaign in the religious press. In a letter to both the *Baptist Advance* and the *Baptist and Commoner*, Comer charged that Smith opposed the marriage laws of the United States when one party in a marriage is of the Catholic faith. Comer noted that the Catholic Church requires a contract that the couple of mixed marriage would rear any offspring in the Catholic faith. Some people, he said, think American Catholics are different from Catholics in other countries, but "there is no such thing as an American Catholic. They are simply Roman Catholics living in America." Smith's election as president, Comer continued, would be a first step toward turning the country over to "the ecclesiastical powers and influences of Rome." The Klan, he concluded, was the only organization of Protestants fighting to prevent the election of a Romanist as president of the United States. In printing Comer's letter, Ben Bogard said that his paper was a Baptist paper, not a Klan paper, but that he was glad "there is an organization with thousands of members ready to present an organized front against RUM AND ROMANISM as represented by Al Smith." Bogard noted that those "who have been guessing that the Klan was dead have another guess coming."[43]

Ben Bogard and the Missionary Baptists had been on the attack against a possible Smith presidency since the Heflin-Robinson debate in January 1928. On February 1, Bogard had praised Heflin for the courage to stand up against the "Roman machine" and said the state was ashamed of Robinson, "who so grossly misrepresented the people of Arkansas." Robinson was simply catering to Catholics for political reasons, Bogard said. Two weeks later he asserted that no Christian or "red-blooded American" could support Al Smith. Throughout the spring, Bogard was plugging *The National Dangers in Roman Catholicism*, a small book by his coworker, the Reverend Doss N. Jackson, of Texarkana's County Avenue Baptist Church. Without naming Al Smith, Jackson detailed the threats to the American political system posed by the Roman Catholic Church, ranging from meddling with government to undermining the public schools and opposing non-Catholic marriages. Using material from the nineteenth-century works of anti-Catholic lecturer P. A. Seguin, Jackson recycled the alleged Catholic oaths and brought up the killing of William Black in Marshall, Texas, in 1915 and the beating of Otis Spurgeon outside of Denver. The booklet finished off by attacking Catholic doctrines such as papal infallibility and the sacramental system. Bogard and the Baptist Press in Little Rock were selling Jackson's booklet for twenty-five cents.[44]

By April, Bogard admitted that Smith would likely get the Democratic nomination. He directed Missionary Baptists to "make up our minds to vote against him in the election and elect a Republican." By mid-May he was announcing a coming special "Rum and Romanism" edition of the *Baptist and Commoner*, and when it appeared on May 30, it was much like his anti-Catholic special edition in 1922.[45]

Bogard's attack on Catholicism, like Jackson's, covered a lot of ground, very little of it original. He led with the old suggestion that the pope was the anti-Christ, linked to the number 666 prophesized in Revelations 13:18. Denunciations of the papacy as a foreign government followed, with a photograph of Pope Pius, who Bogard said would be the real president if Smith were elected. Bogard told readers, "Get familiar with his picture so you will have no trouble recognizing him when he holds out his toe for you to kiss." The paper labeled Al Smith as a liquor man, a Tammanyite who presided over the dens of vice, speakeasies, and houses of ill repute in New York's capital city, Albany. He added a stinging rebuke to the Democratic Party leadership of Arkansas for electing pro-Smith delegates with no regard for the wishes of the people of the state. He directed readers not to go fishing on Election Day but to turn out and vote the Republican ticket. Bogard highlighted a pastor at Malvern's Second Baptist Church, S. C. Hammock, who claimed to have been for thirty years a Catholic and was now available for lectures: "Evils of Roman Catholicism" or "Why Al Smith Should Not Be Nominated on the Democratic Ticket for President of the U.S." Bogard printed extra copies of the issue to sell for ten cents each, or forty for a dollar. A few weeks later, he claimed to have sold two thousand extra copies.[46]

By early June 1928, it appeared a foregone conclusion that Al Smith would become the Democratic nominee. From June 12 to 15, the Republican Party had met in Kansas City and chosen President Coolidge's secretary of commerce, the noted humanitarian Herbert Hoover, on the first ballot, as expected, as its presidential nominee. Senator Charles Curtis of Kansas, a good friend of Joe T. Robinson, became Hoover's running mate. Meanwhile, the anti-Smith forces in Arkansas worked feverishly to prevent a Smith nomination. Bogard, Tull, and other speakers gave a series of anti-Smith speeches at City Park in Little Rock.[47] A group of citizens met at the Columbia County courthouse in Magnolia and resolved that the Arkansas delegation should cast its entire vote for a dry candidate and one "against any principle that savors of the union of Church and State." A local attorney sent the resolution with 500 signatures to Senator Robinson. A similar petition with 105 signatures came from Howard County. Other mail continued to flow in to Robinson's office urging him to use his influence to oppose Smith, including a letter with 27 signatures from the WCTU chapter in Clarksville. The group's leader, Mrs. G. U. Neal, concluded that it seemed impossible "that a man who wished to put his foot on the brass rail and blow the froth from beer could be a safe leader for our great country." The Presbyterian Synod of Arkansas, meeting in early June, directed citizens to vote for no candidates or platforms that were wet.[48]

The bigger question for Houston concerned who would get the vice presidential nomination. But shortly before the convention assembled, that question too was answered as momentum coalesced behind Joe T.

Robinson. He was indeed the perfect complement to Al Smith—a Protestant, dry, southerner, prominent in the party, known to be a good public speaker and campaigner. Several of Robinson's Senate colleagues were pushing for his nomination. A *New York Times* reporter announced on June 19 that it appeared Robinson would get the nomination. And on the day before Robinson left for Houston, a representative of Governor Smith came to Little Rock to give the senator the message personally that Smith wanted him as his vice president. Robinson arrived at Houston on June 24 by way of a train from Little Rock called the "Joe T. Robinson Special," and as the convention opened Robinson's nomination appeared settled.[49]

Southerners celebrated the choice of Houston for the convention, the first time since the Civil War that the party had met in the South. Texans had erected in a short time a grand facility for the meeting, an enormous wood-frame structure with a barrel roof that occupied a full city block and could accommodate twenty-five thousand people. On Tuesday afternoon, before the convention opened on the evening of June 26, the Arkansas delegation caucused. A majority of the state's eighteen delegates planned to cast their votes for Smith. On the next morning, Robinson was sworn in as permanent chairman of the convention, or presiding officer, as he had been at the 1924 convention. His first task at the podium was to call the convention to order and to give a stirring speech, which was made all the more portentous given that the crowd expected him soon to be nominated with Smith.[50]

Robinson's speech aimed to bring the Democratic Party together in the face of obvious division. He called delegates to consider all the issues on which they were in agreement. He specifically asked that the party platform leave out any wet plank. Echoing language he had used frequently throughout the spring, he said the Democratic Party was neither a prohibition party nor an anti-prohibition party. The highlight of the speech, however, was when he strayed off his written script. Robinson alluded to Thomas Jefferson and his ideas of religious freedom, saying that Jefferson gloried in the provision of the Constitution "that declares that no religious test shall ever be required as a qualification for any office of trust in the United States." This comment, coming after his well-known remarks made in the Senate chambers in January, constituted a clear signal for Smith and religious tolerance. A loud cheer erupted, and delegates took to their feet making a round through the cavernous hall holding their state standards. On a second round, the demonstration became disorderly as cheering delegates tried to pull down the flags from some southern states, notably Alabama, Tennessee, and North Carolina, whose delegates remained stubbornly in their chairs. After pushing and shoving, the Houston police intervened to end the struggle. After about twenty minutes, with much rapping of the gavel, Robinson restored order.[51]

The remainder of the 1928 Democratic convention was as quick and smooth as the 1924 convention had been protracted and acrimonious. Discussion of the thirty-three planks of the platform became anticlimactic when the key issue of prohibition was largely ignored. One plank merely pledged support for the enforcement of the Eighteenth Amendment, but took no stand on repealing or preserving it. On June 28, Al Smith won the nomination on the first ballot, receiving seventeen of the eighteen Arkansas votes. The remaining vote went to Senator James A. Reed of Missouri. On the following morning, Senator Pat Harrison of Mississippi was at the podium as chair, a clear signal that the convention was to vote on Robinson as vice presidential nominee. When the votes accumulated in this first ballot, Robinson won the nomination with more than 90 percent of the votes cast. Will Rogers, the humorist from Oklahoma who was covering the convention as special correspondent for the *New York Times,* said, "Joe T. Robinson of Arkansaw got the nomination, with more Democrats agreeing than had ever agreed on any one thing in the history of the party."[52]

As the Democratic convention came to a close, Al Smith's message of acceptance was read to the remaining delegates who were still assembled. Joe T. Robinson had already left Houston for Arkansas. After thanking the convention, Smith's telegram asserted that national prohibition needed to be fundamentally changed, an apparent contradiction to the platform that had been approved just a few days earlier. When the Democratic National Committee met in early July to prepare for the campaign, Smith's choice to become national chairman was John J. Raskob, a Roman Catholic who was well known for his wet position. He was, in fact, the director of the Association Against the Prohibition Amendment and thus had been more active in the drive to end prohibition than Al Smith.[53] Robinson, as the part of the ticket designed to keep southern, Protestant, and dry votes in the Democratic Party, clearly had work to do.

Robinson spent most of July and August campaigning in Arkansas with the exception of a quick trip in July to New York to confer with Smith and another in August to attend the official notification celebration for Smith's candidacy. The first duty of a vice presidential candidate is to carry his or her own state. While Arkansas's electoral votes were relatively few, it would nonetheless embarrass the party if the state went Republican for the first time since Reconstruction, with a favorite son on the ticket. Robinson endeavored to introduce Smith to his Arkansas audience and allay their fears about his religion and position on prohibition. At a Fourth of July rally in Little Rock, Robinson made a plea for religious tolerance and declared that the age of bigotry had passed. At the State Teacher's College in Conway, on July 17, Robinson argued that Smith's election would not endanger public education. "Neither the impairment of the public school system nor priest rule will result from the election of the Democratic ticket," and those who assert that it would, Robinson said, know better. The next day at Geisreiter Park in Pine Bluff, Robinson reviewed the details of Smith's biography and accomplishments as governor of New York. At Hope's Watermelon Festival in early August he castigated preachers who had abandoned the Gospel to preach politics from the pulpit. They invited laughter, he said, when they said that priests would dominate government under a Smith presidency. He noted that Smith's cabinet as governor contained thirteen Protestants, two Catholics, and a Jew. On August 30, Robinson received the official notification of his candidacy at a huge ceremony on the steps of Hot Springs's Arlington Hotel, his campaign headquarters. Thousands mobbed the park, lined the streets of Central Avenue, and hung out of windows of buildings as Robinson formally accepted the nomination in a speech carried over national radio. Al Smith's daughter stood in for the candidate. John Raskob attended to represent the Democratic Party and hear Robinson defend Smith's record and allay concerns about prohibition reform. On the following day, at a homecoming event in Lonoke, Robinson talked about Al Smith's simple, old-fashioned Christian faith. Those who feared that Catholicism would endanger our liberties, he said, should note that Smith's four terms as governor were uninfluenced by the Catholic Church.[54]

Beginning in September and continuing until the election in November, Robinson campaigned in the South, Midwest, and Far West to shore up support for the ticket, while Smith concentrated on his base in the East. On his southern tour, Robinson continually defended Smith's religion, as he had done in Arkansas. In the West and Midwest he concentrated more on other issues, especially the economy. On the advice of his managers, Smith generally avoided the religion issue, addressing it primarily in a speech in Oklahoma City on September 20.[55] Before returning to Arkansas on Monday, November 5, the eve of the election, Robinson had visited thirty states and given sixty major speeches with 157 appearances from the back platform of a train.[56]

Meanwhile, the opposition to a Smith-Robinson ticket mobilized in Arkansas. As before Smith's nomination, the opposition was an alliance between Protestant religious groups and the Ku Klux Klan. Grand Dragon James Comer clearly saw the 1928 election as an opportunity to regain some of the Klan's lost influence. Comer attended the Houston convention, and after returning he announced that the Klan would oppose the Smith-Robinson ticket.[57] In mid-July he launched another letter-writing campaign to former Klansmen throughout Arkansas, urging them to organize the Klan in their districts for a political purpose: to prevent a "Romanist" from being elected as president.[58] Comer boasted that the Klan had taken in many new members because of the Smith candidacy. On July 16, he sent another letter to all candidates for state and district offices, asking them to explain their position toward Smith and his religion. Comer explained the Klan's stand very clearly:

> Every native born Protestant in Arkansas should oppose the election of any man who subscribes to and is loyal to, or is a member of the Roman Catholic Church for the following reasons: First, that the Roman Catholic Church favors the joining of the Church and State. Second, because it does not subscribe to the free public school system. Third, because it is working toward the end of ultimately making America Roman Catholic and subservient to the will of that Institution. Fourth, because the Roman Pontiff by virtue of his alleged apostolic authority claims to have the right to define the doctrine regarding faith and morals and claims to be infallible in all these matters, as well as all others. Fifth because the Pontiff claims to be liberated from all civil subjugation; that he acknowledged no civil superior; that he claims to be the supreme

> judge on earth and the director of the conscience of men, and of what is right and wrong, and because all American Catholics who are loyal to that Institution will be required to project this thought in America and will be guided by the dictation of the Pope.[59]

Comer went on to claim that the Catholic Church controlled the Democratic Party. He asked the candidates not to put party loyalty above America, Protestantism, white supremacy, prohibition, and law enforcement.

One of the Democratic candidates for governor, J. Carroll Cone, passed on Comer's letter to Joe T. Robinson. Another gubernatorial candidate, Ben L. Griffin, charged that the letter contained vicious and premeditated falsehoods. Griffin declared his support for the Smith-Robinson ticket.[60] The head of the Democratic Party organization in Pulaski County announced that Democratic candidates were under no requirement to answer Comer's questionnaire, reminding people that Comer had been a lifelong Republican.[61] Lee Cazort, who had been the Klan's anointed candidate for governor in 1924, won the Democratic nomination for lieutenant governor but ignored the Klan's direction and openly campaigned for the Smith-Robinson ticket.[62] In early September the Klan held a rally in Fort Smith attended by more than two thousand people. Robbie Gill Comer wrote a piece for the Klan magazine, *Kourier*, in October in which she explained how Mrs. Herbert Hoover would be the ideal first lady. Mrs. Comer praised Mrs. Hoover for her education, intelligence, and role as helper to her husband in his many travels around the world as goodwill ambassador. She said nothing about Mrs. Al Smith, who was considered by some to be provincial and unsophisticated.[63] The full extent of the Klan's politicking between July and November is unknown.

After Al Smith singled him out in his Oklahoma City speech, Comer wrote Smith explaining that he opposed him because of his ties to the Roman Catholic Church. Moreover, Comer said he opposed Smith's pronouncements on immigration.[64] Late in October, just before the election, Comer was challenged to a public debate about Al Smith's candidacy by W. P. Strait, a Morrilton lawyer. Strait asked Comer to defend his past association with the Republican Party, which, he said, had tried to use black votes to overthrow white supremacy in the South. He asked what special brand of Christian piety Comer possessed that justified the religious bigotry that attempted to violate constitutional guarantees of religious freedom and the right to participate in government. Comer declined to debate Strait, saying his calendar up to the November 6 vote was filled with other engagements. Moreover, Comer said, Strait was a Catholic and thus could not understand his political views because of his loyalty to his church.[65]

While the Klan may have generally kept its anti-Smith campaign out of the public view, church leaders, particularly representing the Methodist and Baptist churches of Arkansas, used their pulpits and media outlets to influence the election. In the later part of July they formally organized the Anti-Smith Democrats of Arkansas. Ben Bogard, J. S. Compere, the editor of the *Baptist Advance*, and the Reverend Benjamin Asbury Few, the chair of the Methodist Temperance and Social Service Committee, called a meeting to organize this body for July 19. It was postponed until July 25 on account of a similar national meeting in Asheville, North Carolina, taking place on the eighteenth and nineteenth, which A. C. Millar and some other Arkansas Methodists were attending. The Asheville meeting had been called by Bishop James Cannon Jr. of Richmond, the head of the Methodist Episcopal Church, South, and by Dr. Arthur J. Barton, a pastor in Atlanta of the Southern Baptist Convention. Barton was a native of Jonesboro, Arkansas, and formerly a pastor of a Baptist church in Little Rock and editor of the *Baptist Advance*. Two hundred sixty-seven delegates from fourteen states attended this meeting, and they elected Barton as chair and Cannon as secretary of the resulting organization. A. C. Millar and Mrs. John P. Almand of Arkansas were elected to the permanent executive committee. The stated goal of the organization was to oppose Smith's candidacy because of his repudiation of the Houston platform plank on prohibition, his choice of the wet John Rascob as chairman of the party, and Smith's relationship with Tammany Hall. No specific mention was made about his religion.[66]

The Arkansas meeting convened with 225 attending on July 25 at the capital's First Methodist Church, the very church that Joe T. Robinson attended when he was at his Little Rock home. The group elected Dr. Asbury Few as president and I. E. Taylor as secretary and chose an executive committee with members from Little Rock, Pine Bluff, Forrest City, Fort Smith, Brinkley, and Crossett. The committee included Ben

Bogard, Selsus Tull, J. S. Compere, and the pastor of the host church, the Reverend Hubert D. Knickerbocker. A. C. Millar served as head of this committee and would manage a speaker's bureau on behalf of the organization. The meeting declared its dissatisfaction with the manner in which Arkansas delegates to the Houston convention had been chosen. It directed Democrats in the August primary to scratch off the names of pro-Smith candidates and then in November to vote for Hoover. While the declaration concentrated on Smith's wet position and Tammany connections, it made a swipe at the Catholic Church. The statement ended by criticizing Smith supporters who had charged his opponents with religious intolerance. On the contrary, it continued, "Smith's church affiliations identify him with the most intolerant organization that ever existed on earth. It is not intolerant to oppose the representatives of intolerance."[67]

In early September the executive committee of the Anti-Smith Democrats chose a former prosecuting attorney, Andrew A. McDonald of Fort Smith, as campaign manager, and the group opened an office in the Federal and Trust Building in Little Rock. Later in September they opened a second office in Fort Smith, just across the street from the Democratic Headquarters at 922 Garrison Avenue.[68] McDonald challenged Joe T. Robinson to a public debate about Smith, which Robinson ignored, as he was out of the state campaigning.[69] The big event the organization accomplished was a rally on September 18 at Little Rock's Fair Park, featuring Dr. John Roach Straton, the pastor of Calvary Baptist Church in New York City, who had long been sparring with Governor Smith. A. C. Millar, Reverend Knickerbocker, and Ben Bogard also took part in the event at the park's grandstand, which was filled to capacity with some nine thousand people. Straton described with vivid detail the sort of New York environment that made Smith a politician—Tammany corruption, saloons, gambling halls, and houses of ill fame.[70]

To give the Methodists equal billing, Bishop Cannon came to Arkansas in early October. He travelled the state, giving two-and-a-half-hour anti-Smith, pro-Hoover speeches in Fort Smith, Little Rock, Russellville, and Forrest City. Cannon dismissed the charge that opposing Smith constituted religious intolerance. He made clear his view that it was not the religion that he and many others opposed but the "politico-ecclesiasticism of Romanism" that was the problem. He rejected

Cartoon in the 1928 campaign, from *Fellowship Forum* (Washington, D.C.), June 16, 1928.

Sexual predation remained a theme in the 1928 campaign, from *Fellowship Forum* (Washington, D.C.), October 6, 1928.

Robinson's criticism of politics preached from pulpits, saying that Christ himself had been a political preacher and "his preaching brought about his crucifixion." After he left the state, Cannon sent money ($600 in October alone) to Millar to subsidize the dissemination of anti-Smith materials in Arkansas.[71]

As the election neared, the Anti-Smith Democrats organization engaged in a blitz of advertising, curbed only by the limits of its finances. While the organization had appealed for donations since the founding in July, it was unable to advertise in the county papers for lack of funds, with the exception of a few counties where supporters locally purchased the ads.[72] In full-page advertisements in the *Arkansas Methodist* on October 18 and 25, the organization detailed Smith's pro-liquor position, castigated his choice of a wet Catholic as Democratic chair, delineated his ties to Tammany Hall, and declared him to be in favor of changes in immigration law to advantage Catholics and southern Europeans. Smith's position, the group argued, threatened to flood America with illiterate immigrants, "most of whom are ignorant Wet Catholics." The October 18 advertisement bluntly asked readers to consider how Smith's Catholicism would impact his work as a president. Smith and his children had been educated in Catholic schools, and it suggested that under Smith, Catholics would be freed from taxes that support public schools. In Smith's opinion, the ad continued, a couple lived in adultery if not married by a Catholic priest. Besides this appeal to emotions, the advertisement suggested that a Smith victory would threaten white supremacy. Noting that Marcus Garvey's *Negro World* had called for African Americans to support Smith, the article also claimed that Tammany Hall had inverted the races in New York. One high-salaried official of color had a white secretary, and black teachers in New York taught white children. The governor of New York, the Anti-Smith Democrats argued, "favors negro equality" and approved of "marriages of negroes and whites. . . . Smith knows nothing of the fine ideals of the South."[73]

Besides the work of the Anti-Smith Democrat organization, its leaders individually waged their own battles against the Democratic ticket. Robinson's own pastor, the Reverend Knickerbocker, criticized him from the pulpit of First Methodist Church in Little Rock on July 15, saying the senator used the intolerance issue for political purposes. He suggested that Robinson should preach intolerance to the Roman Catholic Church, "where it is most needed." He criticized the state Democratic Committee for pushing aside anti-Smith Democrats, and he called for the support of Hoover. Knickerbocker's sermon topic for July 29 was "Methodism, Prohibition, and Political Preachers," and he declared that Al Smith was prohibition's biggest enemy. Admitting that his attacks on Smith had alienated some members of his congregation, Knickerbocker refused to apologize. He said he would rather be regular with God than with the Democratic Party. By early August all but three members of the Board of Trustees and Board of Stewards, the governing bodies of Knickerbocker's congregation, wrote to Joe T. Robinson apologizing for their pastor's criticism and praising the senator for his stand on intolerance. The presiding bishop of the Arkansas and Oklahoma Conference, Hiram A. Boaz, announced on August 8 that Knickerbocker would be transferred to another conference. Knickerbocker indicated that he had already asked for a transfer because he could not tow the line that some of his members expected.[74] He continued to speak at anti-Smith rallies through the fall campaign season, including at a packed meeting at Little Rock's City Park in late September, at which he attacked Smith and praised Hoover as the "grandest product of modern civilization."[75]

His Methodist colleague, A. C. Millar, worked tirelessly to oppose the Smith-Robinson ticket. His first step after the convention in June was to announce he was no longer a candidate for lieutenant governor. After forty-four years of loyalty to the Democratic Party, he said he could not aspire to be on a ticket that promoted Al Smith for president. Instead of running for office, in fact, Millar said he needed the time to fight Smith's candidacy. He told J. S. Utley, the chair of the state party, that his opposition to Smith-Robinson ticket was all the more painful for it meant defeat of his personal friend and Arkansas's distinguished citizen, whom he had supported for president four years before. He also felt sorry for Robinson, whom he felt was being used "as a cat's paw to get the Southern vote."[76] Millar had the support of Bishop Boaz, who said that withdrawing from the race was all that a man of his convictions could do.[77]

Millar filled the pages of the *Arkansas Methodist* between August and the November 6 election with his own editorials denouncing the Democratic ticket and with reprints of anti-Smith material from other sources. His opposition to Smith was grounded in his sincere opposition to alcohol and years of work as a leader of the Anti-Saloon League. He repeated the report, which he said had never been denied, that Smith drank between four to eight highballs each day. But as the election approached, Millar's rhetoric became more generally anti-Catholic, even desperate. He pointed out that in his appointment of Rascob as head of the Democratic Party, Smith was choosing a fellow Catholic and a Knight of Columbus who, like him, was "the son of foreign parents." By late September he was printing the old charges that the Roman Catholic

Church was un-American and had never practiced toleration of other religions and that it taught that Catholics who marry outside the church are adulterers and their children bastards. In his last issue before the election, Millar said he had tried to stay away from the subject of religion, but "Senator Robinson injected it and Governor Smith emphasized it, and like the prohibition issue, it has been forced upon us." He did not oppose Smith because of his religion, Millar said, "but because his Church is in politics and has always been in politics and we are forced into politics to meet that issue."[78]

By November, Millar, like the Anti-Smith Democrats organization, played the race card. He slammed Smith's Tammany connections for linkages to liquor, prostitution, gambling, and other vices but went further in suggesting that "Tammany has a negro policy that would absolutely ruin the South." Millar continued: "They have thousands of negro members; they have hundreds of negro policemen; . . . they have scores of negroes with white wives, scores of cabarets in which negroes and whites dance and drink together."[79]

As vocal as were Millar and the Reverend Knickerbocker and their Methodist bishops Boaz and Cannon, Millar admitted that Baptists were even more unanimous in their opposition to Al Smith.[80] Southern Baptist Tull and Missionary Baptist leader Bogard headlined a meeting on July 9 at Little Rock's City Park with a crowd estimated between eight and fifteen thousand people. Bogard denounced Robinson for working with Tammany Hall, and he endorsed Hoover and Curtis. Bogard declared his opposition to any Roman Catholic serving in the office because of the Catholic joining of church and state and suppression of all religions but their own. Tull specifically blasted Robinson for labeling many of the very citizens who had elected him as "bigots" because they opposed Smith.[81]

After the Houston convention, Tull revised and reprinted his pamphlet *Should Al Smith Be President?,* adding "A Declaration of the Anti-Smith Democratic Voters League of Arkansas," prepared by a club of anti-Smith Democrats he had organized in Jefferson County. The declaration castigated delegations from southern states, especially Arkansas, for helping nominate Smith in Houston. Calling it party treason, the declaration continued: "Our politicians have treacherously deceived us and upon that blatant fact we proclaim our rebellion against their monstrous perfidity [*sic*]." It labeled Senator Robinson as the tool of Tammany Hall. Smith was a better man than Robinson, the declaration asserted, for he openly declared his faith and support for liquor. "He is a Catholic and is proud of it . . . but Joe T. Robinson has betrayed his constituency." He has become "the stalk-horse of the Roman Catholic Hierarchy and the smoke-screen of the liquor plotters." Tull's declaration concluded, "The Al Smith-Joe Robinson Ticket is a threat to fasten the cloven hand of the Roman Catholic Hierarchy on the administration powers of this Republic." For these reasons Tull and the group of Jefferson County Anti-Smith Democrats renounced the national ticket of the party and pledged their votes to Hoover and Curtis in the November general election.[82]

The *Baptist Advance*, edited by Dr. J. S. Compere, relentlessly opposed the Smith-Robinson ticket from July to the election in the Southern Baptist state paper. Compere, who like Tull and Millar was on the executive committee of the Anti-Smith Democrats of Arkansas, sometimes devoted almost the entirety of issues to political reporting.

But no Baptists could match Ben Bogard and the Missionary Baptists for their zeal in opposing the Smith ticket and the intensity of their anti-Catholic rhetoric. Bogard mobilized his own congregation and denomination. On Sunday morning, July 8, he announced to his congregation, Antioch Baptist Church, at Twenty-second and Brown Streets in Little Rock, his unequivocal opposition to the "Roman Catholic whiskey ticket" and declared he would do all he could to defeat Smith and Robinson in the polls. His congregation gave their unanimous support to their pastor's position by a standing vote. A month later he was trying to rally Missionary Baptists as their local associations, nineteen of them in Arkansas, were about to begin their annual meetings. Bogard advocated that at least two hours of each of these meetings should be devoted to combatting "Rum and Romanism. Set the liquorites and Romanists afire."[83]

Like fellow editors Millar and Compere, Bogard filled his weekly church paper with anti-Smith and anti-Catholic articles. But he increasingly gave attention to Herbert Hoover, somewhat stretching the truth in advocating that Hoover, a Quaker, was the best choice for an evangelical Protestant voter. He said that Hoover was not a strict "party" Republican and that he supported prohibition, an exaggeration, given that Hoover pointedly avoided speaking on the liquor issue. As the election approached, Bogard, like Millar and others, played on racial fears. He called Hoover a "lily-white Republican" who would retain segregation, unlike Al Smith, who believed in Negro equality. As evidence of the "new" Democratic Party's ties with people of color, Bogard cited reports in the Little Rock papers of a black Little Rock physician, Dr. J. M Robinson, who was organizing black Arkansans for Smith. In the October issue Bogard printed a photograph of a black man being served by a white waiter in a northern city. Bogard concluded: "It is a fact that Smith is the negroes' man and that Hoover is the white man's man. No dodging this." Bogard ignored the reality that Robinson, in his campaigning in the Midwest, was frequently challenged by black critics for his opposition to anti-lynching legislation.[84]

Bogard not only wrote tirelessly in the *Baptist and Commoner*, but also travelled around the state giving speeches against the Smith-Robinson ticket. He described one lecture tour through Izard County in the Arkansas Ozarks, where he claimed to have had in Melbourne a crowd of one thousand people. By mid-October he announced he could accept no more speaking invitations because his schedule was full. In late October, Bogard even spoke on radio on the station KGJF, owned by the Nazarene Church of Little Rock.[85]

Besides Smith and Catholicism, Bogard had another issue at stake in the November 6 election. He had drafted a petition and led a successful signature drive to get an initiated act on the ballot to forbid the teaching of evolution in the public schools of Arkansas. Bogard had paid close attention to the evolution issue throughout the 1920s. In 1925, the year that Tennessee famously passed its anti-evolution law that prompted the Scopes trial the next year, Bogard presented a petition on behalf of the Arkansas Missionary Baptist Association, asking the general assembly to enact an anti-evolution law. Two years later, Representative A. L. Rotenberry of Pulaski County introduced such a bill, which passed the House by one vote but was tabled by the Senate and effectively killed. Through the rest of 1927 Bogard called for a public vote on the Rotenberry bill. By May of 1928 he had gathered nineteen thousand signatures, enough to get the initiative on the November ballot. Between his promotion of the anti-evolution measure and his fight against the Smith-Robinson ticket, Bogard was mightily involved in political activities in addition to his religious work in the summer and fall of 1928.[86]

While Millar, Tull, Compere, and Bogard could command a wide audience with high-profile speech making and writings, clergy and laity throughout Arkansas took positions, doubtless, in sermons and conversations that reflected their leaders views. The fragmentary evidence suggests that the opposition to the Smith-Robinson ticket was widespread. The Knights of Columbus complained that someone was again printing and distributing the bogus oath in the Little Rock area. In northeastern Arkansas, an unknown party circulated thousands of handbills with the oath, which were printed by the *Hoxie Tribune*. A Pine Bluff lawyer said the Jefferson County area was flooded with copies of the bogus oath, accompanied by copies of Tull's pamphlet, *Should Al Smith Be President?*[87] Fifteen members of the Protestant ministerial alliance in Fort Smith, including pastors of Baptist, Methodist, Presbyterian, Nazarene, and Disciples of Christ churches, signed a protest statement against Smith's candidacy and called for Christian men and women to "save the nation from this threatening calamity."[88] A hundred leading preachers and laymen of the Pine Bluff District of the Methodist Church pledged to do all in their power to defeat Smith.[89] In his Sunday sermon Dr. J. D. Hammons, pastor of First Methodist Church of El Dorado, declared he would not vote for Smith and would vote Republican for the first time in his life. Conventional Methodist restraint was cast aside, and the pastor was cheered from the pews.[90] Local associations, such as the Harmony Baptist Association of churches in Jefferson, Cleveland, Lincoln, and Desha Counties, passed resolutions opposing any political candidate who would be influenced by the hierarchy of the Roman Catholic Church.[91] Tom Battershall in the 1960s told his grandson how at a small church in Canaan in the hills of Searcy County, the preacher held forth against Al Smith, saying if he was elected everyone would have to become Catholic. He asked everyone who planned to vote for Smith to stand so he could see them. The church grew quiet. Tom, being a strong Democrat, remained seated but looked to the side to see his wife and her family standing.[92]

The three church weeklies printed many letters echoing the editors' stand against the Smith ticket. Robinson received reports from his friends and supporters indicating that preachers were speaking out against the Democratic ticket in Sheridan, Lonoke, Ferndale, Griffithville, Forrest City, Texarkana, Batesville, Smackover, Fort Smith, and Crossett. Upon hearing that a Fayetteville Baptist preacher's sermon topic was "Why Al

Smith Should Not Be Elected President," Robinson's response was that the preacher "who presumes to tell his church members how to vote will soon find himself without a pastorate, and he ought to do so!"[93]

While the opposition to Smith-Robinson was both vocal and widespread, many Arkansans did not share the prejudices against Catholics. For others, loyalties to the Democratic Party trumped any bias against a Catholic candidate. At the anti-Smith rally on July 9, some members of the crowd yelled rebukes to the speakers. One woman shouted out, "Catholic boys fought for this country." Bogard replied to her, "Yes, because they had to. How many of them volunteered?" The woman seemed to know and responded, "Sixty percent." Bogard pretended not to hear her last comment and returned to his prepared remarks.[94] At the September 18 rally featuring the Reverend Straton from New York, Democratic authorities hired an extra one hundred policemen following rumors that some pro-Smith forces planned to egg the speaker.[95] Bogard said at his speeches in Izard County in October he was heckled by Smith supporters and needed protection of the local sheriff. On the very eve of the election, on November 5, Bogard was prevented from speaking in England (Lonoke County) when a crowd assembled and threw eggs at him.[96] A. C. Millar had similar experiences. In one town where he was speaking on a Saturday afternoon, a gang of rude boys under the direction of "a village leader" tried to shout him down. He was scheduled to speak at several churches but declined when laymen in the churches opposed him. Millar said some congregations threatened to take away their pastors' pay if they refused to stop speaking against Smith. Speaking venues, usually granted free to other speakers, were denied to anti-Smith speakers. Hecklers disrupted the Reverend Knickerbocker's anti-Smith speech at city hall in El Dorado in late September. When he asked for officers to restrain the "hoodlums, ruffians, rowdies, and jackasses," as he put it, he found that no city authorities were present to do so.[97]

While many Arkansas Protestants in previous years may have silently shaken their heads at the manifestations of anti-Catholicism, in 1928 this religious prejudice threatened the fate of the Democratic Party and motivated a more active response. The party establishment began work soon after the nomination to counter the work of the anti-Smith preachers. Senator Robinson met on July 31 at the Arlington Hotel with the state's leading Democrats to plan a strategy to oppose the "false and malicious propaganda" that was being spread and to keep Democrats from bolting to Hoover. The meeting chose a chairman for each county to get the county's Democrats to fill out a pledge card of loyalty to the national ticket. By October the Democratic Central Committee of Arkansas refused to place any candidate on the ballot for state and local offices if the person refused to pledge support for the Smith-Robinson ticket.[98] Party stalwarts used the media to defend the ticket and speak against intolerance. Former governor Thomas C. McRae, speaking at Robinson's Little Rock rally, commended the party for "having the courage to strike intolerance, to stand out for religious freedom." Brooks Hays, a candidate for governor in the primary, in a radio address called for people to bury their prejudices.[99]

One Democratic leader, former governor Charles H. Brough, had his loyalties to the party and his church severely tested in 1928. Brough was a prominent Baptist layman but also an intellectual with a PhD from Johns Hopkins University. He had served as a deacon in the First Baptist Church in Fayetteville when he was on the faculty of the University of Arkansas and in Little Rock's Second Baptist Church when he served as governor. In July 1928, he became president of Central College in Conway, a Southern Baptist two-year college for women. As a loyal party man, Brough made several speeches in support of the Democratic ticket after the nomination. In one speech to a special session of the Arkansas General Assembly, he criticized political preachers for delivering the South to the Republican Party. This prompted a response from J. S. Compere, the editor of the *Baptist Advance*, who reminded readers and Brough that as an employee of the Arkansas Baptist Convention he was obligated to conform to the resolution of 1927 pledging opposition to any candidate who was against prohibition. The climax came in late October when Brough was scheduled to speak at a Democratic rally in El Dorado. Compere and J. S. Rogers, the executive secretary of the state Baptist Convention, sent Brough a telegram warning him not to speak for Smith, believing that "our people and the Convention will not stand for it." Brough gave the speech anyway and even told the audience about the ultimatum he had received and denounced the Southern Baptist leaders for their "attempted coercion." In his speech, he criticized Compere for turning the *Baptist Advance* into an organ of the Republican Party and Baptist preachers for using their pulpits as stumps for Hoover. He declared that the election of Smith would be a powerful blow to religious intolerance in the United States. After the October 27 speech, he received many letters and telegrams from people applauding his stand against the preachers, including some from Baptists. But the Baptist leaders kept up the attack. Brough had also spoken against the anti-evolution measure on the November ballot. The *Baptist Advance* reminded readers that the 1924 state convention had passed a resolution opposing the theory of evolution and required that teachers and other employees of the convention's educational institutions sign a copy of the resolution. After the election was over, Brough announced his resignation as president of Central College, effective at the end of the academic year, but he asserted his decision had no relationship to the election controversies. He resigned to take a job as a special publicity agent for the University of Arkansas.[100]

Besides the Democratic political establishment, some clergy and religious lay folk spoke out against the anti-Smith preachers. The Reverend Adolphe H. Poppe, pastor of Little Rock's Evangelical Lutheran Church, said he declined to bring the election into his church, for religion and politics were separate matters. The Rabbi of Little Rock's Temple B'nai Israel, Ira E. Sanders, said the idea of Catholic supremacy was simply a myth. Mrs. John S. Gibson of Hoxie, a Methodist who had been a state president of the WCTU, said that Al Smith "should not be crucified on the cross of intolerance by the fanatics of the South." She opposed churches being turned into "political clubhouses." Even a Baptist pastor, the Reverend A. J. Ashburn, dissented from his church's position against Al Smith. He regretted the irreparable damage to the Baptist cause in Arkansas by the denomination's politicking and the conversion of its paper, the *Baptist Advance*, into an organ for the Republican Party. Another Baptist preacher from Little Rock, E. LeRoy Whidden, wrote to Al Smith and Senator Robinson, telling them that most Baptist ministers are against them and most of them "are Ku Klux who stand for non-Catholicism," but Whidden pledged to work among the ministers for Smith and Robinson.[101] The *Baptist Advance* admitted it lost subscriptions because of the stand it had taken on the election. Even Bogard reported that one subscriber from Hazen cancelled his subscription after the "Rum and Romanism" issue, saying, "I am a Democrat. Stop my paper." But Bogard countered that it was "just one lonesome brother" and that others had ordered extra copies of that issue to distribute in their communities.[102]

The two state daily newspapers subtly worked to oppose the anti-Smith political preachers. While both newspapers continued to hold a dry position on prohibition, they endorsed the Smith-Robinson ticket. Millar accused both papers of refusing coverage of anti-Smith meetings. The *Baptist Advance* charged that the papers refused to present both sides of the presidential race and that the *Gazette* specifically failed to print anti-Smith letters in its "From the People" section.[103] The publisher of the *Arkansas Gazette*, Fred Heiskell, in fact wrote Senator Robinson in late July practically apologizing for giving any space to the political preachers. But he argued that he was using the pages of the *Gazette* for them to "vent" and get it out of their system. Some of Robinson's advisors agreed that it was best to give coverage to the political preachers so that they could not charge that the papers were suppressing the facts. One correspondent from Pine Bluff told Robinson that by getting the issue of religion thrashed out early in the campaign, "the flames will become exhausted and the fire die out. There is no reasoning with those who have narrow religious views."[104]

Some observers suggested that the energy of the religion issue had dissipated by the fall, despite the tireless work by the editors of the three church papers. Vint Miles, a member of the Democratic National Committee, reported in September that in the Fort Smith area the preachers were no longer preaching politics from the pulpits. The Democratic state convention in early October assured candidates that the unfair attacks of the Republican organization based on religious prejudice were back-firing and that Arkansas was now safely in the Democratic column. Robinson, nonetheless, continued to the end to hammer the political preaching. In his last address of the campaign, upon arriving back in Little Rock on the day before the election, he denounced the pastors who tried to control political matters, saying, "No man with hatred in his heart can successfully point out the pathway to eternal life.[105]

On Election Day, November 6, the anti-Smith forces both won and lost. The Democratic ticket carried the state but lost the election. Hoover won by a landslide nationally, with just over 21 million votes to Smith's 15 million. The margin of victory by electoral votes was even more impressive, with 444 for Hoover to 87 for Smith. Smith carried only Massachusetts, Rhode Island, and six southern states: Arkansas, Alabama, Georgia, Louisiana, Mississippi, and South Carolina. Hoover actually won more electoral votes in the "Solid South" than Smith, taking Texas, Virginia, North Carolina, Florida, and Tennessee, as well as all of the border states. Several historians of the 1928 election believe that Smith and the Democrats, with the economic prosperity evident in 1928, had little chance to defeat the Republicans. Some say that the economy, not religion, was the dominant issue in the race. Joan Hoff Wilson's sympathetic biography of Hoover argues that no Democrat could have beaten Hoover in 1928. Ruth Silva's analysis of the 1928 election suggests that Smith's party affiliation was a greater liability to him than his Catholicism and that the liquor issue had virtually no impact. On the other hand, Allan J. Lichtman, who has done the most thorough study of the election results, believes that religion was indeed the most significant single factor influencing votes. But with Smith gaining about as many votes from Roman Catholics as he lost from Protestants, religion's effect on the outcome was negligible.[106]

Arkansas citizens gave 119,186 votes (60.5 percent) for the Smith-Robinson ticket with 77,762 (39.5 percent) going to the Hoover-Curtis ticket. The Republican tally increased substantially from the 40,564 Republican votes cast in the 1924 presidential race, but comparisons are difficult because the total vote in Arkansas was approximately 30 percent greater in 1928 than 1924. Moreover, a third-party candidate in 1924, Robert La Follette, polled over 13,000 Arkansas votes.[107] To estimate the number of traditionally Democratic votes in Arkansas that went from Smith to Hoover, one can compare the presidential vote to the gubernatorial vote on that same day. Arkansas voters gave Hoover 33,829 more votes than they gave the Republican candidate for governor, M. D. Bowers, even though Bowers had declared that he would welcome any Democrat into the Republican Party who opposed Smith on religious grounds. Hoover gained a majority of votes in ten of Arkansas's seventy-five counties, all in the hills of northern and western Arkansas, where Republican loyalties had historically been strongest since the Civil War.[108] One wonders whether Hoover would have carried Arkansas in 1928 had there not been a favorite son on the ticket. Incidentally, the anti-evolution initiated act passed by 108,991 to 63,406 votes, and thus it became illegal in Arkansas public schools to teach evolution. The US Supreme Court would eventually overturn this act, but not until 1968.[109]

With an anti-evolution measure and a wet Catholic from New York City on the ballot, the 1928 election was like the opening of a vein for a number of conservative Protestants in Arkansas. It mobilized their religious prejudices into a flurry of talk and action to oppose feared changes. The Democratic Party in Arkansas was bruised as some thirty-four thousand of the two hundred thousand voters may have bolted from Smith to Hoover. Presumably, some of the traditionally Republican vote (remember Comer was an Arkansas Republican) would have held prejudices against Catholics too. Yet this means that for a large number, even the majority of Arkansas voters, Smith's Catholic religion was not the deciding factor in determining how they voted. Religious prejudice in Arkansas had simply been brought out in the open.

On the day after the election, both of the Little Rock daily newspapers editorialized about the results of the campaign. The *Gazette* said that Smith lost because of his religion and accused many of Smith's opponents of using the prohibition issue as a smokescreen for religious prejudice. The *Democrat* similarly said Democrats had been hurt by "the shadow of the Vatican hanging over the White House."[110] Former governor Brough too believed that Smith would have won the election had he not been Catholic, that his religion hurt him infinitely more than his alleged wetness. Senator and Mrs. Robinson both believed that the election was lost because Al Smith was a Catholic.[111] The Roman Catholic newspaper, the *Guardian*, called the campaign the bitterest in the last forty years of American history but noted that even the church's worst enemies would say that Catholics bore it all silently.[112]

On the other side, the anti-Smith leaders worried that they had failed to win over the majority of Arkansas's voters. A. C. Millar groused after the election about the "unsportsmanlike" tactics of the Democratic machine in applying the party lash. He said some anti-Smith voters were kept from the polls by rumors that they would be imprisoned, fined, or barred from future Democratic primaries if they voted for Hoover. As sore as he was, Millar kept politics out of the *Arkansas Methodist* after the election.[113] Likewise, the *Baptist Advance* retreated from political matters and anti-Catholic writing after the election. The Missionary Baptists, however, did not let the matter drop. The state association met later in the week after the November 6 election and before adjourning approved the following motion: "We recommend that the members of the Churches of this Association, the pastors, and the missionaries use their utmost influence as citizens against the political encroachments of the Papacy. . . . And in order to preserve our religious and civil liberties let us preach, pray, teach, and work against our common enemy at all times and all places."[114] While anti-Catholic rhetoric retreated from the public eye, it would not go away.

CHAPTER 6

A Prejudice Wanes and Waxes, 1929–1960

SOME OBSERVERS BELIEVED that the 1928 election put an end to anti-Catholicism in the United States. Michael Williams, the editor of the Catholic *Commonweal* magazine, who wrote a book about anti-Catholic prejudice culminating in the Al Smith campaign, said soon after the 1928 election that it signaled a decline in bigotry. A Catholic priest in a southern state where the religious strife of the campaign had been particularly bitter had told Williams that the election actually benefitted the Catholic Church. The campaign had precipitated an increase in conversions, the priest said. And, secondly, it had resulted in friendly relations between Catholics, the press, and Protestants repulsed by the vicious attacks of the anti-Catholics. As acrimonious as the rhetoric might have been, Williams noted that there were no acts of physical violence or bloodshed in 1928.[1] Indeed, public displays of hostility toward Catholicism declined in Arkansas and nationally over the next twenty years. In the midst of the "Red Scare" in the late 1940s and 1950s, however, rhetorical attacks against Catholicism rose again. They culminated in a vocal and organized opposition to the presidential candidacy of John Fitzgerald Kennedy. Anti-Catholics were obviously less successful than in 1928, for Kennedy in 1960 became the first Catholic to win the presidency of the United States.

After Smith's defeat in 1928, many anti-Catholics moved forward with the vain confidence that neither party would nominate a Catholic for this high office again. Americans who had been disgusted with the display of religious prejudice, on the other hand, made efforts to improve interfaith relations after 1928. The National Conference of

Christians and Jews was founded during the campaign and in early 1929 had its first conference, which examined the record of religious intolerance of the previous year. With participation of Roman Catholic and mainline Protestant denominations, the name alone suggested a common Christian belief and ethic that stood above the divisions. In the 1990s the organization changed its name to the National Conference for Community and Justice.[2]

Religious conflict in 1929 became overshadowed by an economic crisis that impacted Protestants and Catholics alike. Political energy of the early 1930s centered on relief from the problems of the Great Depression and eventual recovery. In 1928 Herbert Hoover had meant an alternative to a Catholic president, but in 1932 he represented failed economic policies. As the 1930s went on, increasingly threatening foreign affairs and then war dominated people's attention.

The liquor issue, which had added fuel to anti-Catholicism in Arkansas and elsewhere in the 1910s and 1920s, began to wane after 1928. At the Democratic National Convention of 1932 in Chicago, the party staked out an explicitly anti-prohibition position in the platform. In the depths of the Great Depression, Franklin Roosevelt carried Arkansas and the nation in a landslide almost as lopsided as Hoover's win over Smith four years before. Roosevelt won a whopping 86 percent of the Arkansas vote, with a majority in all seventy-five counties.[3] In the summer of 1933, the states began to call conventions to ratify the proposed Twenty-first Amendment, which would repeal the Eighteenth Amendment and end prohibition. Ben Bogard, A. C. Millar, and the Anti-Saloon League folks campaigned against the repeal of prohibition before the statewide referendum on August 1. The United Forces for Prohibition in Arkansas was organized at a meeting at Little Rock's First Baptist Church on June 6, with Millar elected as temporary chairman.[4] For the most part, the campaign against liquor this time omitted the references to Catholicism. Millar did, however, recommend to his readers in the *Arkansas Methodist* an article by Gilbert Nations in the *Civic Bulletin*, entitled "The Vatican Creates and Directs the Repeal Movement."[5] When the vote took place on July 18, the wets won by a three-to-two margin. Arkansas became the first southern state to ratify the Twenty-first Amendment and had the highest percentage of voters favoring repeal of any state of the South. The state remained dry, however, until the next session of the Arkansas General Assembly repealed the state prohibition laws in 1935.[6]

As the 1930s progressed, the economic problems of the Great Depression gave way to international tensions grabbing headlines. While some extremists, like former senator Thomas Heflin or Baptist preacher J. Frank Norris, continued their attacks on Roman Catholicism, they received less attention. Americans came to consider communism as the greatest threat, and the Roman Catholic Church appeared to be a bulwark of defense against the "Red Peril." Pope Pius XI had struck deals with Benito Mussolini's fascist regime in Italy in 1929 and with the Third Reich in July 1933. He and his successor Pius XII vigorously opposed communism. The most publicly visible Catholic cleric in the United States, Father Charles E. Coughlin, in his radio broadcasts of the later 1930s, championed General Francesco Franco's coalition of the Right against the communist-led Left in the Spanish Civil War. Many Americans who saw communism as the worst internal and external threat might conclude that the enemy of my enemy is my friend. After two decades of rampant anti-Catholicism, the 1930s on a national level saw few public manifestations of this prejudice.[7]

As a sign that anti-Catholic attitudes were in decline, the Arkansas General Assembly in March 1937 quietly repealed the Convent Inspection Act of 1915. Representative Lee Nichols of Logan County, where Subiaco Abbey was located, sponsored the bill in the House. Evidently, legislators had forgotten the sexual intent of the law, for Nichols explained that the bill originated from war hysteria before the United States entered the Great War and directed sheriffs to search Catholic institutions such as Subiaco for suspected arms and munitions. The Senate voted unanimously to repeal the law, while the House voted for repeal by a margin of seventy-three to eight.[8]

Anti-Catholicism continued to decline in the 1940s, with World War II dominating the first half of the decade and the beginnings of the Cold War overshadowing the last years of the 1940s. As with the Great War, the call for national unity in a monumental war effort generally muted ethnic and nationalistic distinctions. While Japanese Americans appeared to some as a threat after Pearl Harbor, there were no anti-German outbursts comparable to those of 1917. By 1950 the nativist aspect of anti-Catholicism had significantly declined as the immigration restrictions of the 1920s had done their work. Catholics were increasingly English-speaking, second- or third-generation Americans who had been assimilated into American culture. Their percentage of the population relative to other religions had increased, with Roman Catholicism becoming the largest Christian denomination in the United States by 1940. Hollywood portrayed the Catholic Church and its priests, such as Bing Crosby's characters in *Going My Way* (1944) and the *Bells of St. Mary* (1945), in a flattering, even adoring way. Thomas Merton's *Seven Story Mountain*, his memoir about his life as a Catholic convert and eventually a Trappist monk, became a bestseller at the end of the 1940s.[9]

In Arkansas, the Baptist press still made occasional swipes at Rome in the 1930s but with less frequency and ferocity. As in the country in general, the religious temperature in Arkansas went down in the 1930s and 1940s. The continuing stories of the central figures of this study—Father Boniface Spanke and his nemesis Otis Spurgeon, legislator Robert R. Posey, Missionary Baptist preachers J. A. Scarboro and Ben Bogard, Methodist editor A. C. Millar, newspaperman Herb Lewis, Klan leader James Comer, and Senator Joe T. Robinson—give a sense of what happened to anti-Catholicism after 1928.

Robert Posey, as a young representative in his first term in the Arkansas legislature, introduced the Convent Inspection Bill into the House of Representatives in 1913 and again in 1915, when it passed and became law. This was the legislature that chose Joe T. Robinson, recently elected as governor, to become junior senator for Arkansas. Posey went on to become mayor of his hometown, Sheridan, and served as prosecuting attorney for Grant County. During the Great War he served as the food administrator for the county. In 1924 he moved to Las Cruces, New Mexico, for reasons relating to his wife's health. By 1928 his attitudes about Roman Catholics appear to have changed, for Posey wrote Joe T. Robinson after his vice presidential nomination assuring him of his support for the Smith-Robinson ticket. Posey's grandson, Bob Buckman, who as a teenager cleaned his grandfather's law office and who remembered him well, expressed surprise to learn his grandfather had sponsored anti-Catholic legislation in Arkansas. His grandfather was highly regarded by his many Roman Catholic Latino clients, Buckman said, and was known among his legal peers as a defender of human rights. Posey's daughter Evelyn married a Catholic man, and she converted to the faith. Posey died in Las Cruces in 1968.[10]

Father Boniface Spanke, who vigorously tried to educate Arkansans about Catholicism through his Gospel Wagon ministry and who took on the professional anti-Catholic lecturer Otis Spurgeon in the famous debate of 1914, subsequently retreated from his aggressive posture toward the Protestant community. Bishop John Morris apparently decided that Boniface's assertive style did more harm to Catholicism than good. There was some complaining within the church, but the bishop took the public position of passive silence. After the debate, he shut down the Gospel Wagon and sent Boniface to Texarkana and then out of the diocese, to Wichita Falls, Texas. After seven years Boniface returned to Subiaco, where he assumed a less controversial role as manager of the abbey's farm. He died at the abbey in 1942.[11]

Boniface's nemesis, Otis Spurgeon, who was kidnapped, beaten, and abandoned naked by a gang of Knights of Columbus members in Denver, Colorado, a few months after his debate with Boniface, later ran unsuccessfully as an independent candidate for the US Senate in Iowa and for governor in 1916 on the Prohibition Party ticket. He continued working as a travelling anti-Catholic lecturer until 1915, when he was discharged from the Knights of Luther for dishonesty. He later sued the organization for fraud and graft, and the Knights sued him back for sending out libelous circulars. He served as a chaplain in the Great War and a captain in the 384th Field Artillery officer's reserve.[12] In 1923, Spurgeon surfaced in Poplar Bluff, Missouri, where he pastored the First Baptist Church until he resigned the pulpit to work as Exalted Cyclops of Missouri Klan No. 48 and "travelling patriot," giving anti-Catholic lectures at a yearly salary of $5,000. Poplar Bluff's Knights of Columbus members were looking for information to discredit Spurgeon, for the local newspaper editor, who was not even a Catholic, had vowed to publish such information to run Spurgeon out of town. By the fall he was doing Klan work in Minnesota and Des Moines, Iowa.[13] He lived in Memphis, Tennessee, by 1925, where he worked as a distribution manager for a manufacturing company. When he was arrested for grand larceny for taking some furniture belonging to the former Exalted Cyclops of the Memphis Klan, he was identified as a former Klan orator. After some time in Kansas City, Spurgeon by 1932 worked as a travelling salesman living in Albuquerque, New Mexico. He still had political aspirations, for he was chosen in September 1932 as the vice presidential running mate for Frank E. Webb of San Francisco, running for president for the Liberty Party, a fusion of some socialists, farmers/laborers, and prohibitionists. Spurgeon died in April 1942 of a heart attack in Dallas, Texas, as he was preparing to enter the US Army as an officer.[14] Evidently, after the collapse of the Klan, Spurgeon's anti-Catholic work was insufficient to provide him an income.

Arkansas's leading Klansman, James Comer, also saw his career decline. While he had tried to use the 1928 election as the basis for renewed visibility for the Arkansas Klan, after the election Comer and the Klan slipped into obscurity. At the 1930 census, he and his wife, Robbie Gill Comer, still had sufficient wealth generated from their Klan work to have two live-in black servants at their sumptuous home at 915 Barber Avenue in Little Rock. One of the servants was listed also as a "chauffeur." In 1934 Comer planned to establish an office in Little Rock to begin work to "exterminate Communism," a drive he expected to attract a hundred thousand new members to a revived Klan. There is no evidence, however, that the effort came to any results. Comer died of a cerebral hemorrhage the next year, on August 5, 1935, still identified as Arkansas's Grand Dragon of the Ku Klux Klan. An inventory of property in his will showed that he and Robbie Comer had made a fortune from their Klan work. After Comer's death, Robbie moved to southern California, where she died in 1963.[15]

Nationally, what was left of the Ku Klux Klan disintegrated in the later 1930s. Imperial Commander Hiram Evans liquidated most of the Klan's property. An insurance company purchased the Imperial Palace in Atlanta and, providing some delicious irony, sold it to the Roman Catholic Church. In 1939 Bishop Gerald O'Hara of the Savannah-Atlanta diocese invited Evans to the dedication ceremonies of the new Cathedral of Christ the King, built on the grounds of the former Imperial Palace. Evans accepted the invitation and even toured the rectory in the building he had used for his private office. The Klan organizationally ceased to exist in 1944 when the Internal Revenue Service gave Evan's successor, James A. Colescott, a bill for $685,000 in unpaid taxes on its enormous profits from the 1920s. Colescott was forced to sell the remaining assets, and the Klan went out of business.[16]

Herb Lewis, the editor of the *Gravette News Herald,* who from 1912 to 1925 could scarcely go a week without an attack on the pope, Knights of Columbus, or some aspect of Catholicism, took a ten-year hiatus from newspaper work. He returned to edit the paper in 1935 until his death in 1938. In these years he again was a prolific editorializer, devoting a page each week to air his views on a variety of subjects. While he still made the occasional swipe at Catholicism, communists appeared by the later 1930s as his greatest enemy, as well as the growing threat of fascism in Italy, Germany, and Japan. He frequently laid into Father Coughlin, but less for his Catholicism than for his friendly stance toward fascist dictators and his criticism of President Roosevelt. Lewis praised Joe T. Robinson and served on the planning committee when Gravette prepared for the senator's visit there in August 1936. In his last editorial, published on August 5, 1938, Lewis said nothing of Catholics but ranted against communists, Mussolini, Hitler, and "Jap war lords." He said before closing, "Enough for one dose! See you later." Lewis died at his home of a heart attack before the next week's issue.[17]

As the Klan declined, the career of Senator Robinson, the defender of religious toleration, flourished after 1928. After Robinson's rebuttal to Senator Heflin and his defense of Al Smith, anti-Catholics had threatened that he would be turned out of the Senate at the next opportunity.[18] But when Robinson came before the electorate in 1930, he won handily. Tom Campbell of Randolph County ran against Robinson in the August Democratic primary, and rumors passed around that whatever was left of the Klan was financing his campaign. However, on August 12, Robinson received the largest primary victory in the state's history with nearly 75 percent of the vote. He was unopposed in the November election. When Franklin Roosevelt became president in 1933, Robinson became senate majority leader and pushed Roosevelt's ambitious legislative program, including the New Deal and abolition of prohibition, through the US Senate. He died of a heart attack while he was at the height of his influence on July 14, 1937.[19]

Meanwhile, Alabama senator Thomas Heflin, who had slept with a gun under his pillow in 1928, convinced that Catholics were out to get him, also came up for re-election in 1930. Despite the fact that he had been in Congress since 1904 and the Senate since 1920, the Democratic Party of Alabama barred Heflin from running on the party ticket in the primary because of his public support for Hoover in 1928. He ran as third-party candidate in November but was decisively defeated by the Democratic candidate, John Bankhead. Before his death in 1951, he ran for House or Senate again several times, but never successfully.[20]

The most enduring legacy of anti-Catholicism was probably among the Protestant clergy. Dr. A. C. Millar kept soldiering on against liquor to his death in 1940, still heading the Anti-Saloon League in Arkansas and serving on the executive committee of the national organization.[21] There is no reason to believe that the Reverend Joseph A. Scarboro, who had edited the anti-Catholic *Liberator*, changed his views about Catholics before his death in Georgia in 1932. He and Ben Bogard continued to rail against Catholics in 1929, particularly when the Lateran Treaty between Pope Pius XI and Mussolini made the Vatican a sovereign state of 109 acres. Bogard was so incensed that he declared his opposition to any American Catholic having the right to vote unless the person renounced allegiance to the pope. After Scarboro's death, Bogard eulogized him in a memorial service at Antioch Baptist Church. One of Scarboro's last requests from his deathbed had been for someone to write Bogard with this message: "My love and goodbye; meet me in Heaven."[22]

Bogard's venom against Catholicism calmed somewhat as the 1930s progressed. He announced his opposition to Robinson in 1930, but most of Bogard's political energy in that election focused on the passage of another initiated act that he had written. The Arkansas Bible Bill, alternately known as the Bogard Bible Law, would require the daily reading of the Bible in Arkansas public schools. The bill passed and remained law until invalidated by the US Supreme Court in 1963.[23] As the 1930s progressed, Bogard stepped back some from editing and did more radio broadcasting. Although fewer copies of the *Baptist and Commoner* are extant for the 1930s, it appears that Bogard less often approached the subject of Catholicism, and the angry tone of the 1920s was largely absent. Although Bogard seemed to have softened, one of his seminary students, Albert Garner, authored a small book in the early 1940s, *The Devil's Masterpiece*, proclaiming on the cover: "Romanism is Un-American! Romanism is Un-Christian! Romanism is Idolatry! Romanism is Infidelity!" Garner's book uses the same old material from the 1910s and 1920s, complete with the alleged "Blood Oath of the Knights of Columbus" reprinted from the *Congressional Record* to give the bogus oath some credibility.[24] Bogard retired from directing the seminary and pastoring Antioch Baptist Church in 1947, and four years later he died of a heart attack at age eighty-three.[25]

Albert Garner, either before or after his study under Ben Bogard at the Missionary Baptist Seminary in Little Rock, had been a student at Harding College, which was founded in 1924 in Morrilton and relocated in Searcy in 1934. Harding College, a school associated with the Churches of Christ, was emerging by the 1940s as a center of conservative Christian political thinking. The Churches of Christ, along with the Disciples of Christ, descend from the Restoration movement of the early 1800s, founded by Alexander Campbell and Barton Stone in Kentucky, who wanted to restore what they believed was the practice and teaching of the first-century Christianity. The Churches of Christ split around the turn of the century from the more liberal and ecumenically minded Disciples. The Churches of Christ eschewed denominationalism and had no headquarters, bureaucracy, conventions, or associations. They are perhaps best known for the distinctive prohibition of instrumental music, including pianos and organs, in worship services. The Churches of Christ had their greatest strength in Tennessee, Arkansas, and Texas. In Arkansas, only Methodists, black Baptists, Southern Baptists, and Missionary Baptists surpassed them in numbers. Their congregational autonomy and eschewing of any of the machinery of a denomination meant that they left behind fewer records to track their history. But with the growth of Harding College in the 1930s, Church of Christ leaders began to speak out with a loud voice on issues of national concern, particularly anti-communism but to a lesser degree anti-Catholicism.[26]

One of Harding College's earliest graduates, George S. Benson, returned from missionary work in China to become the college's second president in 1936. Having seen firsthand in China the threats of a strong communist movement, Benson pushed an educational philosophy grounded around the defense of the Christian faith, American democracy, and the free-enterprise economic system.[27] One of his hires in 1944 was another Harding graduate, Dr. James David Bales, fresh from doctoral studies at the University of California–Berkeley. Bales shared with Benson a lifelong opposition to communism, but he also took a strong stand against the Roman Catholic Church. Even before he left Berkeley, he self-published a pamphlet, *Was Peter Pope?*, and authored an article in the Church of Christ weekly *Gospel Advocate*, "Does the Roman Catholic Church Favor Religious Freedom?" As one might expect, he answered his own rhetorical questions with a resounding "No!" After Bales became a professor of Christian doctrine at Harding, one of his first publications was a small book, *Catholicism and Coercion*, which examined the medieval and Spanish inquisitions. Because the Roman Catholic Church claimed that it did not change over time, Bales argued, Catholics might thus use such violence once more against those church officials regarded as heretics. Bales would continue to rail against communism and Catholicism until his retirement from Harding in 1981 and death in 1995.[28]

As Harding College was emerging in the 1940s as a center of ultraconservative Christian thought, anti-Catholic sentiments surfaced again on a national stage. A US Supreme Court decision, *Everson v. Board of Education*, in 1947 allowed parochial school students to ride school buses operated by public schools. Many Americans felt that this ruling, which was supported by the Catholic bishops, violated the constitutional separation of church and state. Many Protestants groups, including the Conference of Methodist Bishops, went on record as opposing the decision. Later in 1947 a group organized as the Protestants and Other Americans United for Separation of Church and State (POAU) to oppose *Everson* and other intrusions of religion into the public sphere. The POAU's founding president, G. Bromley Oxnam, was a Methodist bishop. The organization soon had its own journal, *Church and State*. Catholic bishops and the Knights of Columbus decried the POAU as a renewal of the old anti-Catholicism of the 1920s. The group later dropped "Protestants and Other" from its name, and it still exists today. In the last years of the 1940s the POAU and several Protestant bodies lobbied against several congressional bills to provide federal assistance to parochial education, none of which passed.[29]

The *Everson* case also inspired Paul Blanshard, a former Congregationalist pastor and State Department official who would become the lawyer for the POAU, to write a series of articles for the *Nation* in 1947 and 1948 that criticized Roman Catholicism on a variety of fronts. Blanshard's articles had a similar result to Tom Watson's serialized anti-Catholic pieces of 1911 and 1912 in provoking an angry conversation about the Roman Catholic Church among its detractors and a defensive response from the church itself. Blanshard recycled the old arguments that the Catholic Church threatened democracy, stifled free thought and speech, and sought to become the established religion of the United States and take over the school system. But he added some

Catholicism and Coercion, by Dr. James D. Bales.

new material that would be part of the conversation for years to come: Catholic opposition to sex education, birth control, medically necessary abortions, and divorce. Blanshard revised his articles for publication as a book in 1950, *American Freedom and Catholic Power*. Wildly successful, Blanshard's book went through fourteen printings in its first two years. In 1951, during the heart of the Cold War, Blanshard followed up with another bestseller, *Communism, Democracy, and Catholic Power*. In this book, he made the argument that communism and Catholicism both are authoritarian rather than democratic, use education to indoctrinate their subjects, tend to deify their leaders, and practice a penetrate-and-take-over strategy.[30]

As Blanshard's books were flying off the shelves, another issue renewed anti-Catholic fears of the left and right alike, the diplomatic recognition of the Vatican as a sovereign nation. President Franklin Roosevelt had sent a personal emissary to the Vatican in 1939, Myron C. Taylor, an Episcopalian who was formerly head of US Steel. President Harry Truman reconfirmed him in 1945. After Taylor resigned his post in 1950, Truman asked US Army general Mark W. Clark, also an Episcopalian, to take the position, but as a full ambassador. From October 1951 until February 1952 controversy raged over Truman's proposal. Catholic bishops and the Knights of Columbus lobbied the Senate for the appointment. Mainline Protestant denominations, from Episcopal to Methodist—even the National Council of Churches—joined with Baptists and other fundamentalist groups in opposing Clark and the upgrade of the ambassadorial position. Finally, in early 1952 General Clark asked President Truman to withdraw the nomination. There would be no US ambassador, or even presidential emissary, to the Vatican for the next thirty-three years, until President Ronald Reagan achieved diplomatic recognition of the Holy See as a sovereign state with a regular ambassador appointment in 1984.[31]

The "new" anti-Catholicism of the late 1940s and early 1950s attracted a broad audience of fundamentalists but also more left-leaning Protestants and secularists concerned primarily with building a wall between church and state. Blanshard distinguished his opposition to Catholicism from the type of bigotry that he said had disgraced the country in 1928. The appeal of his argument, he said, "is strongest among the liberals who have always stood most courageously for personal tolerance."[32] However much Blanshard, the PAOU, and others might wish to see their opposition to Catholicism as a liberal position, the renewed attention mobilized again the conservative religious press in places like Arkansas.

The Methodist and Episcopal papers in Arkansas both editorially opposed the diplomatic recognition of the Vatican as a violation of church and state and the granting of preferential status for Roman Catholicism. At a diocesan convention at Little Rock's Trinity Cathedral, Arkansas's Episcopalians drafted a resolution opposing Truman's proposal to send to the president and the state's congressional representatives, who would be asked to appropriate funds for a new embassy for the Vatican.[33] The Clark appointment brought a more vigorous opposition in the Baptist press. The Southern Baptist paper, now renamed the *Arkansas Baptist*, editorialized that the nomination, coming on the heels of the school issue, indicated a new Catholic effort to re-interpret the US Constitution. The paper even complained that most of Baptist president Truman's close personal friends were Roman Catholic. The Reverend Selsus Tull, one of the only veterans left from the anti-Catholic campaign of 1928, authored "The Preacher in Politics," arguing that Baptist preachers should speak out against the threat to the American Constitution with the Clark appointment and tax money going to Catholic schools and hospitals.[34] The Reverend D. N. Jackson, the Missionary Baptist leader who, like Tull, had written against the election of a Catholic president in 1928, argued that Truman's recognition of the Vatican violated the spirit of the Constitution. He warned readers that the pope already had an army and was planning for a Vatican fleet. By January, Jackson's paper, the *American Baptist*, had launched a letter-writing campaign with a goal of fifteen thousand letters to be sent to the president and senators, noting that both Senators William Fulbright and John McClellan of Arkansas opposed the appointment.[35]

The conservative Churches of Christ topped even the Missionary Baptists in criticism of Catholicism. A Church of Christ paper published in Delight, Arkansas, the *Gospel Light*, called for readers to write their senators opposing the Clark appointment. But the *Gospel Light* went further and ran a series of articles, entitled "The Truth About Catholics," opposing Catholic theology. One article, "Holy Hallucinations," tried to expose as frauds the apparitions of Mary, such as to the children of

Fatima, Portugal.[36] From Harding College in Searcy, James D. Bales railed against the diplomatic recognition of the Vatican. If the Holy See was truly a sovereign state, Bales argued, then the church hierarchy and local priests in the United States were really a complex web of spies who were committing treason against this country by sending forward information from America to the Vatican state.[37]

After the *Everson* case and the Clark nomination, no significant national political issue focused attention against the Roman Catholic Church until John Fitzgerald Kennedy's campaign for the presidency in 1960. Kennedy's candidacy would be perhaps the last event in American history to mobilize anti-Catholicism on a significant scale. Catholic-Protestant relations appeared to be improving in the latter half of the 1950s. At the Democratic National Convention in 1956, Kennedy came within a few votes on the third ballot of becoming Adlai Stevenson's vice presidential running mate. After 1956, he appeared to be the leading Democratic contender for the presidential nomination in 1960. Kennedy and the nation had plenty of time to ponder what his Catholic faith might mean for the campaign and presidency. In an article in *Look* magazine early in 1959, Kennedy addressed his religious views in advance of a formal announcement of his candidacy, somewhat like Al Smith's article in the *Atlantic Monthly* in 1927. Kennedy staked out a clear and strong position for the separation of church and state. He opposed diplomatic relations with the Vatican and federal aid to parochial schools. If anything, Kennedy's views may have frightened some Catholics, for he received criticism in the Catholic press. He repeated these positions before a conference of fifty-nine Methodist bishops in Washington, D.C., in mid-April.[38]

The Gallup Agency released a poll in May 1959 on the question "Can a Catholic Win?" Results of the survey indicated that Catholicism had declined as a negative factor for a presidential candidate, but it would still give Kennedy some trouble. While 24 percent of those polled said they would not vote for a Catholic candidate if their party nominated one for president, that was less than the 31 percent who took that position in 1940. In the South, the rate was significantly higher, with 35 percent in 1959 and 40 percent in 1940 taking the anti-Catholic position. The poll indicated that some Catholics would cross parties to vote for a Catholic candidate, but, all in all, a Catholic candidate would be hurt more than benefitted by his or her religion.[39]

Even before Kennedy received the nomination, evangelical church bodies began lining up against him. The Arkansas Baptist Convention at its annual meeting on November 17–19, 1959, at Little Rock's First Baptist Church took a position against a Catholic candidate for president. The national Southern Baptist Convention in Miami, Florida, in May 1960 made a similar stand for the entire denomination.[40] The Missionary Baptists had split into two denominations in 1950 when one group seceded from the American Baptist Association and, at a meeting in Little Rock, became the North American Baptist Association (now the Baptist Missionary Association of America). Arkansas's Missionary Baptists were split fairly evenly between the two denominations. Both groups took strong positions against a Catholic president before Kennedy was nominated. The American Baptist Association in June 1959 meeting in Shreveport, Louisiana, had unanimously passed a resolution opposing any Catholic candidate for president. In June 1960 the church body re-affirmed this stand at a meeting in Kansas City, with the president of the denomination saying, "No man can be loyal to the United States and the Vatican at the same time." The other Missionary Baptist group, at its annual session in Pensacola, Florida, in March 1960, in a unanimous vote opposed any Catholic candidate for president.[41]

In mid-July the Arkansas delegates to the Democratic National Convention in Los Angeles were pledged to support Texas senator Lyndon Baines Johnson, a baptized member of the Disciples of Christ Church, for the presidential nomination. These delegates received more than a hundred telegrams while in Los Angeles, mostly from Baptist preachers in Arkansas, urging them not to support a Roman Catholic for president. Kennedy, who had won all the primaries except for Pennsylvania, was nominated on the first ballot. Johnson, as a Protestant southerner, nicely balanced the ticket as vice presidential nominee. The religion issue did not come up in convention speeches or the platform, unlike in 1928 when Joe T. Robinson addressed religious toleration. Only Kennedy himself mentioned religion in his acceptance speech, acknowledging that the party had taken a risk in nominating someone of his faith. But Kennedy insisted that he would make his public policy decisions on his own—"as an American, a Democrat, and a free man."[42]

Baptists in Arkansas reacted swiftly to Kennedy's nomination. On the Sunday after the convention, the Reverend W. O. Vaught Jr. preached against Kennedy from the pulpit of Immanuel Baptist Church in Little

Rock, a congregation with more than 3,500 members, the state's largest church. Vaught, who had been elected in Miami in May as the first vice president of the Southern Baptist Convention, declared Catholicism and communism to be the two most deadly threats to freedom in the world. The Vatican, he said was determined to make the United States a Catholic nation, and this threat now appeared in the person of Senator Kennedy. The next issue of the *Arkansas Baptist* headlined: "Should a Catholic Be Elected President?" Editor Erwin L. McDonald answered by repeating the long-held views that Rome aspired to take over America. The Catholic Church, McDonald said, was a totalitarian world organization that denied the right of any other religion to exist. No Baptist could support a Catholic for public office, McDonald concluded, any more than a Catholic official could discharge his duties "apart from the will of the Catholic hierarchy."[43]

By early August, the Southern Baptists began to organize against the Kennedy candidacy. The executive board of the Arkansas State Convention met on August 8 and created the Committee on Religious Liberty, whose goal was "to alert Baptists of the state to certain threats to religious liberty should a Catholic be elected President of the United States." Members of this committee included Bernes K. Selph, the president of the Arkansas Convention, O. L. Bayless, pastor of Second Baptist Church of Hot Springs, S. A. Whitlow, the executive secretary of the convention, and Erwin L. McDonald, the editor of the *Arkansas Baptist*. On September 1, the Reverend Vaught sent letters to each of the eight Arkansas presidential electors informing them that Baptists would be carrying their anti-Kennedy campaign to all parts of the state and would hold "religious freedom rallies" in several Arkansas cities, including a special one-day meeting planned for October 3. Vaught told the electors that they could not turn the government over "to a Catholic president who could be influenced by the Pope and by the power of the Catholic hierarchy." With tones of 1928, he concluded, "We cannot be good Americans and on this occasion vote the Democratic ticket." Vaught wrote to the executive director of the POAU that he was working hard to get the Democratic Party in Arkansas to endorse Richard Nixon.[44]

By early September Arkansas fundamentalist leaders began to link up with Republican strategists and national organizations that were opposing Kennedy because of his religion. Orland K. Armstrong, a

Baptist former congressman from Springfield, Missouri, had attended the Southern Baptist Convention in Miami and had helped pass the resolution against a Catholic candidate. By August he was working with the Republican National Committee to lead efforts to exploit opposition to Kennedy's Catholicism. Sometime in August, Armstrong drove from Springfield to Little Rock, where he met with Vaught and other leaders. They planned a Religious Freedom Rally for October 3, at which the keynote speaker would be Glenn Archer, the executive director of the POAU. Armstrong also met with William R. Smith, a Church of Christ plantation owner and businessman from Lake Village, who served as an advisor for Governor Orval Faubus and was a member of the Arkansas Development Commission. Smith had been one of the Arkansas delegates to the Democratic National Convention in Los Angeles, and he came back disgusted at the Kennedy nomination and Johnson's willingness to accept the vice presidential slot. Smith introduced Armstrong to influential pastors in the Churches of Christ and some laymen with deep pockets.[45] Smith's Churches of Christ took a particularly strong stand against Kennedy in 1960.

Church of Christ and Baptist representatives from Arkansas attended a series of meetings in Washington, D.C., in early September that rallied anti-Catholic opposition to the Kennedy ticket. The POAU held a conference on September 6 with delegates from many liberal and conservative Protestant denominations and notables such as Orland Armstrong and Paul Blanshard. Glenn Archer had personally invited the Reverend Vaught to attend this meeting, and Erwin McDonald of the *Arkansas Baptist* was slated to attend. Vaught was travelling to D.C. also to attend the Baptist Joint Affairs Committee meeting, which also strategized ways to influence the outcome of the election.[46]

These two meetings were overshadowed by a meeting on September 7 at the Mayflower Hotel, under the chairmanship of Dr. Norman Vincent Peale, the well-known author and pastor of Marble Collegiate Church in New York City. The conference came out of a gathering in mid-August in Montreux, Switzerland, at the conclusion of a Billy Graham crusade, at which Graham, Peale, and other Protestant leaders planned a response to a Kennedy candidacy. They formed an organization called the Citizens for Religious Freedom, which put on the conference at the Mayflower Hotel, most often since known as the Peale meeting. The 150 leaders at the Mayflower represented thirty-seven Protestant denominations and other organizations such as the POAU and the National Association of Evangelicals. Press members were not allowed inside the assembly, but the organizers released a two-thousand-word manifesto of concern about the possibility of having a Catholic in the White House. Historian Shaun Casey believes that part of the manifesto had been written before the meeting by activists working for the Republican National Committee. A reporter for *Newsday*, although excluded from the meeting, was able to sit in a nearby sound room and listen to the speeches. She shared her material with the *Washington Post*. Their news reports presented the view that Peale and the newly organized Citizens for Religious Freedom were repeating the stale anti-Catholic positions of the past and were working to defeat Kennedy on the basis of his religion. The negative press damaged Peale, who resigned from the Citizens for Religious Freedom and offered to give up his pulpit. With all the media attention on Peale and the meeting, Nixon disavowed it publicly the following Sunday on a national television talk show.[47]

The Reverend Whitlow and Erwin McDonald, of Arkansas Southern Baptist's Committee on Religious Liberty, attended the Peale meeting. Church of Christ layman William R. Smith attended and was the second of the seven speakers at the event. Historian Shaun Casey believes that Smith, a relatively unknown layman among prominent religious leaders, was added to the program at the last minute as a reward for his organizational assistance. By virtue of his membership on the Arkansas Industrial Development Commission, where he worked with wealthy Republican Winthrop Rockefeller, Smith was able to facilitate the use of Rockefeller's airplane to transport preachers around the southwestern states to talk against Kennedy. Smith also had introduced Armstrong to James Walter Nichols, perhaps the Churches of Christ's most visible leader as editor of a paper, the *Christian Chronicle*, and a television program, the *Herald of Truth*. Smith's connections had brought to Washington a wealthy Church of Christ Texas oilman who had subsidized a large portion of the costs of the meeting. Smith's talk was entitled "A Layman Looks at the Issue."[48]

The Peale meeting and the massive media attention it received shocked the Kennedy campaign and convinced the candidate and his advisers that he must address the religion subject forcefully. Casey argues that someone involved in the Washington meetings leaked to the Kennedy campaign information about the role of Armstrong and the Republican National Committee in using the religion issue to organize conservative Protestants. Kennedy had an invitation to address the Ministerial Alliance of Houston, Texas, on September 12 and decided to use the occasion to clear the air about his Catholic faith. From the dais of the Houston's Rice Hotel, where Joe T. Robinson had stayed when attending the 1928 Democratic National Convention, Kennedy gave a short speech that has been widely regarded as a masterpiece of rhetoric and a possible turning point in the campaign. He repeated his position about the separation of church and state with the strongest language and made clear that as president he would make decisions according to his own conscience and the national interest, not considering any outside religious dictates. If faced with a conflict between his duties as president and any demands of his church, Kennedy said he would resign the presidency. One of his most memorable lines for a Texas audience referred to the Alamo, which he had visited earlier that day on the way to Houston. For those who died there, he said, "no one knows whether they were Catholics or not. For there were no religious tests there." Kennedy's speech met applause from clergy who clearly had arrived with much skepticism. He received a generally favorable treatment by the press. Kennedy's Houston speech ranks with his performance in the two televised debates with Nixon as the shining moments of his campaign. One historian of the 1960 election, W. J. Rorabaugh, considers the oration the most effective speech by either candidate during the entire race.[49]

In Arkansas, the Democratic political establishment mobilized behind Kennedy, while the Baptist and Church of Christ preachers continued to oppose him. Arkansas governor Orval Faubus, who had acquired a national reputation as a segregationist for his role in the Central High Crisis of 1957, did not attend the Democratic National Convention in July, but he asked the Arkansas delegates to cast their votes for Lyndon Johnson. After Kennedy received the nomination, however, Faubus reluctantly supported the Democratic ticket. He and state Democratic leaders hosted a luncheon in Little Rock for the Speaker of the House, Sam Rayburn, and Rayburn took the opportunity to speak against Baptist groups, in particular, who were working against Kennedy on account of his religion. Later that same day at the state Democratic convention in Little Rock, the chairman and keynote speaker, Dr. J. Lex Moore, a dentist from Harrison, denounced the "wicked fraud" of religious prejudice, which he said had been injected already into the campaign. Any religious leader who tries to embroil the church in political affairs, Moore said, "is in deed and fact disloyal to the highest American ideals." Moore's speech met with warm applause from the assembled delegates.[50] Despite Faubus's profession of support for the national ticket, Kennedy snubbed him a week later, the day after Kennedy's speech to the Houston Ministerial Alliance, when he made a campaign appearance in Texarkana. Faubus, some other state officials, and Senator William Fulbright, were part of a crowd variously estimated as between fifty and one hundred thousand people who assembled to greet Kennedy. But when Faubus went to the Texarkana airport to see Kennedy off after the event, the candidate hurried onto the plane without saying goodbye to the governor. A photographer was there intent on getting a picture of Kennedy and Faubus shaking hands to circulate in the African American press. Kennedy pointedly avoided a photo opportunity that would hurt him with black northern voters. So much for "Profiles in Courage," Faubus would later say of the incident.[51]

Meanwhile, the Baptists continued to work against Kennedy. On the evening of October 3, at Little Rock's Robinson Auditorium, the Religious Liberty Rally kicked off with an invocation led by Reverend J. Albert Gatlin, pastor of Gardner Memorial Methodist Church, apparently on the program to lend an ecumenical flavor to the meeting. The music minister of Immanuel Baptist Church led the crowd of five to six hundred in singing "America the Beautiful," the Reverend Vaught opened the meeting, and Erwin McDonald introduced the speaker, Glenn Archer, executive director of the POAU. Archer attacked the Catholic Church's "subversion of religious liberty," the parochial school system, and the overrepresentation of Catholics in Congress and statehouses. Besides prayers, singing, and speeches, the evening included the premier of a film produced by the POAU entitled *Boycott*, which described the problems created in a small New England town when public funds began to be used to support parochial schools. A variety of pamphlets were distributed in the foyer of the auditorium, and copies of Archer's speech were handed out for attendees to take away with them. At least two Catholics attended the event, for the *Arkansas*

Democrat reporter, Bobbie Forster, was a communicant member of St. Andrews Cathedral. The *Guardian*'s managing editor, William W. O'Donnell, attended and noted the twenty-five hundred empty seats in the auditorium.[52]

Religious leaders continued the anti-Kennedy work right up to the November 8 election. Southern Baptists, who had sponsored the October 3 rally, kept the message going in pulpits and editorial columns of the *Arkansas Baptist.* On October 17 the Reverend Vaught spoke at an anti-Kennedy rally at First Baptist Church in Forrest City, and on the same day Dr. Robert Smith of Pine Bluff provided the oration at a similar meeting at First Baptist in Fayetteville. Erwin McDonald, in a sermon at an association meeting in Harrisburg on October 18, responded to Kennedy's stand of separation of church and state, saying that Catholic authorities had not affirmed his position. McDonald concluded, any Catholic who sits in the White House would be joined to the Pope and the Vatican by "iron bands."[53]

Arkansas's Missionary Baptists also continued to take a hard line in opposing Kennedy. At the American Baptist Association's state meeting in Springdale just before the election, the delegates affirmed the resolution opposing any Catholic candidate for president made by the national meeting in Kansas City in June. The Central Arkansas Association of the North American Baptist Association (NABA), the other Missionary Baptist group, without a dissenting vote affirmed the anti-Catholic stand of its national association.[54] Albert Garner appears to have republished his anti-Catholic *Devil's Masterpiece* in 1960. The two NABA papers in Arkansas kept a relentless series of articles going against Kennedy and Catholicism in the fall of 1960. D. N. Jackson wrote a lengthy article in August in his *American Baptist*, which he was selling as a pamphlet, twenty copies for a dollar, under the title *Twelve Reasons Why I Will Not Vote for a Catholic for President.* Almost all of his twelve reasons were recycling the old arguments he had discussed in his 1928 pamphlet *National Dangers of Roman Catholicism.* One original point was reason number nine: that a Catholic president would enable communists to infiltrate the country more readily. In Jackson's view, the great inequities and authoritarian governments characteristic of Catholic countries provided the breeding grounds for communist movements. Jackson told readers to not believe Kennedy's claims that he would keep church and state separate, for the candidate was a member of the Knight of Columbus. Jackson directed readers not to boycott the election, but to vote the Nixon-Lodge ticket.[55] One NABA preacher in Newark, Arkansas, Jurl Mitchell, agreed with Jackson, saying that Kennedy was simply lying when he said he would preserve the separation of church and state. He quoted a purported Catholic source that said that it was morally legitimate to make false statements if the lies were made to someone who had no right to the truth. So in other words, one cannot believe anything candidate Kennedy would say on the subject of religion.[56]

Some Missionary Baptist preachers during the fall campaign even recycled the old bogus oath of the Knights of Columbus. Carl Johns, a Clarksville preacher who had his own fifteen-minute daily radio program, read on-air from the oath and announced he would send copies of the oath to anyone who asked for it. Another Missionary Baptist preacher in neighboring Russellville, the Reverend R. H. Adams, preached about the oath in a radio program and from his pulpit, and he enclosed a copy of the oath in his church bulletin on August 18. Under the advice of Knights of Columbus national leaders, a Catholic attorney in Conway, Francis Donovan, along with priests from Conway and Russellville, visited Adams and threatened to seek prosecution for libel unless he made a public apology and retraction. Adams did nothing, apparently feeling he was in a strong position, for he had called the oath after all an "alleged bloody oath." After repeated threats of prosecution by Donovan, Adams finally on October 20 placed a "retraction" in his church bulletin, which simply said that the Knights of Columbus denied the authenticity of the oath. Donovan and the Knights apparently let the matter drop.[57] The bogus oath turned up in print or in radio broadcasts during the 1960 campaign also in Fort Smith, Manila, Newport, and Blytheville.[58]

Pastors of the Churches of Christ took perhaps the strongest anti-Catholic position in 1960. The Church of Christ papers, *Christian Chronicle*, *Gospel Advocate*, and *Firm Foundation*, published a barrage of articles and editorials in the weeks leading up to the election, warning Church of Christ followers away from John Kennedy. The *Christian Chronicle* even had its cartoonist depict the threats from a Catholic president. Arkansas's own *Gospel Light* spoke in the strongest language, calling the Catholic Church "the name of sin . . . the son of perdition . . . the mother of harlots and of the abominations of the earth." In

October the paper took up the argument made by Jurl Mitchell, that of the credibility of any assertion made by a Roman Catholic seeking public office. At the Kennedy meeting with the Houston Ministerial Alliance on September 12, one Church of Christ pastor, V. E. Howard of Greenville, Texas, had badgered Kennedy in the question-and-answer session concerning the issue of Catholic teaching about truth-telling. Howard read several quotes from Catholic sources that implied that Catholics might be required to lie under certain circumstances to protect their church, and he asked Kennedy if he subscribed to these sources. Several members of the audience stood up and shouted for the moderator to move on to the next question. Kennedy astutely recognized he was being set up to either profess disloyalty to his church or admit that he could be lying whenever he talked about his religion. Kennedy made clear he was unfamiliar with the quotes and without the context of such quotes and reading the sources in full, could not comment on a hypothetical meaning. Howard later learned that all but one television station that covered the meeting had edited out his exchange with the candidate. He kept pushing his case, sending several telegrams to Kennedy asking him to affirm or deny the quotations. Writing in the *Gospel Light*, the Reverend Howard rebutted two of Kennedy's claims in his prepared speech. When Kennedy said he would resign the presidency if he were presented with a conflict between his role as president and member of the Catholic Church, Howard claimed this demonstrated that his ultimate allegiance is to the pope, for he had not said he would resign from the Catholic Church. And to Kennedy's assertion that there was no religious test at the Alamo, Howard said indeed there was, for the Texas Declaration of Independence had declared itself not just against the Mexican government and Santa Anna, but also the Catholic priesthood.[59] Howard authored a thirty-two-page pamphlet entitled the *White House: American or Roman?* and he claimed four hundred thousand copies of it were circulating in the fall of 1960. Howard had pastored congregations at Hot Springs and Conway, Arkansas, before moving to Texas and had attended Arkansas State University and Harding College. Harding's James Bales, in the closing days before the election, added a parting shot when he wrote the *Arkansas Gazette* suggesting that the Kennedy campaign itself was keeping the religious issue inflamed with the intent to win Catholic votes.[60]

Cartoon from the *Christian Chronicle* (Oklahoma City, OK), August 5, 1960. Courtesy of Oklahoma Christian University.

Not all Protestants in Arkansas followed the lead of the Baptists and Churches of Christ. As established above, the Arkansas Democratic Party fell into line with the national ticket. An informal survey of Little Rock clergy by the *Arkansas Democrat* found that while Baptist and Church of Christ pastors took a strong public stand against a Catholic president, Methodist, Episcopal, and Disciples of Christ pastors were reluctant to bring politics into the pulpit. Rabbi Ira Sanders of Temple B'Nai Israel objected to the injection of religion into the presidential campaign.[61] One Protestant woman from Searcy, who had lived in Arkansas for ten years, wrote in to the *Arkansas Democrat*, saying: "If anyone would have told me there was so much religious bigotry in Arkansas, I surely wouldn't have settled here." Even some Baptists publically disagreed with their leaders. A notable exception to the norm was former Arkansas congressman Brooks Hays, who had from 1957 to 1959 served as the president of the Southern Baptist Convention, one of the few laymen to do so. Hays had supported Al Smith in 1928 and given radio speeches arguing that Smith's Catholicism should not be an excuse to oppose him. Hays had lost his seat in Congress in 1958 when Governor Orval Faubus orchestrated a write-in campaign to turn him out of office after he won the Democratic nomination, replacing him with Little Rock ophthalmologist Dale Alford. Alford was a Faubus protégée and staunch segregationist who had served on the Little Rock School Board during the Central High Crisis. Brooks Hays met with Kennedy after his nomination at Los Angeles to advise the candidate on how to handle the issue of his religion among Baptists. Hays even claimed to have convinced evangelist Billy Graham not to endorse his close friend, Vice President Nixon. After Kennedy's election, Hays would receive an appointment as assistant secretary of state for congressional affairs, and after ten months in this post he became a member of Kennedy's staff at the White House.[62]

When the election finally arrived, Kennedy won by the narrowest of margins, just 112,803 popular votes, 49.7 percent to Nixon's 49.6 percent. Nationally, Kennedy won 34 percent of the white Protestant vote, about the same percentage that had gone for the Democratic nominee, Adlai Stevenson, in 1956. But he carried 83 percent of the votes of Roman Catholics, up from Stevenson's 45 percent in 1956. His Catholicism thus may have helped him in the North more than it hurt him in the South. Johnson's presence on the ticket helped Kennedy win the electoral votes of Texas and possibly the Carolinas.[63]

In Arkansas the vote was less close. After all the hubbub, as in 1928, the Democratic candidate won handily, with Kennedy receiving just over 50 percent of the state's popular vote, to Nixon's 43 percent, with the National States Rights ticket garnering 7 percent. Nixon carried nearly two dozen of Arkansas's seventy-five counties, most of them in the Ozark and Ouachita Mountain regions, which often voted with the GOP. When one compares the Democratic versus Republican votes for 1960 to the 1956 Stevenson-Eisenhower race, the Democratic ticket in Arkansas actually gained a half percent against the Republicans. However, one can only speculate that many of the States Rights voters also opposed a Catholic candidate.[64]

Clearly, anti-Catholic prejudice had declined after the 1928 presidential election. While anti-Catholicism obviously had not gone away, it was generally relegated to private expression and opinion. Well-publicized national events, such as the controversy over diplomatic recognition of the Vatican or ultimately the presidential campaign of a Roman Catholic, were required to bring anti-Catholic attitudes out of the shadows and back into the public arena. But even then Catholics did not rival communists as the greatest antithesis to traditional American values. Attempts by some to link anti-Catholicism and anti-communism ultimately failed. And as strident as were some attacks on John Kennedy's religion in 1960, they never matched the pitch and tenor of anti-Catholic rhetoric in the 1928 election, in Arkansas and elsewhere.

CHAPTER 7

Postlude: After 1960

THE ELECTION OF a Catholic president in 1960 ended a chapter in anti-Catholicism, if it did not actually slam the book shut. Fundamentalist Protestants, who were the last holdouts of anti-Catholic attitudes, became conflicted in their views about Catholics as time wore on. Eventually, the prejudices against Catholicism eroded further as fundamentalists came to see Catholics as allies in a common opposition to a greater enemy, secular humanistic liberalism.

After the 1960 election, Baptist editor Erwin McDonald was still licking his wounds. Arkansas Baptists, he said, were unhappy with the results of the vote and had not changed their feelings about a Catholic president. However, the Arkansas Baptist Convention that met in Fayetteville on the week following the election vowed to give the president-elect prayers and support.[1] Similarly, Missionary Baptist leaders called for their followers to put aside their personal choices, to pray for the new president, and to come to respect him. D. N. Jackson looked at the Kennedy victory as a glass half full, for the campaign, he said, had forced the president-elect to adopt a "Protestant" position of strict separation of church and state. But he warned Americans not to relax their vigil, for Rome's "artful schemes and frauds . . . require persistent watch over liberty."[2]

Kennedy's actions as president may have allayed fears. Early in his presidency Kennedy supported a bill for federal aid to education, but he specifically opposed inclusion of aid to parochial schools. He promised not to create any ambassadorial position for the Vatican. He opposed other policies traditionally championed by the Catholic hierarchy. Kennedy took a more strict interpretation of the separation of church and state than presidents before him, perhaps the strictest position in American history.[3]

The anti-Catholic reporting in the Baptist press declined after 1960, disappearing entirely in 1961 from the *Arkansas Baptist.* In 1962 editor McDonald offered to lend the use of the paper's equipment to print an issue of the *Guardian* when the Catholic paper purchased a new offset press and was not sure that the transition would be complete in a week's time. When Kennedy was assassinated the next year, McDonald eulogized the great loss to the nation without mention of the president's religion.[4] Brooks Hays, the former president of the Southern Baptist Convention and Arkansas congressman, authored a piece for a Baptist newsletter about the slain president entitled "A Sincere and Practicing Christian."[5] Hays had met with Pope John XXIII in 1961 when he was working in the Kennedy administration. The pope told him: "I too am Baptist," referring to his name John, and said, "We are brothers in Christ." This Arkansas Baptist layman a few years later would have a private audience also with Pope Paul VI. In 1968 Hays was asked by Wake Forest University, the Baptist school in Winston-Salem, North Carolina, to head the Ecumenical Institute, specifically designed to promote dialogue between Baptists and Roman Catholics. Through the 1970s the institute planned yearly meetings between Catholic and Baptist scholars, clergy, and laity to discuss common ground and differences.[6]

As Baptists softened their stance toward Catholics, the Roman church itself changed dramatically in the 1960s with the second Vatican Council, which met between 1962 and 1965. Protestant representatives were invited to observe the council's sessions, even Paul Blanshard, perhaps the Catholic Church's most influential American critic. The council's most visible result was to place worship into vernacular languages instead of Latin. The center of gravity within Catholicism moved away from the church hierarchy toward the laity. And the council changed the church's stance toward other religions, officially recognizing Protestants as fellow Christians. The Roman Catholic Church that emerged from Vatican II was one much less alien to American Protestants.

As the Catholic Church changed, eight years of the ascendancy of the Democratic Party, 1961–1969, left its mark on the country as well. Conservative Protestants had feared the collapse of the wall between church and state, but several important Supreme Court rulings made that wall more inflexible in the 1960s. Arkansas's laws requiring daily Bible reading in public schools and prohibiting the teaching of evolution, both authored by Ben Bogard as initiated acts, were made unconstitutional by court rulings *Abington School District v. Schempp* and *Epperson v. Arkansas*.[7] Religious conservatives reacted to cultural changes in the 1960s with the arrival of the birth-control pill and legal abortion in some states, a counter-culture lifestyle among young people, and more relaxed standards of public morality.

By the 1970s secular humanism, rather than Catholicism, appeared to be the great enemy for many fundamentalist Christians. Between *Roe v. Wade* in 1973 and the election of Ronald Reagan in 1980, there was a sea change in the posture of conservative Protestants toward politics and society. The Southern Baptist Convention, ironically, had taken a more tolerant position toward abortion in the late 1960s and early 1970s, perhaps seeing opposition to abortion as a "Catholic" position. The 1971 convention even passed a resolution urging states to liberalize their abortion laws. One of the Baptist-Catholic dialogues, in November 1975, by Brooks Hays's Ecumenical Institute concerned the subject of abortion. As the 1970s went on, fundamentalist Protestants and the Roman Catholic Church began to converge into the "Christian Right." Conservatives took control of the Southern Baptist Convention in 1979 and reversed the denomination's stand on abortion and passed resolutions denouncing pornography, homosexuality, and the teaching of human evolution. The landslide that was Ronald Reagan's victory in 1980, defeating the Southern Baptist incumbent Jimmy Carter, no less, cemented the identification of the conservative evangelicals with the Republican Party.[8]

Illustrative of the transition in the 1970s and 1980s were the two issues that caused such a fuss thirty years before: federal aid to education and an ambassador for the Vatican. A Catholic senator from New York, Daniel Patrick Moynihan, introduced a bill in 1978 to provide tuition tax credits for parents of children in parochial schools. The generally liberal *Arkansas Gazette* in 1978 criticized Moynihan's position through a cartoon by the paper's celebrated editorial cartoonist, George Fisher. He showed Moynihan as a Roman pontiff dangling the incense of federal aid to church schools over a toga-clad lady-liberty figure who represented the US Constitution. As the clerical figure puckered to kiss the sumptuous female figure, the cartoon was eerily reminiscent of *Menace* cartoons of the 1910s portraying priests and young women in the confessional. Some *Gazette* readers saw the resemblance and accused the paper of being anti-Catholic.[9]

But in 1982 it was President Ronald Reagan who proposed tuition tax credits for private and parochial education. The Southern Baptist

Cartoon from the *Arkansas Gazette* (Little Rock), April 16, 1978. *Courtesy of the* Arkansas Democrat-Gazette.

Convention and numerous state conventions went on record as opposing this measure, and the bill got nowhere in Congress.[10] But then two years later Reagan appointed a Roman Catholic convert, William A. Wilson, as ambassador to the Vatican, with full diplomatic recognition for the Holy See. The Baptist press of Arkansas noted statements by some Baptist leaders and efforts of Baptist senator Jesse Helms of North Carolina to oppose this measure. The *Arkansas Methodist* reported about three Methodist leaders who spoke against the appointment to the Senate Foreign Relations Committee. Otherwise, there was little reaction. Succeeding presidents after Reagan have continued the practice of choosing a Roman Catholic as ambassador to the Vatican.[11]

Since Al Smith and John Kennedy, the two major parties have only once nominated a Roman Catholic for the presidency, Senator John Kerry in 2004. Kerry received opposition, not for being Catholic, but for not being Catholic enough. Fundamentalist voters and conservative Roman Catholics, as well as some members of the Catholic hierarchy, criticized Kerry for his stand for abortion rights, in contradiction to the teachings of his church.[12] In Arkansas, George W. Bush won with 54 percent of the vote to Kerry's 45 percent. But Kerry's Catholicism did not seem to be an issue; the state's Southern Baptist, Missionary Baptist, and Church of Christ papers never even mentioned it during the fall campaign. The Baptist papers were full of commentary, however, about a proposed state constitutional amendment on the November ballot that defined marriage in the state of Arkansas as being between one man and one woman. That amendment passed with 75 percent of the vote. The state convention of Southern Baptists passed a resolution praising Arkansas voters for enacting this law.[13]

A good example of the transition among Arkansas evangelicals would be Mike Huckabee, Baptist preacher cum Arkansas governor, presidential candidate, and conservative pundit. Born in Hope in 1955 to working-class parents who were southern-style Democrats, Huckabee grew up in a small Missionary Baptist church and graduated from Ouachita Baptist University. From 1980 to 1992 he was a minister in Southern Baptist congregations in Pine Bluff and then Texarkana. In the early 1990s he was elected president of the Arkansas Baptist Convention, the youngest president in the convention's 150-year history. Under Huckabee's leadership in the 1990s, Arkansas's Southern Baptists regularly enacted resolutions against alcohol, pornography, abortion, gay rights, and the distribution of contraceptives in public schools. After a two-year presidency of the convention, he moved from the pulpit to politics as a conservative Republican. Huckabee has explained that the Democratic Party of his childhood represented the party of the workingman while the Republican Party was the party of the "button-down, wealthy few." But in his adult life, Huckabee said, "Democrats had become the party of pro-abortionists, gay rights supporters, and others who ignore the bedrock tenets of biblical integrity and long-cherished American traditions."[14] After his two-year term as president of Arkansas's Southern Baptists, he was elected as lieutenant governor, and then served as governor from 1996 to 2007. As a Republican presidential candidate in 2008, he championed "traditional family values" and sought the support of the Christian Right. Huckabee surprised the nation when he won the Iowa caucus. He went on to win Republican primaries in Alabama, Arkansas, Georgia, Louisiana, and Tennessee, as well as caucuses in Kansas and West Virginia.

In the next presidential election of 2012, it was a Roman Catholic senator from Pennsylvania, Ric Santorum, who targeted the same block of voters. Taking a strong position against abortion and gay marriage, Santorum had success with evangelical Protestant voters as well as Roman Catholics. Like Huckabee, he won the Iowa caucus, but also Republican caucuses in Colorado and Minnesota, as well as primaries in North Dakota, Missouri, Oklahoma, Louisiana, Mississippi, Alabama, and Tennessee. Had Santorum not dropped out of the race in April before Arkansas's May 22 primary, one suspects that this Catholic Republican would have won in Arkansas too, given that he carried each bordering state except Texas, whose primary was the week after Arkansas's. With the exception of 1992 and 1996, when favorite son Bill Clinton carried the state, Arkansas has gone Republican in every presidential election since 1972.

Thus, as we get to the present, anti-Catholic attitudes seem like a distant memory to older Americans and incomprehensible to the young. In southern states, such as Arkansas, fundamentalist Protestants increasingly perceive Catholics as kindred Christians who have much the same agenda on the important moral questions. Anti-Catholicism has been relegated, like the Ku Klux Klan, to what most people would consider an extremist fringe. One example is Tony Alamo, the stage name for a

California entertainer turned religious cult leader, who in 1975 moved the headquarters of his ministry to Dyer, his wife's hometown in western Arkansas. The Alamo ministry was known for vicious anti-Catholic slurs made in tracts left on car windshields. One six-page tract distributed in 1985 in central Arkansas accused the Vatican of controlling the Communist Party, Nazis, the Mafia, the FBI, the press, numerous government agencies, the United Nations, and President Ronald Reagan. A 1990 Alamo publication accused Pope John Paul II of being a Nazi war criminal and printed a picture of President George H. W. Bush appearing to kiss a nun on the lips. The Arkansas branch of the National Conference of Christians and Jews denounced the ongoing distribution of this anti-Catholic material by the Alamo group.[15] It remained active until Alamo himself was arrested in 2008 and then tried, found guilty, and sentenced to 175 years in prison for taking underage girls across state lines for the purposes of sexual activity.

In 1960, as a Catholic Democratic presidential nominee from the Northeast was balanced by a Protestant running mate from the South, the discussion about Catholicism and politics repeated much of what was said in Arkansas thirty-two years before, in 1928. Fast forward another thirty-two years and a Baptist governor of Arkansas received the Democratic nomination, but by this time issues of religion and region seemed less important in balancing a ticket. The balance came from a Washington insider, Senator Al Gore, another Baptist from a contiguous state. In recent presidential elections, balancing a ticket has become more a matter of gender, race, or ideology. In the 2012 election, Republican nominee Mitt Romney, who came from the business progressive wing of the GOP, chose Congressman Paul Ryan as a vice presidential running mate not because he was Catholic and from Wisconsin, but because he represented the conservative Tea Party wing of the party. This ticket of a Mormon and a Catholic carried Arkansas and the rest of the South, with the exception of Virginia. Ben Bogard, who had denounced Mormons as not even Christian in his columns of the *Baptist and Commoner*, would have rolled over in his grave as Arkansas's Missionary Baptists voted for this ticket.

Two scholarly books have examined anti-Catholicism in the United States in recent years, Mark Massa's *Anti-Catholicism in America* and Philip Jenkins's *The New Anti-Catholicism*, and both use the same subtitle: *The Last Acceptable Prejudice.* Both Massa and Jenkins argue that anti-Catholicism was a pervasive prejudice throughout American history that has never gone away. Massa devotes some attention to the new "old" type of anti-Catholicism, called, in this book, fringe extremism. Both Massa and Jenkins, however, concentrate on the liberal secular critique of Catholicism, of the sort that emerged with the work of Blanshard and the Protestants and Other Americans United for Separation of Church and State (POAU). Jenkins particularly argues that liberals, the news media, and even Hollywood have increasingly portrayed the Roman Catholic Church, with its opposition to abortion, contraception, women's ordination, and gay rights, as a relic from a past era. Adding to negative images of the Catholic Church were the much publicized priest sex scandals of the 1990s and 2000s, which titillated the public with accounts of clerical abuse of children and cover-ups by bishops who often simply moved offending priests to other parishes where they continued to prey on children. Jenkins argues that media accounts of these priestly sex scandals are modern-day versions of Maria Monk. Liberal critics, Jenkins believes, have stereotyped devout Catholics as anti-feminist gay-hating bigots and have mocked Catholicism in ways that would be considered hate speech if directed toward other groups.[16] This left-wing critique of Catholicism has held little sway in conservative Arkansas, a place where fundamentalists might perceive a similar victimization at the hands of politically correct liberals.

This book has examined how a prejudice evolved in a community over time. The small state of Arkansas was not unique in harboring anti-Catholic attitudes in the twentieth century. Yet Arkansas typified the area in the United States where anti-Catholicism was strongest in the 1910s and 1920s and where it lasted the longest thereafter. The South, and particularly the upper southern states from Tennessee to Arkansas, southern Missouri, Oklahoma, and Texas, may have had the deepest antipathy toward Catholicism. There were reasons that Al Smith chose Oklahoma City in 1928 and John Kennedy chose Houston in 1960 as the location for their speeches in defense of their presidential candidacies as Roman Catholics.

Two strands of anti-Catholicism were apparent in early twentieth-century Arkansas. In the 1910s anti-Catholicism revolved around fears of priests as sexual predators who persuaded women to reveal their sexual thoughts and actions in the confessional or used housekeepers in rectories or nuns in convents as personal harems. This preoccupation with sexuality, so central to nineteenth-century anti-Catholicism, reflects a Victorian-style repression that channeled acceptable discussion of sex into the condemnation of a sexual "other." Christian men in small-town or rural Arkansas who might not be able to talk to their wives, or each other, about whores, impure confessions, sexual torture, and rape could pay ten cents to hear the "Men Only" talk by a professional anti-Catholic lecturer, who would describe in lurid detail these acts by priests and nuns. Missionary Baptists considered the Roman Catholic Church to be the Whore of Babylon, whose drunken sexual perversions are described in the book of Revelations. How arousing it must have been. The pornographic quality of this anti-Catholicism was understood by the postmaster general of Canada, who banned distribution of the *Menace* in that country's mail as "indecent." Father Boniface Spanke in his much publicized debate of 1914 may have fed these sexual fears, as a young, handsome, charismatic priest going to battle for his faith. Bishop John Morris perhaps wisely called off Boniface, recognizing that silence sometimes was a more effective response than a crusade.

The French theorist and historian Michel Foucault suggests that sexual norms are put in place not so much by repression as by the postulations of what is "not normal," a sexual "other." And the discourse about what is deviant, Foucault argues, brings a feeling of socially acceptable pleasure. Celibate priests and nuns defied the norms, as did consensual interracial sexual relationships. Irrational fear about priests as sexual predators is reminiscent of the fear of black male sexuality that motivated many rape accusations and lynchings in the late nineteenth- and early twentieth-century South. We might scratch our heads at such "irrational" fears, but nonetheless the ideas worked powerfully on the white male Protestant imagination.[17]

Another strand of anti-Catholicism evident in the 1910s that came to full expression in the 1920s was anxiety about authentic American culture. Folks of Anglo-Saxon descent in small-town and rural Arkansas watched from afar as Catholic immigration and urban industrial society transformed the face of America. Paranoia over the loss of traditional identity to a multicultural American society became a foundation of the new wave of anti-Catholicism in the 1910s. But the organizational genius of the Ku Klux Klan, its penetration into the local life of Arkansas communities, and the effective propaganda of its journals, speakers, and programs took this call for authentic American culture to a new level in the early 1920s. As with sexual norms discussed above, "authentic" American values were defined by the construction of an inauthentic "other," a phantom mirror-image who displayed the opposite of these values. Catholicism as imagined by the Klan provided the antithesis of "One Hundred Percent Americanism." In 1928 the candidacy of Al Smith, with his New York swagger and Irish Catholic persona, again personified this other perfectly. Moreover, Smith represented an imagined attempt by the Roman Catholic Church to take over the government of the United States and transform its institutions, most notably the public school.

After the 1928 election, visible expressions of anti-Catholic prejudice declined. The success of immigration reform in the 1920s sucked away some energy within anti-Catholicism, for the Johnson-Reed law was enacted at the height of the Klan's influence in 1924 and was in full effect by 1929. The flood of Catholic immigration thereafter became a trickle. The repeal of the Eighteenth Amendment in 1933 further weakened anti-Catholicism, for one could no longer argue that prohibition was an authentic American value. Anti-Catholic attitudes by the 1930s were moving from the public arena back to the private domain. John Higham in *Strangers in the Land* brilliantly demonstrates how nativist movements waxed and waned according to specific conditions, the intersection of personal prejudices with external situations that brought attitudes to the surface like cream rising in milk. In the 1930s and 1940s conservative Americans increasingly perceived communists as the other who threatened American values. Efforts to provide federal aid to parochial education and diplomatic recognition for the Vatican brought anti-Catholic sentiments temporarily back to the forefront. Even though the papacy historically had been the staunchest opponent to communism in Europe, some, like Paul Blanshard or Erwin McDonald in his editorials in the *Arkansas Baptist*, tried to link Catholicism with communism and make the two others essentially one. Finally, the Kennedy election of 1960 once more transformed anti-Catholic attitudes into an organized movement.

Anti-Catholicism, like any prejudice, moved back and forth on a continuum, ranging from vague emotions and privately expressed language to an organized movement, to social action that could influence law or governmental actions that negatively impacted the target group. Fortunately, this prejudice rarely progressed to the point of physical violence against property or persons. One of the only instances of violence of property came in 1923 when someone scrawled two crosses and KKK in red paint on the walls of the Catholic Church in Rogers. But the Rogers Klan offered a fifty-dollar reward for the apprehension and conviction of the "yellow cur" who committed this act.[18] Unlike white racism in Arkansas, anti-Catholic prejudice was mostly a war of words. Nor would it take the final step on the continuum, as in Nazi Germany or Rwanda, to become genocide.

Arkansas's anti-Catholicism cannot be understood outside of the context of Protestant religious sensibilities. The *Menace*, the professional anti-Catholic lecturers, and Herb Lewis's newspaper had no formal relationship with a church body, although the lecturers and editors were most often members of Protestant churches. Some of the "professionals," such as Otis Spurgeon, Billy Parker, and William Black, appear to have been motivated by the chance to make money off of people's prejudices. James and Robbie Gill Comer made a fortune from their cut in the Klan's pyramid schemes. But many Arkansas Protestants espoused anti-Catholic views from sincere religious convictions. The Reverend Joseph Scarboro gave up a comfortable income as pastor of Magnolia's First Baptist Church only to lose his life savings publishing an anti-Catholic newspaper, the *Liberator*. While the Klan is often regarded as a social organization, it was also a religious one. Kelly J. Baker brings the religious dimensions of the Klan to our attention in her recent book, *The Gospel According to the Klan*. The requirement that one be Protestant to join, the money gifts made to churches made by white-robed members, and the ceremonial use of Christian prayers and hymns—*Onward Christian Soldiers* was a favorite in Arkansas and elsewhere—all belie the nature of the Klan as a religious movement. The role of church leaders and the Protestant press in opposing Al Smith's candidacy in 1928 and Kennedy's in 1960 shows a particularly religious face to anti-Catholicism in Arkansas.

The fundamentalist religious climate in Arkansas contributed to intense anti-Catholic sentiments. Fundamentalism was just emerging as a Protestant movement in the early twentieth century as some leaders and church bodies staked out positions rejecting theological and scientific challenges to traditional teachings. Leaders listed several propositions that were considered "fundamental" to the Christian faith, such as the divinity of Christ and the Bible as the inerrant authority for Christian truth. In a general way, fundamentalism was a reaction against modernity. Anti-Catholicism provided a way for fundamentalists to claim the social and political status quo as urbanization, immigration, and ethnic diversity threatened it on a national level. It makes sense that fundamentalists would be the most anti-Catholic of Protestants. That said, fundamentalists did not agree on much, even on how many fundamentals there were.[19]

Baptists were and are today the largest fundamentalist group in Arkansas and the United States. And in the 1920s Arkansas was one of the most Baptist states in the country. While the largest white Baptist denomination, the Southern Baptist Convention, consistently held anti-Catholic positions, from the convent inspection legislation of the 1910s to the 1928 and 1960 presidential campaigns, it was the Missionary Baptists who took the most extreme stand against Catholicism. Ben Bogard had led followers to walk away from the Southern Baptist Convention by 1905, and the denomination had its greatest concentration in Arkansas.[20] Arkansas's only single-purpose anti-Catholic newspaper, the *Liberator*, was published from 1912 to 1915 by a Missionary Baptist leader, the Reverend Joseph Scarboro. After Scarboro left the state and Ben Bogard returned to Arkansas and became editor of the *Baptist and Commoner*, Bogard launched the most insistent and outlandish campaign against Catholicism in the 1920s.

Something about the very nature of the Missionary Baptist movement would make it more disposed to oppose Catholicism. The hallmark of the Missionary Baptists' identity was congregational autonomy. In fact, the denomination split from the Southern Baptist Convention because of opposition to the convention's Board of Missions and other expressions of a denominational bureaucracy. Missionary Baptists insisted that only individual congregations should send missionaries, not a convention or associational organization, hence the name "Missionary" Baptist. They championed the local, the anti-hierarchy. Thus, Roman Catholicism, with its top-down polity, represented the exact opposite of the Missionary

Baptist ideal. Bogard's greatest insult when he sparred with Southern Baptist leaders was to label the convention Baptists as "like the Catholics" for having a church bureaucracy. Missionary Baptists were also insistent upon being direct descendants from the first-century Christian Church. As Missionary Baptists viewed history, Roman Catholics were the first group to split off from them in the sixth century. The Catholic hierarchy then persecuted the true remnant for a thousand years, with these authentic Baptist Christians continuing as a direct line through the Waldensian movement in the Middle Ages, through the Anabaptists in Reformation times, until finding relative toleration on this side of the Atlantic. Therefore in the Missionary Baptist worldview, the Roman Catholic Church had been their true enemy for millennia.

A similar argument might be made about anti-Catholicism within the Churches of Christ. This religious tradition began in the early 1800s as an anti-denomination, calling itself the Restoration movement, attempting to take Christianity back to the ways and teachings of the early church, before the divisions into separate bodies. Like the Missionary Baptists, the Churches of Christ were congregationalist in polity, so much so, in fact, that they allowed for no denominational hierarchy or bureaucracy at all. One of the early leaders of the Churches of Christ, probably the most influential figure during the time that the Churches of Christ was separating from the Disciples of Christ, was David Lipscomb in Tennessee. He strongly urged followers and congregations to withdraw from worldly and political affairs. Any opposition to Catholicism within the Churches of Christ in the 1910s and 1920s generally thus stayed within the realm of pulpits and personal attitudes and did not attach to political or public activity.[21] That position evolved beginning in the 1930s for the Churches of Christ in general, but especially in Arkansas. George S. Benson became president of Harding College in 1936 and served until 1965. In his tenure, he made the college a bastion of anti-communism and pro-Americanism. Benson became a nationally prominent figure, promoting patriotism and godliness in education, speaking before Congress, preaching on his own radio program, and writing a syndicated column for some twenty-five hundred small-town newspapers. He even produced a documentary film in the early 1960s, *The Truth About Communism*, narrated by the Hollywood actor Ronald Reagan. Harding's Professor James Bales by the 1940s wrote in the strongest language against Catholicism and communism. World War II firmly put an end to the pacifist streak in the Churches of Christ.[22] By the later 1940s when Church of Christ leaders began to speak out on political and social issues, they rivaled Baptists in their stridency against Catholicism. As with the Missionary Baptists, Arkansas had a particular concentration of members of the Churches of Christ. If one considers this non-denomination a denomination, it would be the fourth-largest white Christian group in Arkansas at the 1926 religious census, behind the Methodist Episcopal Church South, the Southern Baptists, and the Missionary Baptists. Only Tennessee and Texas had more members of the Churches of Christ.[23]

The religious form of anti-Catholicism had a long life in Arkansas, a state with some of the highest levels of measurable religiosity in the United States.[24] But even here, anti-Catholic paranoia became mostly a memory of those who can recollect life before the 1960s. What has continued is the postulation of a group believed to subvert authentic Christian American values. From the 1930s through the Cold War, communists were another other, but the definition continues. Historian Allan Lichtman in *White Protestant Nation* has argued convincingly that American conservatism today, including the Christian Right, stems from an ethos that began in the 1920s. The Ku Klux Klan organized the movement on a grassroots level to oppose pluralistic, diverse, and cosmopolitan forces that threatened the national identity. The 1920s Klan faded away after a short life, but the 100 percent Americanism perspective did not. Since the Reagan years, the internal enemy has become secular liberals who hold radically different views of what constitutes a moral order. Illegal immigration, gay marriage, Muslim extremism/terrorism, abortion—these issues have held the power to energize conservativism in recent years. The easiest group to call other might be homosexuals. Michel Foucault has explained that in the last 150 years, Western culture has redefined homosexuality from being an act to being an essence.[25] In this view, all aspects of a gay person's identity and personality are attributable to his or her sexual preference. Thus, for conservative heterosexuals, homosexuals might appear fundamentally different, like a square peg trying to force its way into the round hole of Christian American culture. And the projection of an other becomes all the more powerful when infused with sexuality, as with talk of a Whore of Babylon.

In February 1915, the Arkansas General Assembly, controlled by Democrats, passed Act 130, the Convent Inspection Act, which called for county sheriffs to inspect convents to make sure women there were not being kept as the sex slaves of lecherous priests. One hundred years later, in its 2015 session, the Arkansas General Assembly had Republican majorities in both House and Senate for the first time since Reconstruction. The legislature passed Act 137, which prohibited a county or city government in Arkansas from establishing any ordinance to prevent discrimination against homosexual or transgendered individuals. In a more controversial measure, the general assembly went on to pass a "Religious Freedom" bill whose purpose was widely believed to allow businesses or individuals on the basis of religious convictions to refuse service to gay or transgendered people. Following national criticism, public protests, and calls from the Arkansas business community, including the state's biggest company, Walmart, Republican governor Asa Hutchinson asked the legislature to rewrite the law. The general assembly did so in a manner closely following the federal religious freedom law of 1993. While they were at it, legislators passed a law, Act 1231, to place a monument to the Ten Commandments on the grounds of the state capitol. It is no surprise that the language of the Ten Commandments approved by the general assembly was the version used by fundamentalist Protestants rather than the one embraced by Roman Catholics.[26] This choice of wording probably reflects simply the version familiar to legislators, rather than anti-Catholic sentiments. Yet, it demonstrates that conservative Protestants still dominate Arkansas politics. The culture wars of the 1910s and 1920s show no signs of ending in twenty-first-century Arkansas.

NOTES

CHAPTER 1 • Prelude: Before 1913

1. See the Magnolia, Arkansas, *Liberator*, October 2, 16, 1913. These two issues are the only ones known to exist. They are archived at the Arkansas History Commission, Little Rock. For a scholarly discussion of the history of the coupe glass and its association with feminine sexuality, see Adrienne Mayor, "Libation Titillation: Wine Goblets and Women's Breasts," *Studies in Popular Culture* 16, no. 2 (April 1994): 61–71.

2. John Higham, *Strangers in the Land: Patterns of American Nativism, 1860–1925* (New Brunswick, NJ: Rutgers University Press, 1955); Justin Nordstrom, *Danger on the Doorstep: Anti-Catholicism and American Print Culture in the Progressive Era* (Notre Dame, IN: University of Notre Dame Press, 2006).

3. For an interesting study of how anti-Catholicism manifested itself in a southern community, motivating a murder in Birmingham, Alabama, in 1921, see Sharon Davies, *Rising Road: A True Tale of Love, Race, and Religion in America* (New York: Oxford University Press, 2010); for an examination of anti-Catholicism in another southern state, see Robert B. Rackleff, "Anti-Catholicism and the Florida Legislature, 1911–1919," *Florida Historical Quarterly* 50 (April 1972): 352–65.

4. For more information on the long history of anti-Catholicism in the United States, see Donald Louis Kinzer, *An Episode in Anti-Catholicism: The American Protective Association* (Seattle: University of Washington Press, 1964); Mark S. Massa, *Anti-Catholicism in America: The Last Acceptable Prejudice* (New York: Crossroads, 2003); and Nordstrom, *Danger on the Doorstep*.

5. John Higham, in *Strangers in the Land*, 81, suggests that the American Protective Association made little headway below Kentucky. Southerners, he said, viewed the organization as the tool of the Republican Party. However, a Catholic priest, Johan Eugen Weibel, who founded several parishes in northeastern Arkansas in the late 1800s, said that American Protective Association had a large membership in Jonesboro. After he started a school there for black children in the early 1890s, he received mail threatening to burn down the church, convent, and school if he continued to educate Negroes, he said. He paid the threats no attention. But in May 1896 the church, convent, and rectory burned to the ground. Weibel blamed the fire on the American Protective Association. See Father E. J. Weibel, *Forty Years Missionary in Arkansas*, trans. Sister M. Agnes, OSB (Jonesboro, AR: Holy Angels Convent, 1968), 126, 135–37; a translation of *Vierzig Jahre Missionaer in Arkansas* (Lucerne, Switzerland: Verlag von Raeber und Cie, 1927). Later, parishioners in Jonesboro would assert that the church burned because of a lightning strike on the bell tower. With scant evidence, it is difficult to assess how active the American Protective Association was in Jonesboro or elsewhere in Arkansas. See Sr. Henrietta Hockle, OSB, *Parish on the Ridge: A History of Blessed Sacrament Parish, 1885–2005, Jonesboro, Arkansas* (Jonesboro: Pinpoint Publishing, 2007), 11.

6. James M. Woods, *Mission and Memory: A History of the Catholic Church in*

Arkansas (Little Rock, AR: Diocese of Little Rock, 1993), 22–23, 25–27; Jeannie M. Whayne, Thomas A. DeBlack, George Sabo III, and Morris S. Arnold, *Arkansas: A Narrative History* (Fayetteville: University of Arkansas Press, 2002), 22, 28–32.

7. For the authoritative work on Arkansas Post, see Morris S. Arnold, *Colonial Arkansas, 1686–1804* (Fayetteville: University of Arkansas Press, 1991); Morris S. Arnold, *The Rumble of a Distant Drum: The Quapaws and Old World Newcomers, 1673–1804* (Fayetteville: University of Arkansas Press, 2000); and Kathleen DuVal, *The Native Ground: Indians and Colonists in the Heart of the Continent* (Philadelphia: University of Pennsylvania Press, 2005).

8. Woods, *Mission and Memory*, 47, 52–53, 66, 110–11, 115.

9. Ibid., 115, 126–38, 266–68. For more information about the founding of Catholic institutions, see Scott Jones, "Monastic Missionaries in the New Wilderness: A History of Catholic Monasticism in Arkansas, 1878–1998" (PhD dissertation, University of Arkansas, 1998). For information on the Holy Ghost Order in Arkansas, see Henry J. Koren, CS Sp., *The Serpent and the Dove: A History of the Congregation of the Holy Ghost in the United States, 1745–1984* (Pittsburgh, PA: Spiritus Press, 1985), 105–24.

10. James Hennesey, SJ, *American Catholics: A History of the Roman Catholic Community in the United States* (New York: Oxford University Press, 1981), 173.

11. See Robert F. Zeidel, *Immigrants Progressives and Exclusion Politics: The Dillingham Commission 1900–1927* (DeKalb: Northern Illinois Press, 2004).

12. Bureau of the Census, *Thirteenth Census of the United States, 1910* (Washington, DC: Government Printing Office, 1913), vol. 2: 118–31.

13. One can assume that North Carolina's Catholic percentage was smaller than that of Arkansas, for it was so small that it was not singled out for enumeration, but instead included in the designation "all other denominations." Bureau of the Census, *Special Reports: Religious Bodies, 1916* (Washington, DC: Government Printing Office, 1919), 112.

14. *Acts of Arkansas, May–June, 1911* (Little Rock, AR: Democrat Printing, 1911), 460–61; *Southern Guardian*, October 14, 1911, October 9, 1915.

15. Nordstrom, *Danger on Our Doorstep*, 10, 62–66.

16. Still the seminal biography of Watson is C. Vann Woodward's book, written not long after Watson's death, *Tom Watson: Agrarian Rebel* (New York: Oxford University Press, 1963, first published 1938).

17. Woodward, *Tom Watson*, 420. In February 1911, *Watson's Jeffersonian Magazine* became simply *Watson's Magazine*.

18. *Watson's Magazine*, October 1911, 523.

19. These newspapers are noted in Nordstrom, *Danger on the Doorstep*, 56, 64. Dates of their publication were ascertained through WorldCat.

20. *The Ozark Region: Its History and Its People*, 3 vols. (Springfield, MO: Interstate Historical Society, 1917), 2:211–12; Higham, *Strangers in the Land*, 180.

21. *Glenwood (AR) News*, quoted in the *Southern Guardian* (Little Rock), September 16, 1911.

22. Excerpts from these papers were printed in the *Menace* (Aurora, MO), July 13, August 31, 1912. The *Wilmot (AR) Weekly*, edited by Edward J. Doyle, appears to have had a short life of a few months in 1912; see Fred W. Allsopp, *History of the Arkansas Press for a Hundred Years and More* (Little Rock, AR: Parke-Harper, 1922), 58.

23. *Southern Guardian*, March 8, 1913. For the founding of the Guardians of Liberty, see Reuben Maury, *The Wars of the Ungodly* (New York: McBride, 1928), 254–56. By August 1912, the Guardians of Liberty claimed to have 126,000 members nationwide.

24. For biographical information about Lewis and Veach, see Dallas Herndon, *Centennial History of Arkansas*, 3 vols. (Chicago: S. J. Clarke, 1922), 2:146–47; Allsopp, *History of the Arkansas Press*, 69–70, 597–98.

25. Herb Lewis's first long diatribe against Catholicism was in the *Gravette (AR) News Herald*, July 28, 1911. See also issues of February 23 and May 3, 1912.

26. *Gravette News Herald*, August 30, 1912.

27. Ibid., January 17, 24, 31, February 14, 1913.

28. *Menace*, November 9, 1912, October 11, 1913, January 13, 1914; *Liberator*, October 2, 1913; *Gravette News Herald*, September 13, 1912.

29. *Menace*, January 4, August 23, November 15, 1913. The first mention of the *Liberator* in the *Southern Guardian* was in April 6, 1912, and Herb Lewis seems to have discovered it by May 3, 1912, *Gravette News Herald*. The *Baptist* (Little Rock), September 16, 1914. Joseph Scarboro claimed a circulation of 8,000 in 1914 and 15,000 in 1915 in *N. W. Ayer and Son's American Newspaper Annual and Directory, 1914*, 2 vols. (Philadelphia, PA: Ayer and Son's, 1914), 2:52; and *N. W. Ayer and Son's American Newspaper Annual and Directory, 1915*, 2 vols. (Philadelphia, PA: Ayer and Son's, 1915), 2:52. The Ayer listings claim the editorial stance of anti-Roman Catholic. In the *Liberator* issue of October 2, 1913, Scarboro said most subscribers were in the South and West. Biographical information about Scarboro can be found in Robert Ashcraft, ed., *History of the American Baptist Association* (Texarkana, TX: American Baptist Association, 2000), 554–57.

30. Bureau of the Census, *Religious Bodies in 1916*, 112.

31. J. P. Robinson, *Why Believers Should Be Baptised and Catholicism Exposed* (Nashville, TN: National Baptist Publishing Board, 1911), preface, 74–75.

32. *Baptist Advance*, articles against Mormons and Jehovah's Witnesses, January 5, 1911, and July 25, 1912; anti-Catholic articles appearing October 19, December 7, 21, 1911, and January 18, February 1, 15, 29, March 7, April 4, 18, 1912.

33. J. S. Rogers, *History of Arkansas Baptists* (Little Rock: Arkansas Baptist State Convention, 1948), 218.

34. Allen Hill Autry, *Warning Signals or Romanism an American Peril* (Little Rock, AR: Doctrinal Interpreter, 1911); Rogers, *History of Arkansas Baptists*, 218.

35. For more information about the Landmark movement, see Paul Harvey, *Redeeming the South: Religious Cultures and Racial Identities among Southern Baptists, 1865–1925* (Chapel Hill: University of North Carolina Press, 1997), 8, 86–90; Rogers, *History of Arkansas Baptists*, 596–600, 630; and Todd Everett Lewis, "Ben Bogard and the Crusade against Evolution, Rum, and Romanism in Arkansas, 1926–1928" (MA thesis, University of Arkansas, 1989), 1–5.

36. For a Missionary Baptist version of these events, see *Pioneer Faith: The History of Missionary Baptist Associations and Churches in Arkansas from 1818 to 1920* (Malvern, AR: History and Archives Committee of State Association of Missionary Baptist Churches of Arkansas, 1994), 439–44. For a Southern Baptist perspective, see Rogers, *History of Arkansas Baptists*, 578–86; and E. Glenn Hinson, *A History of Baptists in Arkansas, 1818–1978* (Little Rock: Arkansas Baptist State Convention, 1979), 174–79.

For a more balanced view, see C. Fred Williams, S. Ray Granade, and Kenneth M. Startup, *A System and Plan: Arkansas Baptist State Convention, 1848–1998* (Franklin, TN: Providence House, 1998), 167–73; and Christopher Bart Barber, "The Bogard Schism: An Arkansas Baptist Agrarian Revolt" (PhD dissertation, Southwestern Baptist Theological Seminary, 2006), 139–58.

37. *Pioneer Faith*, 441–44. *Proceedings of the Arkansas Baptist State Convention at Little Rock, November 12–14, 1919* ([n.p., n.d.], 69, Special Collections, Riley-Hickingbotham Library, Ouachita Baptist University, Arkadelphia, Arkansas) indicates that three-fifths of Arkansas's Baptists walked out with the Landmark movement. Membership figures for 1921 show 1,135 Southern Baptist congregations with 98,376 members in Arkansas and 507 Missionary Baptist congregations with 34,271 members; from Hinson, *A History of Baptists in Arkansas*, 180. For Barber's conclusion and quote, see Barber, "The Bogard Schism," 214.

38. Allen Autry Hill suggested that more personal motivations pushed Bogard and Scarboro to lead the defection from the Southern Baptist Convention. He said Scarboro was passed over for a job by the Georgia Convention and had fought the convention ever since. Bogard, Autry said, became angry at the Arkansas Convention when Ouachita College, a Southern Baptist school in Arkadelphia, Arkansas, turned him down in a bid for an honorary Doctor of Divinity degree. Although he lacked a college degree, he did eventually receive the honorary doctorate from Southwest Baptist College in Bolivar, Missouri. See Allen Hill Autry, *Grapeshot and Canister: From the Arsenal of Truth in Mission Methods* (Little Rock, AR: Doctrinal Interpreter, 1911), 160–75.

39. For biographical material about Bogard, see Lewis, "Ben Bogard," 9–14; Barber, "The Bogard Schism," 125–38; and J. Kristian Pratt, *The Father of Modern Landmarkism: The Life of Ben M. Bogard* (Macon, GA: Mercer University Press, 2013), 2–57.

40. *Watson's Jeffersonian Magazine*, May 1910, 409–11, and August 1911, 323–26.

41. *Liberator*, October 2, 16, 1913; *LaFayette County Democrat* (Stamps, AR), June 7, 1912.

42. *Liberator*, October 2, 16, 1913.

43. Ibid., October 2, 1913; *Baptist*, September 16, 1914.

44. In its February 14, 1914, issue, the *Menace* listed eight professional anti-Catholic lecturers, including William Lloyd Clark of Milan, Illinois; W. H. Boles of Marion, Illinois; Otis L. Spurgeon of Des Moines, Iowa; Augustus Barnett of Philadelphia, Pennsylvania; Walter Sims of Bay City, Michigan; C. W. Bibb of Minneapolis, Minnesota; P. A. Seguin of Stevens Point, Wisconsin; and Anna M. Lowry of Ritzville, Washington.

45. Clark's lectures in Hope were described by the local priest, Father P. J. Higgins, in the *Southern Guardian*, January 13, 1912; Scarboro presented the anti-Catholic perspective, including letters from a couple of Hope Protestants who attended the lectures, in a piece entitled "Clark Hits, and Higgins Howls," in William Lloyd Clark, *Reminiscences of a Reformer's Life, Or Twenty-Five Years on the Skirmish Line Against Political Romanism* (Milan, IL, 1913), 21–45. The *Menace* printed a list of anti-Catholic books; see issue of September 7, 1912.

46. *Southern Guardian*, April 6, May 11, 1912. Father Higgins served most of southwestern Arkansas's Roman Catholics. Besides his parish in Hope, he led churches in Stamps and Prescott and missions in Washington, Columbus, Magnolia, Nashville,

McNeil, Beirne, Gurdon, Roseboro, Glenwood, Arkadelphia, Malvern, Bento, Bauxite, and Fulton. A "mission" involved saying mass in the home of a local Catholic family. *Southern Guardian*, February 1, 1913.

47. *Souvenir of the Dedication of St. Agnes New Church, October 16, 1922, Commemorating the Silver Jubilee Year of the Ordination to Priesthood of the Very Rev. A.P. Gallagher, V.F.* (Mena, AR: Star Printing, ca. 1922), 10–13.

48. *Menace*, March 1, 1913.

CHAPTER 2 • Sex and the Sisters, 1913–1915

1. *Arkansas Gazette*, May 14, 15, 1892.

2. *Menace*, December 21, 1912; see also *Arkansas Gazette*, January 18, 1913. Posey, a Methodist, had trained as a teacher at Arkansas State Normal School in Conway, today's University of Central Arkansas, and had taught school for seven years and recently married before his election to the Arkansas House of Representatives. For biographical information, see Herndon, *Centennial History of Arkansas*, 3:771–72.

3. Holt's bill was introduced as Senate Bill number 132, *Arkansas Gazette*, February 6, 1913; the full text of the bill can be found in the *Southern Guardian*, February 22, 1913.

4. Marie Anne Pagliarini, "The Pure American Woman and the Wicked Catholic Priest: An Analysis of Anti-Catholic Literature in Antebellum America," *Religion and American Culture: A Journal of Interpretation* 9 (Winter 1999): 99.

5. See the discussion of the book in Nordstrom, *Danger on the Doorstep*, 38–39; and Pagliarini, "The Pure American Woman and the Wicked Catholic Priest," 99–100. Ray Allen Billington has done the most extensive study of Maria and her tale; see his "Maria Monk and Her Influence," in *Catholic Historical Review* 22 (October 1936): 283–96. The Maria Monk book remains in print today, including a free download as an e-book.

6. *Arkansas Gazette*, February 21, 1913.

7. Ibid., March 2, 1913. Representative Heartsill Ragon of Johnson County charged that Posey's bill was actually drawn up by the editor of an anti-Catholic newspaper. The death of the Posey bill was discussed in the *Southern Guardian*, March 15, 1913.

8. See the discussion of the votes in the *Arkansas Gazette*, February 21, March 2, 1913.

9. *Baptist Advance*, February 6, 1913; *Southern Guardian*, March 1, 1913; *Gravette News Herald*, February 21, 28, 1913.

10. *Baptist Advance*, January 23, 30, February 20, 27, 1913. For a history of the Knights of Columbus, see Christopher J. Kauffman, *Faith and Fraternalism: The History of the Knights of Columbus, 1882–1982* (New York: Harper and Row, 1982).

11. *Southern Guardian*, July 12, 1913; *Gravette News Herald*, July 11, 25, 1913.

12. *Southern Guardian*, April 5, 12, 26.

13. *Menace*, July 26, 1913.

14. Father Hugh Assenmacher, in his centennial history of Subiaco Abbey, devotes a chapter to the colorful Father Boniface, entitled "The Happy Warrior of the Lord." Father Hugh Assenmacher, *A Place Called Subiaco* (Little Rock: Rose Publishing, 1977), 244–55. Fr. Jerome Kodell has told this story in "The Gospel Wagon of Father

Boniface Spanke, O.S.B.," *American Benedictine Review* 61 (March, June, September 2010): 257–85. Kodell's article includes excerpts he translated from the German and edited from the abbey's in-house newsletter "Der Klausner von Subiako" ("The Subiaco Hermit"). Father Boniface's problems in Fort Smith are described in Boniface to Rev. P. John Niss, OSB, Munday, Texas, January 25, 1933, folder XIV.D1.2YA, box XIV 1–100, Archives of Subiaco Abbey.

15. Kodell, "The Gospel Wagon of Father Boniface Spanke," 259.

16. See Wilma Rugh Taylor, *This Train Is Bound for Glory: The Story of America's Chapel Cars* (Valley Forge, PA: Judson Press, 1999), with chapters 11 and 12 concerning Catholic chapel cars.

17. *New York Times*, March 16, 1913.

18. The "Gospel Wagon" was described in the Subiaco newsletter, "Der Klausner von Subiako," June, July, August, September 1913, in Kodell, "The Gospel Wagon of Father Boniface Spanke," 261–67. *Southern Guardian*, September 27, October 4, 1913. Acetylene (also known as carbide) lamps combined water with calcium carbide to yield flammable acetylene gas that burned to provide light. The lamps were popular in the early twentieth century before being supplanted by electricity.

19. "Der Klausner von Subiako," August, September 1913, in Kodell, "The Gospel Wagon of Father Boniface Spanke," 263–67. "Der Klausner" also quoted extensively from the *Southern Guardian*, the Fort Smith *Southwest American*, and the *Kansas City Star*.

20. *Gravette News Herald*, September 5, 1913.

21. Information about Illigen was obtained from his World War I draft registration card, the New York Passenger Lists, and the 1940 census, Ancestry.com (accessed June 26, 2013).

22. *Southern Guardian*, September 27, 1913. The paper published Boniface's lengthy, newsy accounts of his mission work weekly throughout the fall of 1913. See also typescript article, "Gospel Wagon Experiences of Father Boniface," folder XID. D1–25A, box XIV 1–100, Archives of Subiaco Abbey.

23. *Southern Guardian*, October 4, 11, 25, 1913.

24. Ibid., October 25, 1913.

25. Ibid., November 8, 15, 22, 29, 1913.

26. Ibid., October 11, 18, November 22, December 6, 1913.

27. Ibid., December 6, 1913; Conway *Log Cabin Democrat*, November 25, 26, 1913.

28. *Menace*, April 18, 1914. Father Noll was collecting information about Spurgeon and his family in order to discredit the professional anti-Catholic lecturer. Noll corresponded with J. E. Fenton, a grocer in Spurgeon's hometown of Boone, Iowa, to learn that Spurgeon family members were known for criminal tendencies. His father had a court record for bootlegging, and his brother and two sisters had spent time in the penitentiary. While Otis Spurgeon had no police record, Fenton said, the family in those parts went by the nickname of "chicken thieves." J. E. Fenton to Noll, May 29, 1915, Anti-Catholic Collection, Archives of the Diocese of Fort Wayne/South Bend, Fort Wayne, Indiana.

29. *Southern Guardian*, December 6, 1913; Michael Lensing, "Father Boniface vs. Spurgeon in the Great Debate," *Abbey Message*, February 1957, p. 7, in folder XIV. DI-25A, box XIV 1-100, Archives of Subiaco Abbey.

30. *Southern Guardian*, December 13, 2012. The Conway *Log Cabin Democrat*,

December 6, 1913, reported that Father Boniface would lecture on the *Menace*, "Thirty Minutes in Hell," and Maria Monk. The paper provided no commentary about the lectures. The *Menace*, December 13, 1913, printed the agreement/rules for the debate in its entirety, with the predictable commentary, and expressed hope that the bishop would not intervene and "spoil the show."

31. "Der Klausner von Subiako," January 1914, in Kodell, "Gospel Wagon of Father Boniface Spanke," 281. Evidently, the editor of "Der Klausner," Father George Binkert, OSB, made comments about Boniface's whereabouts from personal knowledge.

32. *Southern Guardian*, October 11, 1913. Boniface indicated he had Bishop Morris's direction to engage in the debate in his letter to the Rev. P. John Nigg, January 25, 1933, folder XIV.D1.2YA, box XIV 1-100, Archives of Subiaco Abbey.

33. *Menace*, December 13, 1913, January 14, February 7, 1914; Assenmacher, *A Place Called Subiaco*, 250; *Arkansas Gazette*, January 14, 1914. The Conway *Log Cabin-Democrat* (January 14, 1914) estimated attendance at from twelve hundred to three thousand, including a large contingent from Conway, while the *Southern Guardian*, January 17, 1914, downplayed the debate, estimating attendance around five hundred. Morrilton's population figures came from "Morrilton," *The Encyclopedia of Arkansas History and Culture*, http://www.encyclopediaofarkansas.com (accessed April 19, 2012.)

34. On the first day of the debate the jury was chosen to include J. B. O'Neal, merchant; J. A. Eades, lawyer; G. H. Taylor, ex-postmaster; C. R. Wood, merchant; A. E. Poteete, seed dealer; H. R. Osborne, marble worker; J. M. Rhodes, laborer; J. V. Rhoden, barber; Joe Michau, farmer; E. E. King, blacksmith; J. E. Tolbert (or Talbert), occupation unknown; and C. R. Street, photographer. The jury chose its own chair, G. H. Taylor, who had served a term in the 1880s as the county judge of Conway County. *Arkansas Gazette*, January 14, 1914. Occupations are listed in *Southern Guardian*, January 17, 1914.

35. For the entirety of the debate, I rely on the extensive account in the *Menace*, January 31, 1914, and the *Arkansas Gazette*, January 14, 15, 17, 20, 21, 22, 1914. The debaters took Sunday off as an observance of the day of worship, but Spurgeon apparently took the Sunday train to Little Rock, where he lectured on Roman Catholicism to a crowd at the Immanuel Baptist Church. *Baptist Advance*, January 22, 1914.

36. *Menace*, January 31, 1914. Chiniquy had claimed before his death in Montreal in 1899 that Jesuits had assassinated President Abraham Lincoln.

37. The convent to which Boniface was referring was most probably the Sister of Mercy convent in downtown Little Rock. In 1908 it was moved to its present location in Pulaski Heights. Woods, *Mission and Memory*, 271; *Menace*, January 31, 1914.

38. *Menace*, January 31, 1914.

39. Ibid.

40. Ibid.

41. For more about Father Schmidt, see Mark Gado, *Killer Priest: The Crimes, Trial, and Execution of Father Hans Schmidt* (Westport, CT: Praeger, 2006). Gado argues that Schmidt was in modern terms a sex addict who used unsuccessfully the insanity plea in his defense. The *Liberator* in its issue of October 2, 1913, shortly after Schmidt's arrest, used the disgraced priest as an example: "The priest gets the license and marries himself to the woman, puts the license away and when he decides he

cannot afford to corrupt his priestly office by a marriage which he performed himself, he kills the woman, chops her body to pieces, throws her in the river and goes back to his job of hearing confessions and forgiving sin! 'Once a priest always a priest!'"

42. *Menace*, January 31, 1914.

43. Ibid.

44. Ibid.

45. Little Rock *Arkansas Echo*, February 5, 1914.

46. Besides calling him "dung-beetle Spurgeon" (in German, "Mistkfel Spurgeon"), the *Echo* referred to him as "Dreckmichel Spurgeon," the German equivalent of "Joe-shit Spurgeon," see *Arkansas Echo*, February 5, 1914; *Menace*, January 31, 1914.

47. *Menace*, January 31, 1914; *Southern Guardian*, January 24, 1914; Boniface to Rev. P. John Nigg, OSB, January 25, 1933.

48. Unfortunately neither the Morrilton *Headlight* nor *Democrat* is extant for 1914, so one can only infer by the *Menace*'s (February 7, 1914) praise of the *Headlight*'s "American attitude and enlightened method" and criticism of the editor of the *Democrat* for posing as a censor, dishing out a "Romanistic" perspective. The *Arkansas Echo* (February 5, 1914) lauded the *Democrat*'s editor for behaving intelligently and courteously toward Catholics.

49. *Arkansas Echo*, February 5, 1914; P. Olfen, "Morrilton. Rèsidence du Sacrè-Coeur (1912–1914)," item 12, folder D, file 7, Sacred Heart Reports, Spiritan Archives, Bethel Park, Pennsylvania. Just as several parishes in the western part of the Arkansas River Valley were served by Benedictine priests, parishes from Atkins to Conway were served by priests of the Holy Ghost Order. With its headquarters outside Paris, the language of the business of the order was French, and Olfen reported in French to the North American headquarters in Pittsburgh. Olfen had replaced Father Haas, who was the pastor of Sacred Heart during the debates. Haas had come down with appendicitis and died on April 27, 1914.

50. Assenmacher, *A Place Called Subiaco*, 251; Boniface to Nigg, January 25, 1933, p. 23; *Southern Guardian*, January 24, 1914. Even the *Baptist Advance*, February 5, 1914, commented on the five inches of space devoted to the debate when the *Southern Guardian* had "allowed Priest Boniface to say much about the proposed debate at Morrilton before it came off." Boniface returned to Subiaco in the 1920s and remained there, serving as the abbey's farm manager until his death on December 11, 1942.

51. *Southern Guardian*, January 31, 1914; *Arkansas Echo*, February 5, 1914.

52. *Arkansas Gazette*, April 7, 1914; *Menace*, April 18, 1914. The *Southern Guardian*, on December 19, 1914, crowed about Spurgeon's defeat after running on an anti-Catholic platform.

53. Little Rock *Landmark Baptist*, April 29, 1914.

54. *Southern Guardian*, May 23, 1914; *Baptist Advance*, June 4, 1914.

55. *Proceedings of the 66th Annual Session, held at Little Rock, November 12–14, 1914* (Little Rock, 1914), 62, Special Collections, Riley-Hickingbotham Library, Ouachita Baptist University, Arkadelphia, Arkansas; *Baptist Advance*, February 25, 1915.

56. *Menace*, January 31, 1914. For Lewis's full platform, see *Gravette News Herald*, January 16, 1914; for election returns, see the April 3, 1914, issue.

57. *Southern Guardian*, September 26, 1914; *Baptist Advance*, September 17, 1914.

58. *Baptist Advance*, September 17, December 17, 1914.

59. *Southern Guardian*, January 24, 1914; *Gravette News Herald*, February 4, 13, 20, 1914.

60. *Gravette News Herald*, August 14, 21, 28, September 4, 1914. Newton had provided one of the testimonials about Clark's lectures in Hope, published in Joseph Scarboro's "Clark Hits, and Higgins Howls," in Clark, *Reminiscences of a Reformer's Life*, 43–45. Newton had apparently given anti-Catholic lectures at Mena in 1914, according to the *Southern Guardian*, August 22, 1914.

61. *Gravette News Herald*, November 14, 1913, April 17, 1914; *Southern Guardian*, October 3, December 26, 1914; *Menace*, October 24, 1914, October 2, 1915. On July 7, 1916, the *Gravette News Herald* reported that Veach moved his printing press to Joplin, Missouri, to found a new weekly newspaper, the *Interstate Gazette*, to cover news of Arkansas, Missouri, Kansas, and Oklahoma. But by 1917, Veach was back in Benton County, Arkansas, starting up a newspaper in Sulphur Springs (Allsopp, *History of the Arkansas Press*, 72). In the 1930 census he was living with his wife again in Gravette (1930 census, Ancestry.com, accessed June 15, 2012).

62. *The Baptist*, September 16, 1914.

63. *Southern Guardian*, August 22, November 15, 1914.

64. *Souvenir of the Dedication of St. Agnes New Church*, 13.

65. *Southern Guardian*, January 16, 1915.

66. Ibid., January 30, 1915.

67. *Arkansas Gazette*, February 2, 1915; the letter was also published in the *Daily Texarkanian*, January 28, 1915, and the *Menace*, February 21, 1915.

68. *Southern Guardian*, January 23, 30, 1915.

69. Ibid., January 30, 1915; Asschenmacher, *A Place Called Subiaco*, 233–34; *Menace*, February 6, 1915.

70. *Baptist Advance*, February 11, 1915.

71. Ibid., February 25, 1915.

72. *Marshall (TX) Messenger*, February 6, 9, 1915, *Arkansas Gazette*, February 4, 1915.

73. *Marshall Messenger*, February 9, 1915; *Baptist Advance*, February 4, 1915; *Southern Guardian*, April 3, 1915.

74. *Southern Guardian*, January 16, 1915.

75. *Baptist Advance*, January 14, 1915; *Southern Guardian*, January 16, 23, 30, February 13, 1915; *Arkansas Gazette*, February 4, 1915.

76. Kauffman, *Faith and Fraternalism*, 169; Michael Williams, *Shadow of the Pope* (New York: McGraw Hill, 1932), 299. The entirety of the oath can be found in Kauffman, *Faith and Fraternalism*, 169–71; and *Southern Guardian*, February 23, 1915.

77. Kauffman, *Faith and Fraternalism*, 172–75. The *Southern Guardian* (February 23, 30, 1915) publicized the verdict of the California Masons and noted that it had previously been reported in the *Arkansas Gazette* on November 21, 1914.

78. *Southern Guardian*, January 23, March 27, 1915.

79. *Baptist Advance*, February 4, 1915; *Arkansas Democrat*, February 4, 1915; *Southern Guardian*, February 6, 1915.

80. *Southern Guardian*, February 13, 1915. Bishop Donahue of the Diocese of Wheeling confirmed that no one in the diocese had ever heard of Black serving as a priest. P. J. Donahue to F. P. Kenkel, February 16, 1915, folder 2, box 7, Catholic Central Verein Collection, University of Notre Dame Archives, South Bend, Indiana.

A later Catholic source would claim that Black was an outright imposter who had never been a Catholic priest and, moreover, was a crook. Father Noll's publishing company, Our Sunday Visitor, in Huntingdon, Indiana, kept files on anti-Catholic lecturers and newspaper editors. Sometime in the early 1920s, the company published *Defamers of the Church: Their Character* (Huntingdon, IN: Our Sunday Visitor, 1925), which claimed Black was never a priest, nor even a Catholic. The book (ibid., 12–14) said that in 1912 Black had been preaching in a "Campbellite" church in Rifle, Colorado, for just a few weeks before he skipped town owing several people money. This issue used, published in 1925, indicated that it was the enlarged seventeenth edition, so it is not clear when the account was first published.

81. *Guardian*, January 17, 1925; Woods, *Mission and Memory*, 273.

82. *Marshall Messenger*, February 5, 1915; *Arkansas Democrat*, February 4, 1915; *Arkansas Gazette*, February 4, 5, 1915.

83. *Arkansas Gazette*, February 4, 1915; *Marshall Messenger*, February 5, 1915. Sadie talked about Baptist preacher "Brother DeWitt," who must be the Rev. Charles DeWit mentioned in the *Menace*, on May 29, 1915, as leading the campaign of a "pro-American" candidate for mayor of Hot Springs against the candidate backed by the Knights of Columbus. Bishop P. J. Donahue, the bishop of Wheeling, said that Black represented himself when in the South as the grandnephew of Robert E. Lee. Donahue to F. P. Kenkel, folder 2, box 7, Catholic Central Verein Collection.

84. *Arkansas Gazette*, February 5, 1915; *Marshall Messenger*, February 6, 1915.

85. *Marshall Messenger*, February 5, 6, 1915. The Marshall Council of the Knights of Columbus denied that the Catholic men were under the direction of the council when they called on Black. They were simply acting as citizens and Catholics out of outrage at the statements made by Black in his lecture. F. Ludolph, financial secretary of the Marshall Council number 1422, to William J. McGinley, Supreme Secretary of the Knights of Columbus, quoted in letter from John Donahue to Aquinas Knopf, September 20, 1928, Anti-Catholic Collection, Archives of the Diocese of Fort Wayne/South Bend, Fort Wayne, Indiana.

86. *Arkansas Gazette*, February 5, 7, 1915; *Marshall Messenger*, February 4, 5, 6, 9, 1915.

87. *Arkansas Gazette*, February 4, 1915, October 26, 1916; *Marshall Messenger*, February 6, 1915.

88. *Marshall Messenger*, February 9, 1915; *Menace*, February 27, 1915.

89. *Marshall Messenger*, February 9, 11, March 8, 1915; *Southern Guardian*, April 3, 1915; *Arkansas Gazette*, October 25, 26, 28, 29, 1915; *Arkansas Democrat*, December 13, 1915, October 28, 1916; *The Day* (New London, CT), November 1, 1916.

90. *Menace*, February 27, 1915; *Daily Texarkanian*, February 4, 5, 1915.

91. *Menace*, February 27, 1915; *Daily Texarkanian*, February 6, 1915.

92. *Menace*, February 27, 1915; *Arkansas Gazette*, February 5, 13, 1915. The 1920 manuscript census returns (Ancestry.com, accessed June 23, 2012) show a twenty-two-year-old Sadie Black, who was born in Arkansas, living in Chicago, boarding with a couple who had emigrated from Norway. Sadie is listed as a nurse, working in a hospital. One of Sadie's patients was a flyer injured in the Great War, David Bergenham, a graduate of Northwestern University and son of a prosperous Chicago family. David and Sadie married in 1921, had a daughter, Lillian, and moved to Dallas, Texas, where Sadie's parents had moved by the later 1920s. Sometime after 1930 they

moved to Marcellus, Michigan, where Sadie died of cancer on December 12, 1932; information from Jim Bergenham, Kentwood, Michigan, telephone interview, July 5, 2012. Mr. Bergenham is the son of David Bergenham by his second wife, Alice, who nursed Sadie during her terminal illness. Mr. Bergenham says he never heard any account of the adventures of Sadie and William Black from his father, who lived on until 1982.

93. *Arkansas Gazette*, February 4, 1915; *Southern Guardian*, January 30, 1915. The *Southern Guardian* recorded the roll-call vote to postpone, in-effect kill, the bill on January 25, and the comment regarding town/rural breakdown of the vote concerns this motion. The vote on January 25 was 35 to 60, almost identical to the February 4 vote on the bill itself, which was 60 to 34. I could find no record of individual votes for the February 4 House vote.

94. The *Gravette News Herald*, February 12, 19, 1915, quoted the *Sheridan Headlight*; *Southern Guardian*, February 6, 13, 20, 1915.

95. The *Southern Guardian*, February 27, 1915, printed the petition, signed by A. B. Grace, John M. Elliot, C. M. Philpot, W. B. Sorrells, T. Y. Murphy, E. W. Freeman, John H. Shelby, J. W. Chawford, J. G. Taylor, S. G. Seabrooks, A. C. Jordan, V. O. Alexander, and E. D. Russell. *Menace*, March 13, 1915.

96. In addition to Jones and Going, the six other opponents were W. C. Adamson (Pulaski, Perry), I. C. Burgess (Pope, Johnson), C. C. Calvert (Sebastian), Harry C. Harris (Arkansas, Monroe), John I. Moore (Phillips, Lee), and Samuel N. Vann (Cross, Woodruff). *Arkansas Gazette*, March 3, 1915; *Daily Texarkanian*, March 3, 1915; *Southern Guardian*, March 6, 1915; *Acts of Arkansas, 1915* (Little Rock: Democrat Printing, 1915), 505-08.

97. *Southern Guardian*, April 3, May 27 (erroneously labeled May 22), 1915. The April 3 issue said Oregon and Colorado legislatures passed inspection laws, but the May 27 issue said that such bills did not pass in these states. The *Menace*, May 1, 1915, also indicated that Arkansas was the first state to pass a convent inspection law. For Georgia, see the *Southern Cross*, July 20, 2006, 3.

98. *Baptist Advance*, June 17, 1915; *Southern Guardian*, May 27, 1915, and this issue printed both Sherriff Finger's report and the *Dixie Press's* account; *Mena Weekly Star*, May 20, 1915. Doyle had taken an anti-Catholic stance three years before when he edited the *Wilmot Weekly*, and apparently his stint as editor in Mena lasted no longer than it had in Wilmot. For Doyle's editorial career, see Allsopp, *History of the Arkansas Press*, 58, 297.

99. *Menace*, June 19, 1915; Assenmacher, *A Place Called Subiaco*, 233–34; "Der Klausner von Subiako," December 1915, translated by Fr. Jerome Kodell, Archives of Subiaco Abbey.

CHAPTER 3 • Liquor and War, 1915–1919

1. *N. W. Ayers and Son's Newspaper Annual and Directory, 1915*, 1:502, 674.

2. Paul Donley, *Tracks to the Past: A Pictorial History of Aurora, Missouri* (Marceline, MO: D-Books, 1998), 29–34.

3. *Defamers of the Church*, 3.

4. *Report of Commission on Religious Prejudices, 1915* (N.p.: Knights of Columbus, 1915), 20–23; Nordstrom, *Danger on the Doorstep*, 184.

5. Nordstrom, *Danger on the Doorstep*, 184–85; Benjamin O. Flowers, *The Story of the Menace Trial: A Brief Sketch of This Historic Case, with Reports of the Masterly Addresses by Hon. J. L. McNatt and Hon. J. I. Sheppard* (Aurora, MO: United States Publishing, 1916.)

6. *Report of Commission on Religious Prejudices, 1915*, 24–25.

7. Kauffman, *Faith and Fraternalism*, 182–83.

8. *Report of Commission on Religious Prejudices, 1915*, 5, 19–23, 28–31.

9. Leon Hutton, "Catholicism and Civility: John Francis Noll and the Origin of *Our Sunday Visitor*," *U.S. Catholic Historian* 15 (Summer 1997): 11–15; Ann Ball, with Father Leon Hutton, *Champion of the Church: The Extraordinary Life and Legacy of Archbishop Noll* (Huntingdon, IN: Our Sunday Visitor, 2006), 58–62.

10. On the last week of December of each year the *Menace* posted the following subscription figures:

1911 – 37,763
1912 – 445,512
1913 – 1,119,624
1914 – 1,424,171
1915 – 1,250,597

The circulation peaked at the April 17, 1915, issue, which claimed 1,507,923 subscriptions. Circulation began a steady decline until the November 20, 1915, issue, which listed 1,298,979 subscribers. The paper thereafter no longer listed subscription figures. The *Ayers and Son's Newspaper Annual and Directory* gives circulation figures for the *Menace* beginning in 1914:

1914 – 662,358
1915 – 1,469,400
1916 – 1,350,000
1917 – 1,250,000
1918 – 750,000
1919 – 750,000
1920 – 750,000

It is not clear what date within a year corresponds to the circulation figure. Also note that these numbers beginning in 1916 appear to be rounded estimates, and one wonders about their accuracy.

11. *Menace*, August 5, 1916; *Gravette News Herald*, August 4, 1916.

12. *Southern Guardian*, January 30, 1915, reported that Scarboro was leaving Arkansas with plans to publish the *Liberator* from Atlanta, Georgia. There is no evidence that the *Liberator* existed after 1915. Nettie Hicks Kilgore's *History of Columbia County* ([Magnolia, AR: n.p., ca. 1947], 89) says the *Liberator* was not a financial success and that it ceased publication in 1916. Scarboro reflected on his past in *Baptist and Commoner* (Little Rock), January 22, 1919.

13. See the excellent discussion in Ben F. Johnson III, *John Barleycorn Must Die: The War Against Drink in Arkansas* (Fayetteville: University of Arkansas Press, 2005), 42–50.

14. George Murrell Hunt, "A History of the Prohibition Movement in Arkansas" (MA thesis, University of Arkansas, 1933).

15. See the discussion of Southern Baptist prohibition activities and figures on discipline in Hinson, *A History of Baptists in Arkansas*, 205, 217–19; *Proceedings of the*

Baptist State Convention, 64th Annual Session, held at Hot Springs, Arkansas, November 14–17, 1912 (Little Rock, 1912), 11.

16. The Prohibition or Temperance Committees were noted in each of the association meetings from 1902 to 1920; see *Pioneer Faith*, 445–81; *Baptist* (Little Rock), March 27, April 3, 1912.

17. Johnson, *John Barleycorn Must Die*, 52.

18. Ibid., 52–54; see also the discussion of these prohibition measures in Whayne et al., *Arkansas: A Narrative History*, 284–87; and Hunt, "A History of the Prohibition Movement in Arkansas," 135–38. The Baptist take on Moose's ruling was uttered in the *Proceedings of the Baptist State Convention, 65th Annual Session, held in Monticello, Arkansas, November 13–16, 1913* (Little Rock, 1913), 58, Special Collections, Riley-Hickingbotham Library, Ouachita Baptist University, Arkadelphia, Arkansas. In his opinion of November 13, 1913, Moose actually spelled out that "white" would include a swarthy Caucasian while it would exclude any person with some admixture of Negro blood, no matter how light was the complexion. See *Biennial Report of the Attorney General of Arkansas, 1913–1914* (Little Rock: Democrat, 1915), 164–65. The only extant copy of this report appears to be at the attorney general's office in Little Rock. Jeannie Whayne has demonstrated that race was not a primary factor in determining the local success or failure of prohibition efforts. See Jeannie Whayne, "Caging the Blind Tiger: Race, Class, and Family in the Battle for Prohibition in Small Town Arkansas," *Arkansas Historical Quarterly* 71, no. 1 (Spring 2012): 44–60.

19. *Southern Guardian*, August 24, September 7, 1912.

20. Autry, *Warning Signals*, 22–24.

21. Hinson, *History of Arkansas Baptists*, 218–19; *Baptist Advance* (Little Rock), February 5, 1914.

22. *Baptist*, November 11, 1914.

23. *Gravette News Herald*, August 2, November 13, December 19, 1913; *Liberator*, quoted in *Gravette News Herald*, May 3, 1912.

24. Anti-Prohibition votes can be found in the *Arkansas Gazette*, February 2, 1915; the *Southern Guardian* published the votes on the Convent Inspection Bill, April 3, 1915. In addition, votes against both inspection and prohibition were cast by representatives from several delta counties, including Poinsett, Prairie, Lincoln, and Chicot.

25. *Baptist Advance*, October 12, November 9, 16, 1916; *Gravette News Herald*, October 27, 1916.

26. Hunt, "A History of the Prohibition Movement in Arkansas," 149; Johnson, *John Barleycorn Must Die*, 56; *Guardian*, January 13, 27, 1917. The *Southern Guardian* dropped "Southern" from its title and became simply the *Guardian* on June 26, 1915.

27. *Guardian*, January 13, February 3, 1917; *Baptist Advance*, January 18, 1917; *Gravette News Herald*, January 26, 1917.

28. *Guardian*, September 15, 1917; *Gravette News Herald*, January 4, 1918.

29. LaVern J. Rippley, *The German-Americans* (Latham, MD: University Press of America, 1984), 180–82; Richard O'Conner, *The German-Americans: An Informal History* (Boston: Little, Brown & Co., 1968), 377.

30. *Southern Guardian*, November 28, 1914, August 7, 1915.

31. Ibid., September 26, 1914.

32. Ibid., September 5, 1914; *Guardian*, September 4, 1915, October 14, 1916.

33. *Gravette News Herald*, August 27, October 20, 1916.

34. *Baptist Advance*, December 17, 1914; *Gravette News Herald*, October 3, 1913, March 26, April 23, August 13, 1915.

35. *Gravette News Herald*, November 21, 1913.

36. *Guardian*, April 14, 1917.

37. Woods, *Mission and Memory*, 176–77; *Guardian*, April 13, 1918.

38. *Guardian*, November 3, 1917, March 23, 1918.

39. Assenmacher, *A Place Called Subiaco*, 238; "Der Klausner von Subiako," April 9, 1917, Archives of Subiaco Abbey.

40. *Guardian*, November 15, 1924; *Souvenir of the Dedication of St. Agnes New Church*, 14.

41. For a discussion of the anti-German hysteria following the American entry into the war, see chapter 8, "Superpatriotism in Action: 1917," in Frederick C. Luebke's *Bonds of Loyalty: German Americans and World War I* (Dekalb: Northern Illinois University Press, 1974), 226–65. For more about the crack-down on dissent by the Wilson administration, see David M. Kennedy, *Over There: The First World War and American Society* (New York: Oxford University Press, 1980), 23–26; and William H. Thomas Jr., *Unsafe for Democracy: World War I and the U.S. Justice Department's Covert Campaign to Suppress Dissent* (Madison: University of Wisconsin Press, 2008).

42. Shirley Schuette, "The Germans," *Encyclopedia of Arkansas History and Culture*, http://encyclopediaofarkansas.com (accessed August 30, 2012); Michael Dougan, *Arkansas Odyssey* (Little Rock, AR: Rose Publishing, 1994), 378. The information about Curtis Ackermann can be found in Joseph Carruth, "World War I Propaganda and Its Effects in Arkansas," *Arkansas Historical Quarterly* 56 (Winter 1997): 392–93; and the *Arkansas Gazette*, August 9, 10, 11, September 12, 1917. See Shirley Schuette's excellent discussion in "Intolerance on the Homefront: Anti-German and Anti-Black Sentiment during the War Years and Beyond," in *To Can the Kaiser: Arkansas and the Great War*, edited by Michael D. Polston and Guy Lancaster (Little Rock: Butler Center Books, 2015), 108–20.

43. Assenmacher, *A Place Called Subiaco*, 237–38; "Der Klausner von Subiako," April 13, 1917, January 2, April 1, 9, 1918, Archives of Subiaco Abbey; *Guardian*, April 13, 1918.

44. Weibel, *Forty Years Missionary in Arkansas*, 209; *Centennial History of St. Joseph's Parish (1879–1979), Paris, Arkansas* (Hot Springs: Hall Printers, 1979), 89.

45. Carruth, "World War I Propaganda," 395; *Arkansas Gazette*, March 28, 29, 30, 1918; *Fort Smith Times Record*, March 28, 1918.

46. Carruth, "World War I Propaganda," 392; *Arkansas Gazette*, March 29, April 22, 1918. A correspondent from Hartman wrote to the German-language *Arkansas Echo* to suggest that that *Arkansas Gazette* had misrepresented local feelings toward Mr. Oberle, saying the opinion of the "better people" in Clarksville was sympathetic toward Oberle ("die Meinung der bessern Leute zu Gunsten von Herrn Oberle gewendet"); *Arkansas Echo*, April 11, 1918.

47. Steven Teske, "World War I," *Encyclopedia of Arkansas History and Culture*, http://encyclopediaofarkansas.net (accessed August 30, 2012).

48. Luebke, *Bonds of Loyalty*, 279; Luebke describes the lynching of Robert Prager on pages 3–14.

49. *Gravette News Herald*, August 27, October 5, December 21, 1917.

50. Ibid., January 11, 1918.

51. Ibid., July 6, September 14, 1917, February 1, October 11, 1918.

52. Ibid., October 25, November 29, 1918. Wyric Lewis had previously been part of an Arkansas National Guard unit from northwestern Arkansas that in June 1916 had been sent to Fort Roots, North Little Rock, for training and then in August was shipped to Deming, New Mexico, to defend the borders as the US army entered Mexico to chase Pancho Villa. The Arkansas unit arrived back in Little Rock in early March 1917 and was mustered out of duty. Wyric worked for his father at the newspaper office just a couple of months before his unit was called up again. *Gravette News Herald*, June 30, August 10, 1916, March 10, 1917.

53. *Baptist Advance*, August 2, 1917.

54. *Baptist and Commoner*, November 14, 1917.

55. *Guardian*, November 3, 10, 1917.

56. *Baptist Advance*, November 15, December 6, 1917, April 4, June 27, 1918.

57. *Guardian*, February 2, May 4, July 13, August 10, September 28, 1918.

58. Ibid., September 28, 1918.

59. *Baptist Advance*, August 1, 8, 15, September 5, 19, 1918.

60. Ibid., September 19, 1918; *Guardian*, September 21, November 2, 1918.

61. *Baptist and Commoner*, March 13, 20, October 16, 1918.

62. Ibid., March 20, May 29, 1918. This newspaper resulted from a merger in 1917 of the two Missionary Baptist papers, the *Baptist*, published in Little Rock, with the *Baptist Commoner*, published in Texarkana. The *Baptist* was the continuation of the *Arkansas Baptist*, which dropped "Arkansas" from the title in 1912.

63. *Baptist and Commoner*, April 10, October 16, 1918.

CHAPTER 4 • Catholics and the Ku Klux Klan, 1921–1925

1. *Arkansas Gazette*, July 1, 5, 1924; *Arkansas Democrat*, July 4, 5, 1924.

2. Thomas R. Pegram, *One Hundred Percent American: The Rebirth and Decline of the Ku Klux Klan in the 1920s* (Chicago: Ivan R. Dee, 2011), 7–10, 15–16. See also the description of the founding of the Klan in Wyn Craig Wade, *The Fiery Cross: The Ku Klux Klan in America* (New York: Oxford University Press, 1987), 119–66.

3. Charles C. Alexander, *The Ku Klux Klan in the Southwest* (Lexington: University of Kentucky Press, 1966), 51–52; Charles C. Alexander, "White-Robed Reformers: The Ku Klux Klan Comes to Arkansas, 1921–1922," *Arkansas Historical Quarterly* 22, no. 1 (Spring 1963): 14. For more information on Comer, see Todd E. Lewis, "From Bull Mooser to Grand Dragon of the Ku Klux Klan: James A. Comer of Little Rock," *Pulaski County Historical Review* 43, no. 2 (Summer 1995): 26–41.

4. *Conway Weekly News*, January 13, 1922.

5. Alexander, "White Robed Reformers," 8–9; *Arkansas Gazette*, February 11, 1922. The *Gazette* account was reprinted in the Conway *Log Cabin Democrat*, February 11, 1922. The April meeting is described in the *Arkansas Gazette*, April 28, 1923.

6. Alexander, *Ku Klux Klan in the Southwest*, 53.

7. *Jonesboro Evening Sun*, July 24, 1922.

8. *Log Cabin Democrat*, August 20, 1923, noted that the Quitman Klan was number 135.

9. Kathleen M. Blee, *Women of the Klan: Racism and Gender in the 1920s* (Berkeley: University of California Press, 1991), 2.

10. Donald B. Holley, "A Look Behind the Masks: The 1920s Klan in Monticello, Arkansas," *Arkansas Historical Quarterly* 60, no. 2 (Summer 2001): 139–43.

11. *Jonesboro Evening Sun*, June 27, 1922. Membership lists have survived for the majority of the Indiana Klan and have been analyzed by Leonard J. Moore in *Citizen Klansman: The Ku Klux Klan in Indiana, 1921–1928* (Chapel Hill: University of North Carolina Press, 1991). Moore's work is largely responsible for establishing the view of historians of the 1920s Klan as a middle-class phenomenon.

12. *Jonesboro Daily Tribune*, August 26, 1922. Accounts of Klansmen making dramatic gifts to churches are ubiquitous.

13. Alexander, "White Robed Reformers," 15.

14. Pegram, *One Hundred Percent American*, 238.

15. *Jonesboro Evening Sun*, June 14, 1922; *Gravette News Herald*, March 6, 1925.

16. *Jonesboro Daily Tribune*, February 15, 1922.

17. Alexander, "White-Robed Reformers," 22–23.

18. *Jonesboro Evening Sun*, November 17, 1922.

19. *Jonesboro Daily Tribune*, June 25, 1922.

20. See Brooks Blevins's discussion of Klan activity in the Ozarks in relationship to the MN&A strike. Brooks Blevins, "The Strike and the Still: Anti-radical Violence and the Ku Klux Klan in the Ozarks," *Arkansas Historical Quarterly* 42, no. 4 (Winter 1993): 405–25.

21. Blevins, "The Strike and the Still," 420; Alexander, *Ku Klux Klan in the Southwest*, 64.

22. Pegram, *One Hundred Percent American*, 33, 57–59, 69–70; Wade, *The Fiery Cross*, 199.

23. Nancy McLean, *Behind the Mask of Chivalry: The Making of the Second Ku Klux Klan* (New York: Oxford University Press, 1994), 99; Blee, *Women of the Klan*, 21–23.

24. For the most thorough account of Simmon's ouster from power in the Klan, see Wade, *The Fiery Cross*, 186–92.

25. A flyer for the book featured a blurb from the *Arkansas Methodist*, saying, "All Protestants should study this problem with the help of this book. It will enlighten those . . . who think that Romanists are just like themselves." Folder: Klan Publications, Advertisements, 1920s, box 1, Ku Klux Klan, Mecosta County, Michigan, Collection, Clarke Historical Library, Central Michigan University, Mount Pleasant, Michigan.

26. David M. Chalmers, *Hooded Americanism: The First Century of the Ku Klux Klan, 1865–1965* (Garden City, NY: Doubleday, 1965), 57–58, 106; Charles C. Alexander, "White Robes in Politics: The Ku Klux Klan in Arkansas, 1922–1924," *Arkansas Historical Quarterly* 22, no. 3 (Autumn 1963): 196–98; Alexander, *Ku Klux Klan in the Southwest*, 100–103.

27. *Imperial Night Hawk* (Atlanta, GA), March 28, 1923.

28. Alexander, "White Robes in Politics," 198–203.

29. *Guardian*, August 5, 1922, January 20, 1923.

30. *Jonesboro Evening Sun*, June 7, 1922.

31. Ibid., May 6, 1922.

32. *Baptist and Commoner*, June 14, 1922.

33. L. D. Foreman and Alta Payne, *Life and Works of Benjamin Marcus Bogard*, 3 vols. (Little Rock, AR: Foreman and Payne, 1966), 1:128, 150–53, 220–21; Pratt, *The Father of Modern Landmarkism*, 81.

34. *Guardian*, October 1, 8, 1921; *Baptist and Commoner*, October 19, 1921.

35. *Baptist and Commoner*, June 14, 1922; Ben M. Bogard, *Ku Klux Klan Exposed: Inside Facts Laid Bare and Explained* (Little Rock, AR, n.d.). The only extant copy of this work is housed at the Rare Book Collection in the library of the University of North Carolina, Chapel Hill. Bogard advertised this lecture to be given from the courthouse steps in Sheridan on April 10, 1922. *Sheridan Headlight*, March 30, 1922. Bogard clearly served in some semi-official capacity as a Klan lecturer, for only officers, lecturers, and political candidates made their Klan membership publicly known.

36. These publications were advertised weekly in the *Baptist and Commoner;* see, for example, the issue of October 22, 1924.

37. *New York Times*, September 23, 1923, p. 9; *Washington Post*, September 23, 1913, p. 18. Wade (*The Fiery Cross*, 165) presents the initiation in the White House as fact, while Harding biographers have found no evidence of it.

38. Basil E. Newton, *K.K.K. vs. Enemies* (n.p., n.d.). The only extant copy of this booklet is located at the Wisconsin Historical Society in Madison.

39. *Arkansas Traveller*, October 22, November 5, 1923, folder 166, box 280, Anti-Catholicism: Bogus Oath Collection, Knights of Columbus Supreme Council Archives, New Haven, Connecticut, hereafter cited as Bogus Oath Collection. These two issues of the *Arkansas Traveller* appear to be the only extant issues of the newspaper. The newspaper calls Moore a national lecturer and says he was previously pastor of a leading church in Hot Springs.

40. *Gravette News Herald*, June 26, 1925. Gravette Klan's membership of two hundred was insinuated by Lewis in an editorial of June 27, 1924.

41. See the discussion of anti-Catholic lecturers and the Klan in Blee, *Women of the Klan*, 86–91; and Kelly J. Baker, *Gospel According to the Klan: The KKK's Appeal to Protestant America, 1915–1930* (Lawrence: University of Kansas Press, 2011), 149–55.

42. *Baptist and Commoner*, March 8, 1922.

43. *Guardian*, May 20, June 10, 1922.

44. For more information about Jackson and King, see Blee, *Women of the Klan*, 89–91; Baker, *Gospel According to the Klan*, 149–55; and *Defamers of the Church*, 9–12, 98–99.

45. *Guardian*, February 3, 1923; *Gravette News Herald*, May 25, June 1, 8, 1923.

46. J. M. Maus to Central Bureau of the Central Verein, March 10, April 22, 1924, folder 1, box 7; James R. Wilson deposition before J. A. Worsham, Atkins, Arkansas, April 15, 1924, folder 3, box 7, Catholic Central Verein Collection, Archives of the University of Notre Dame, South Bend, Indiana.

47. *Defamers of the Church*, 35. Newspaper clippings from the *Western American*, May 23, 1925, and the *Catholic Citizen*, May 16, 1925, in Anti-Catholic Collection, Archives of the Diocese of Fort Wayne/South Bend. The 1920 census, available via a search in Ancestry.com (July 26, 2012), shows Gerald Sheehan lived in Memphis, Tennessee, in 1920, at age forty-three serving as pastor of the Rowan Baptist Church. The census reports that he was born in Scotland, as were his mother and father, and

that he came to this country at the age of eighteen, which makes his claim about the priesthood even more doubtful.

48. *Defamers of the Church*, 33–34. Robert Hull to the Reverend. A. A. Malloy, December 4, 1923, Anti-Catholic Collection, Archives of the Diocese of Fort Wayne–South Bend, Fort Wayne, Indiana, reported that he was claiming to be an ex-priest.

49. This biographical material for Reeb came from city directories, decennial censuses, and other sources in Ancestry.com (accessed July 26, 2012). Christian Henry Reeb shows up in records under various forms and spelling of his name: C. H. Reeb, C. Henry Reeb, Christian H. Reeb, and Henry Reeb. Occasionally, the Reeb name was transcribed incorrectly as Ruel, Reed, and Roebb.

50. Robert Hull, an associate editor of *Our Sunday Visitor*, wrote to Dr. L. C. Scarborough, the president of Reeb's seminary, suggesting that he ask the Reverend Reeb when, where, and by whom he was ordained to the Catholic priesthood as he was claiming. Anti-Catholic Collection, Archives of the Diocese of Fort Wayne/South Bend.

51. Roger Daniels, *Guarding the Golden Door: American Immigration Policies and Immigrants since 1882* (New York: Hill and Wang, 2004), 45–49; Higham, *Strangers in the Land*, 308–11.

52. *Gravette News Herald*, January 20, May 19, 1922.

53. Bogard, *Ku Klux Klan Exposed*, 4–5.

54. Harry G. Knowles, *Eight Cs for Klanswomen* (n.p., ca. 1924?), 31. This pamphlet was provided by Special Collections, Shields Library, University of California, Davis.

55. Newton, *K.K.K. vs. Enemies*, 8, 35.

56. *Gravette News Herald*, May 19, 1922, January 11, 1924.

57. Ibid., May 19, 1922.

58. *Races Trust Influence Knowledge Kindling Leadership Unity Brains-Brawn-Breadth: Pamphlet No. 3 of the Tri-K Klub Series* (Little Rock, AR: Women of the Ku Klux Klan, n.d.), 4–5, 9, Pamphlets and Emphera Collection 2145, Arkansas History Commission, Little Rock.

59. The *Imperial Night Hawk*, September 19, 1923, and the *Arkansas Gazette*, August 28, 1923, announced the charter of the American Krusaders; and Comer gave a lengthy interview explaining the new organization to the *Gazette*, September 2, 1923. See also information about the Krusaders in Chalmers, *Hooded Americanism*, 217.

60. *Fellowship Forum* (Washington, DC), December 27, 1924; Craig Fox, *Everyday Klansfolk: White Protestant Life and the Ku Klux Klan in 1920s Michigan* (East Lansing: Michigan State University Press, 2011), 103–8.

61. Daniels, *Guarding the Golden Door*, 4, 351–58; Mae M. Ngai, *Impossible Subjects: Illegal Aliens and the Making of Modern America* (Princeton: Princeton University Press, 2005), 22–30; Higham, *Strangers in the Land*, 316–24.

62. *New York Times*, April 19, 1924; *Congressional Record*, 68th Congress, 1st Session, 1924, 65, pt. 4–6: 6257–6258.

63. *Kourier* (Atlanta, GA), December 1924.

64. Newton, *Eight C's for Klanswomen*, 13; *Gravette News Herald*, February 27, 1925.

65. See the discussion of the law in Pegram, *One Hundred Percent American*, 91–92, 116; *Gravette News Herald*, May 18, 1923.

66. *Acts of Arkansas, General, 1923* (Little Rock: Democrat Printing, 1923), 479–89. Act 614 also required that any college degree awarded in Arkansas include one course

in American history or government, a policy still in effect for public universities in the state today. *Gravette News Herald*, March 30, 1923.

67. *Log Cabin Democrat*, June 10, 1922; *Conway Weekly News*, June 9, 1922. The Conway schools had nearly closed the year before because tax revenue was insufficient to pay the teachers. Pegram, *One Hundred Percent American*, 98.

68. *Imperial Night Hawk*, June 6, 1923; *Gravette News Herald*, March 10, 1922.

69. *Arkansas Traveller*, October 15, 1923.

70. *Baptist and Commoner*, June 14, October 11, 1922.

71. *Guardian*, June 17, 1922.

72. Newton, *Eight C's for Klanswomen*, 15–16.

73. Ibid., 13; *Gravette News Herald*, December 7, 1923.

74. *Gravette News Herald*, January 23, 1925.

75. Kauffman, *Faith and Fraternalism*, 262–68.

76. *Gravette New Herald*, August 12, December 2, 1921, January 20, 1922; Newton, *Eight C's for Klanswomen*, 23.

77. *Gravette News Herald*, May 12, 1922.

78. Kauffman, *Faith and Fraternalism*, 267–72.

79. Ibid., 278; *Baptist and Commoner*, June 14, 1922.

80. A. P. Coolidge, Grand Knight of the Helena Council, to James A. Flaherty, Supreme Knight, August 9, 1922; Luke Hart, Supreme Advocate, to Coolidge, August 18, 1922; L. B. Barry, Jr., Grand Knight of the Fort Smith Council, to Hart, April 20, 1923; Hart to Barry, April 25, 1923, all in folder: Luke Hart Correspondence, Arkansas, 1922–1927, folder 164, box 280, Bogus Oath Collection.

81. L. B. Barry, Jr., to A. P. Coolidge, August 3, 1923; Luke Hart to Coolidge, September 5, 1923, folder 164, box 280, Bogus Oath Collection.

82. Ray H. Siegfried to Luke Hart, October 29, 1923; Hart to Siegfried, October 30, 1923; Hart to Joseph C. Carroll, Jr., October 30, 1923; Carroll to Hart, November 2, 1923; folder 164; box 280, Bogus Oath Collection; and *Arkansas Traveller*, October 15, 1923, and November 5, 1923.

83. C. L. Burris to Catholic Church Extension Society, Chicago, April 13, 1924; William D. O'Brien to Knights of Columbus headquarters, April 16, 1924, folder 164, box 280, Bogus Oath Collection.

84. *Baptist and Commoner*, June 21, 1922, April 6, 1923; *Gravette News Herald*, October 21, 1921, February 2, 1923.

85. *Gravette News Herald*, October 21, 1921, December 5, 1922, August 10, 1923; *Imperial Night Hawk*, April 23, 1924. For an extended version of the Klan perspective of the Knights of Columbus, see the pamphlet authored by the Grand Dragon of New Jersey, Arthur H. Bell, entitled *The Ku Klux Klan or the Knights of Columbus Klan* (Milan, IL: The Rail Splitter, ca. 1924).

86. Bogard, *Ku Klux Klan Exposed*, 6; Newton, *K.K.K. vs. Enemies*, 8.

87. *Baptist and Commoner*, June 14, 1922; *Gravette News Herald*, August 25, 1922.

88. *Baptist and Commoner*, June 1, 1921, 14, 1922.

89. Knowles, *Eight C's for Klanswomen*, 29–30; *Baptist and Commoner*, June 1, 1921, June 14, 1922.

90. For more about Smith, see Richard O'Conner, *The First Hurrah: A Biography of Alfred E. Smith* (New York: G. P. Putnam's Sons, 1970); and Matthew Josephson and Hannah Josephson, *Al Smith: Hero of the Cities* (Boston: Houghton Mifflin, 1969).

91. *Gravette News Herald*, May 16, 23, 1924.

92. *New York Times*, June 22, 1924; Robert K. Murray, *The 103rd Ballot: Democrats and the Disaster in Madison Square Garden* (New York: Harper and Row, 1976), 107–9.

93. *Arkansas Gazette*, June 21, 1924.

94. For a discussion of the politics surrounding the platform debate and vote, see Murray, *The 103rd Ballot*, 153–64. For the vote of the Arkansas delegation, see *Arkansas Gazette*, June 29, 1924.

95. For McAdoo's biography, see Murray, *The 103rd Ballot*, 38–50.

96. Alexander, *Ku Klux Klan in the Southwest*, 163; A. W. Parke to Joe T. Robinson, April 6, 1924, folder 4, box 31, subseries 3, series 4, Joseph Taylor Robinson Collection, Special Collections, University of Arkansas Libraries, Fayetteville; *Arkansas Gazette*, June 21, 1924.

97. Murray, *The 103rd Ballot*, 124–25; Cecil Edward Weller Jr., *Joe T. Robinson: Always a Loyal Democrat* (Fayetteville: University of Arkansas Press, 1998), 101. The full text of Brough's two-minute speech can be found in the *Arkansas Gazette*, June 26, 1924.

98. Murray, *The 103rd Ballot*, 203–7; *Arkansas Gazette*, July 8, 1924.

99. *Baptist and Commoner*, October 22, 1924.

100. Murray, *The 103rd Ballot*, 253.

101. Alexander, *Ku Klux Klan in the Southwest*, 186–91.

102. See Lewis, "From Bull Mooser to Grand Dragon of the Ku Klux Klan," 36–37.

103. *Fellowship Forum* (Washington, DC), May 1, 1926.

104. Blee, *Women of the Ku Klux Klan*, 28–29, 60–61; Charles C. Alexander, "Defeat, Decline, Disintegration: The Ku Klux Klan in Arkansas, 1924 and After," *Arkansas Historical Quarterly* 22 (Winter 1963): 323–25. For more details of the court case, see A. B. Cloud et al. v. Robbie Gill Comer et al., Pulaski County Chancery Court, no. 34369, box 1344, Pulaski County Courthouse, Little Rock.

105. Undated newspaper clipping, folder 2, subseries 3, series 2, Lawrence Brooks Hays Papers, Special Collections, University of Arkansas Libraries, Fayetteville.

106. Alexander, "Defeat, Decline, Disintegration," 326–27.

107. For the sordid details of this episode and its impact on Klan membership, see Wade, *The Fiery Cross*, 239–47.

CHAPTER 5 • Al Smith, Joe T. Robinson, and the 1928 Election

1. See Douglas B. Craig, *After Wilson: The Struggle for the Democratic Party, 1920–1934* (Chapel Hill: University of North Carolina Press, 1992), 93–103.

2. Charles C. Marshall, "An Open Letter to Governor Smith," *Atlantic Monthly* 139 (April 27, 1927): 540–49; Alfred Smith, "Catholic and Patriot: Governor Smith Replies," *Atlantic Monthly* 139 (May 27, 1927): 721–28.

3. See Thomas J. Shelley, "'What the Hell Is an Encyclical?': Governor Alfred E. Smith, Charles C. Marshall, Esq., and Father Francis P. Duffy," *U.S. Catholic Historian* 15, no. 2 (Spring 1997): 87–107. It is unclear exactly how much of the beautifully crafted response Al Smith actually wrote. Shelley says Smith asked his advisor, Judge Joseph Proskauer, to write the article for him with advice from Father Francis Duffy, pastor of Holy Cross Church in midtown Manhattan. When Smith read Marshall's discussion of various papal encyclicals, he reportedly responded, "What the hell is an encyclical?"

4. *Baptist Advance*, May 26, 1927. For a discussion of Cardinal Bonzano's visit to the United States for the Eucharistic Congress in Chicago, and the anti-Catholic response it inspired, see Edmund A. Moore, *A Catholic Runs for President: The Campaign of 1928* (New York: Ronald Press Co., 1956), 44–45.

5. *Baptist and Commoner*, September 1, 21, 1927. See Todd Lewis's discussion of Bogard's editorials in Lewis, "Ben Bogard," 56–59. The Ku Klux Klan disseminated quotable misinformation about Catholicism through a pamphlet, *Facts for Patriotic Americans*, folder 29, Clifford N. Taylor Papers, Yale Collection of Western Americana, Beinecke Rare Book and Manuscript Library, Yale University, New Haven, CT.

6. *Baptist Advance* (Little Rock), September 1927.

7. *Proceedings of the Arkansas Baptist State Convention in Its 74th Annual Session, Jonesboro, November 16–18, 1927* (n.p., n.d.), Special Collections, Riley-Hickingbotham Library, Ouachita Baptist University, Arkadelphia, Arkansas.

8. Unidentified newspaper clipping, February 8, 1927, folder 167; copy of House Bill no. 269, folder 168, box 280, Bogus Oath Collection; *Arkansas Democrat*, February 8, 1927.

9. "Address of Mrs. Robbie Gill Comer," *Kourier Magazine*, September 1927, 15–23.

10. *Out of Their Own Mouths Shall They Be Condemned*, Pamphlets and Ephemera 6830, 1927, Arkansas History Commission, Little Rock.

11. For biographical information about Robinson, see Weller, *Joe T. Robinson*, 1–63; and Nevin Emil Neal, "A Biography of Joseph T. Robinson" (PhD dissertation, University of Oklahoma, 1958), 1–92.

12. Weller, *Joe T. Robinson*, 66–108; Neal, "A Biography of Joseph T. Robinson," 93–233.

13. Weller, *Joe T. Robinson*, xiii, 50–51, 106.

14. *Southern Guardian*, January 18, 1913; *Guardian*, October 30, 1920, June 30, 1925.

15. *Congressional Record—Senate, 70th Congress, 1st Session* (Washington, DC: Government Printing Office, 1928), 1649–59. See the accounts in *New York Times*, January 19, 1928; and *Arkansas Gazette*, January 19, 1928.

16. In a burst of anger, Robinson had knocked a man unconscious at the 1920 Democratic convention. He was once kicked out of a Chevy Chase, Maryland, country club for fighting on the golf course. Weller, *Joe T. Robinson*, xii–xiii.

17. Robinson's debate with Heflin is recorded in *Congressional Record—Senate, 70th Congress, 1st Session*, 1659–65.

18. Weller, *Joe T. Robinson*, 110–11; Cal Ledbetter, "Joe T. Robinson and the Presidential Campaign of 1928," *Arkansas Historical Quarterly* 45, no. 2 (Summer 1986): 101–3.

19. Weller, *Joe T. Robinson*, 111.

20. The correspondence relating to Robinson's speech is grouped together in folders 2–5 of box 36, and folder 1 of box 37, Robinson Collection. Robinson ignored the critical letters but responded with appreciation to most of the letters of support.

21. J. R. Sterling to Joe T. Robinson, January 19, 1928, folder 2, box 36, Robinson Collection.

22. As a sample, I reviewed thirty-six newspapers available in the microfilm collections of the libraries of the University of Arkansas and the University of Central Arkansas and two whose clippings were embedded in the Robinson Collection.

23. *Arkansas Democrat*, January 20, 1928; *Arkansas Gazette*, January 20, 1928; *Malvern Daily Record*, January 21, 1928; *Springdale News*, January 27, 1928; *Newark Journal*, January 26, 1928; *Dardanelle Post Dispatch*, January 19, 1928.

24. Ledbetter, "Joe T. Robinson and the Presidential Campaign of 1928," 104.

25. Lucille Harwood Mills, "The Presidential Campaign of 1928 in Arkansas" (MA thesis, University of Arkansas, 1948), 11; Speech Given before the Friendly Sons of St. Patrick, Philadelphia, March 17, 1928, folder 6, box 37, Robinson Collection.

26. Mills, "The Presidential Campaign of 1928," 12; Joe T. Robinson to J. S. Utley, March 16, 1928, folder 5, box 38, Robinson Collection.

27. Mills, "The Presidential Campaign of 1928," 13–14; Michael Richard Strickland, "'Rum, Rebellion, Racketeers, and Rascals': Alexander Copeland Millar and the Fights to Preserve Prohibition in Arkansas, 1927–1933" (MA thesis, University of Arkansas, 1993), 41–42. Tull described his resolution in the *Baptist Advance*, March 29, 1928.

28. J. S. Utley to Joe T. Robinson, April 25, 1928, folder 1, box 37, Robinson Collection.

29. Strickland, "'Rum, Rebellion, Racketeers, and Rascals,'" 15–24, 117.

30. "The Oral Memoirs of S. E. Tull: An Interview Conducted August 28, 1965, by Robert A. Baker, in Pine Bluff, Arkansas," in the Selsus E. Tull Collection, Moody Library, Baylor University, http://digitalcollections.baylor.edu/cdm/ref/collection/buioh/id/1236 (accessed January 20, 2015); obituary of Tull in *Arkansas Gazette*, January 27, 1973.

31. *Baptist Advance*, February 2, 1928; Mills, "The Presidential Campaign of 1928 in Arkansas," 57.

32. *Baptist Advance*, January 26, 1928; *Kourier Magazine*, April 1928, 9–10.

33. Neal, "A Biography of Joseph T. Robinson," 237; Selsus E. Tull to Joe T. Robinson, January 24, 1928, folder 5, box 36, Robinson Collection.

34. *Baptist Advance*, February 2, 1928; Selsus E. Tull, *Should Al Smith Be President?* (Pine Bluff: National Druggists Printing Supply Company, [1928]). Bogard, in an unusual show of Baptist brotherhood, plugged Tull's pamphlet in the *Baptist and Commoner*, March 14, 1928.

35. *Baptist Advance*, March 15, 1928.

36. *Baptist and Commoner*, April 11, 1928.

37. Strickland, "'Rum, Rebellion, Racketeers, and Rascals,'" 42–43; Mills, "The Presidential Campaign of 1928 in Arkansas," 15–16; *Arkansas Gazette*, March 25, 1928.

38. A. C. Millar to Joe T. Robinson, June 8, 1928, and Robinson to A. C. Millar, June 12, 1928, folder 5, box 38, Robinson Collection; Strickland, "'Rum, Rebellion, Racketeers, and Rascals,'" 45–46.

39. Strickland, "'Rum, Rebellion, Racketeers, and Rascals,'" 47–48; Mills, "The Presidential Campaign of 1928 in Arkansas," 17–18.

40. *Guardian,* March 10, 1928; Alexander, *Ku Klux Klan in the Southwest*, 234. Reuben Maury, in *The Wars of the Ungodly*, 311, says the Knights of the Green Forest represented an attempt by Hiram Evans to prepare for a campaign against an Al Smith candidacy. The new degree instituted the unmasking of Klansmen, a measure that neutralized one of the greatest criticisms of the Klan. Knights of the Green Forest also were to pay one dollar to the Klan treasury, creating a new income stream for the order.

41. Letter of March 29, 1928, folder 42, Ku Klux Klan Materials, MSS 04-30, Butler Center for Arkansas Studies, Central Arkansas Library System, Little Rock.

42. Mills, "The Presidential Campaign of 1928 in Arkansas," 64. For more about the Oklahoma speech, see Moore, *A Catholic Runs for President*, 183.

43. *Baptist Advance*, March 29, 1928; *Baptist and Commoner*, April 18, 1928.

44. *Baptist and Commoner*, February 1, 15, March 14, 1928; D. N. Jackson, *National Danger in Roman Catholicism* (Texarkana: Baptist Sunday School Committee, 1928).

45. *Baptist and Commoner*, April 18, May 16, 1928.

46. The special anti-Catholic edition of the *Baptist and Commoner* was May 30, 1928; his boast of sales is found in the June 20, 1928, edition. See also Lewis's discussion, "Ben Bogard," 69–72.

47. Lewis, "Ben Bogard," 72.

48. Henry Stevens to Joe T. Robinson, June 15, 1928, folder 5, box 38; the Howard County petition is in folder 3, box 39; Mrs. G. U. Neal to Joe T. Robinson, June 13, 1928, folder 8, box 31, Robinson Collection; *Arkansas Gazette*, June 9, 1928.

49. Weller, *Joe T. Robinson*, 112–13; Ledbetter, "Joe T. Robinson and the Presidential Campaign of 1928," 104–7.

50. Weller, *Joe T. Robinson*, 113–14; Mills, "The Presidential Campaign of 1928 in Arkansas," 21–23.

51. Weller, *Joe T. Robinson*, 114; Mills, "The Presidential Campaign of 1928 in Arkansas," 23–24. Printed copies of the speech (in folder 4, box 39, Robinson Collection) were prepared for dissemination to the press as soon as it was delivered, and these copies did not contain the most celebrated statement.

52. Mills, "The Presidential Campaign of 1928 in Arkansas," 26–36; the Rogers quote appears in Ledbetter, "Joe T. Robinson and the Presidential Campaign of 1928," 108.

53. Mills, "The Presidential Campaign of 1928 in Arkansas," 37–40; Roy V. Peel and Thomas C. Donnelly, *The 1928 Campaign: An Analysis* (New York: Arno Press, 1974), 39.

54. The Conway, Pine Bluff, Hope, and Lonoke speeches are in folder 6, box 37, Robinson Collection. Neal, "A Biography of Joseph T. Robinson," 273–75; Weller, *Joe T. Robinson*, 115–17. The Democratic National Committee later published a pamphlet detailing all the appointments Governor Smith made for his state's departments and divisions, as well as to judicial and county offices; see folder 2, box 38, Robinson Collection.

55. Mills, "The Presidential Campaign of 1928 in Arkansas," 63; for a lengthy discussion of Smith's Oklahoma City speech, see Williams, *Shadow of the Pope*, 206–17.

56. Ledbetter, "Joe T. Robinson and the Presidential Campaign of 1928," 117.

57. *Arkansas Gazette*, July 2, 1928.

58. A Little Rock friend sent Robinson a copy of the letter, and he passed it on to Henry Moskowitz at Democratic Headquarters in New York. Joe T. Robinson to Henry Moskowitz, July 17, 1928, folder 2, box 32, Robinson Collection.

59. James A. Comer to J. Carroll Cone, July 16, 1928, folder 3, box 32, Robinson Collection.

60. Harry Lee Williams to Joe T. Robinson, writing on letterhead for the Cone campaign, July 24, 1928, enclosing the letter of Jas. A. Comer to J. Carroll Cone, July 16, 1928, folder 3, box 32, Robinson Collection; Mills, "The Presidential Campaign of 1928 in Arkansas," 89; *Arkansas Gazette*, July 21, 1928.

61. Ibid., July 19, 1928.

62. Alexander, *Ku Klux Klan in the Southwest*, 238.

63. Ledbetter, "Joe T. Robinson and the Presidential Campaign of 1928," 112; *Kourier Magazine*, October 1928, 31–33.

64. *Arkansas Democrat*, October 29, 1928.

65. Ibid., October 31, 1928.

66. See the discussion of the Asheville meeting in Mills, "The Presidential Campaign of 1928 in Arkansas," 69–70; Strickland, "'Rum, Rebellion, Racketeers, and Rascals,'" 57–58; Millar's report in *Arkansas Methodist*, July 26, 1928; and *Arkansas Gazette*, July 26, 1928. Information about Barton can be found in Lucien Lamar Knight, *A Standard History of Georgia and Georgians*, 6 vols. (Chicago: Lewis Publishing, 1917), 5:2439.

67. Ledbetter, "Joe T. Robinson and the Presidential Campaign of 1928," 115; *Arkansas Methodist*, August 2, 1928.

68. *Arkansas Methodist*, September 13, 1928; form letter from Arkansas Anti-Smith Democrats, folder 4, box 33, Robinson Collection; W. E. Womble to Robinson, September 25, 1928, folder 1, box 34, Robinson Collection.

69. Ledbetter, "Joe T. Robinson and the Presidential Campaign of 1928," 115.

70. Nevin Emil Neal, "The Smith-Robinson Arkansas Campaign of 1928," *Arkansas Historical Quarterly* 19 (Spring 1960): 8; Mills, "The Presidential Campaign of 1928 in Arkansas," 49–53. For a discussion of Straton's campaign against Smith in New York, see Moore, *A Catholic Runs for President*, 136–44.

71. *Arkansas Methodist*, October 11, 1928; Mills, "The Presidential Campaign of 1928 in Arkansas," 65. For a discussion of Bishop Cannon's anti-Smith work throughout the fall campaign, see Moore, *A Catholic Runs for President*, 169–71.

72. *Arkansas Methodist*, November 15, 1928.

73. Ibid., October 18, 25, 1928.

74. Neal, "The Smith-Robinson Arkansas Campaign," 8–9; Ledbetter, "Joe T. Robinson and the Presidential Campaign of 1928," 114–15. Little Rock's First Methodist Church boasted a membership of 2,500 in 1928; *Arkansas Methodist*, November 15, 1928.

75. *Arkansas Democrat*, September 26, 1928. Knickerbocker gave a radio broadcast from a Baptist Church in Fort Worth, Texas, in late September at which he bragged that the anti-Smith rallies in Arkansas attracted bigger audiences than had Joe T. Robinson's acceptance ceremony in Hot Springs. *Arkansas Democrat*, October 1, 1928.

76. Strickland, "'Rum, Rebellion, Racketeers, and Rascals,'" 54–57; A. C. Millar to J. S. Utley, June 30, 1928, folder 8, box 31, Robinson Collection. Millar printed his letter to Utley in the *Arkansas Methodist*, July 12, 1928.

77. *Arkansas Methodist*, August 16, 1928. Boaz had written Senator Robinson on June 21, 1928, just before the convention urging him, as a personal friend, to do all he could to prevent Smith from getting the nomination. Folder 8, box 31, Robinson Collection.

78. *Arkansas Methodist*, July 19, September 20, November 1, 1928.

79. Ibid., November 1, 1928.

80. Ibid., October 4, 1928.

81. Lewis, "Ben Bogard," 73; Neal, "The Smith-Robinson Arkansas Campaign," 7; *Baptist and Commoner*," July 18, 1928. Bogard published the full text of his speech in the *Baptist and Commoner*, August 1, 1928.

82. Tull, *Should Al Smith Be President?*, 26–31.

83. *Arkansas Gazette*, August 7, 1928; *Baptist and Commoner*, July 11, August 15, 1928. The August 15 issue listed the schedule of the associational meetings, including nineteen in Arkansas, six in Oklahoma, three in Texas, and one each in Alabama, Missouri, Mississippi, Georgia, Florida, and Tennessee.

84. Lewis, "Ben Bogard," 76–79; *Baptist and Commoner*, October 3, 1928. For Robinson's response to criticism of his record on the anti-lynching bill, see his speech at East St. Louis, October 31, 1928, in folder 1, box 38, Robinson Collection. In October a rumor was passing around in black districts in northern cities that Robinson had once said that upon waking and feeling ill, that he "killed a couple of negroes before breakfast" to feel better. As outrageous as this accusation might seem, Robinson had to react to it, and he arranged for several prominent black Arkansans to write testimonials indicating the respect he had among black voters in Arkansas. See Weller, *Joe T. Robinson*, 119. For more about the racial politics of the 1928 election, see Allan J. Lichtman, *Prejudice and the Old Politics: The Presidential Election of 1928* (Lanham, MD: Lexington Books, 2000, originally published in 1979), 147–59; and Donald J. Lisio, *Hoover, Blacks, and Lily Whites* (Chapel Hill: University of North Carolina Press, 1985), 72–92.

85. Lewis, "Ben Bogard," 44, 76; *Baptist and Commoner*, October 24, 1928.

86. For a thorough discussion of Bogard's fight against evolution, see Lewis, "Ben Bogard," 18–52; or see the summary of Lewis's work in Pratt, *The Father of Modern Landmarkism*, 9–109.

87. *Guardian*, October 20, 1928. Edmund Moore, in *A Catholic Runs for President*, 153–54, suggests that the bogus oath appeared in all parts of the country in the 1928 campaign. Boas E. Gibson of Hoxie, to Martin H. Cormody, October 18, 1928, folder 165; William J. McGinley to Edwin J. Kerwin, October 17, 1928; Kerwin to McGinley, January 23, 1929, box 280; J. T. Ryan to John B. Donahue, September 21, 1928; Luke Hart to Ryan, September 29, 1928, folder 117, box 279, Bogus Oath Collection. Hart and Ryan assumed that the National Druggists Printing Supply Company of Pine Bluff had printed the bogus oath, given that its name appeared as printer on the Tull pamphlet. Hart and Ryan were considering seeking prosecution of the company for criminal libel.

88. *Arkansas Methodist*, August 16, 1928; Neal, "The Smith-Robinson Arkansas Campaign," 8.

89. A. C. Millar to J. S. Utley, June 30, 1928, folder 8, box 31, Robinson Collection; Mills, "The Presidential Campaign of 1928 in Arkansas," 72.

90. *Arkansas Methodist*, March 29, 1928.

91. *Arkansas Gazette*, September 7, 1928. J. S. Compere was the chief speaker at this association meeting.

92. Tom Falls, grandson of Tom Battershall, to author, October 3, 2012.

93. Carroll Wood to Joe T. Robinson, no date; Robinson to Wood, July 23, 1928, folder 3, box 32, Robinson Collection. The correspondence about the political preachers can be found in folders 2–4, box 32; folder 2, box 33; and folders 1–2, box 34, Robinson Collection.

94. Lewis, "Ben Bogard," 74; *Arkansas Gazette*, July 10, 1928.

95. Neal, "The Smith-Robinson Arkansas Campaign of 1928," 8.

96. *Baptist and Commoner*, October 24, 1928; Lewis, "Ben Bogard," 74, 76.

97. *Arkansas Methodist*, October 4, 1928; *Arkansas Democrat*, September 28, 1928.

98. Neal, "The Smith-Robinson Arkansas Campaign," 5–7.

99. Mills, "The Presidential Campaign of 1928 in Arkansas," 54–55.

100. This story is well told in Foy Lisenby, "Brough, Baptists, and Bombast: The Election of 1928," *Arkansas Historical Quarterly* 32, no. 2 (Summer 1973): 120–31. See also his biography of Brough: Foy Lisenby, *Charles Hillman Brough: A Biography* (Fayetteville: University of Arkansas Press, 1996).

101. Mills, "The Presidential Campaign of 1928 in Arkansas," 52–53; Whidden to Al Smith, August 28, 1928, folder 2, box 33, Robinson Collection.

102. *Baptist Advance*, August 9; *Baptist and Commoner*, June 13, 1928.

103. Strickland, "'Rum, Racketeers, Rebellion, and Rascals,'" 50, 61; *Baptist Advance*, September 27, 1928.

104. Heiskell to Joe T. Robinson, July 31, 1928, folder 3, box 32; E. J. Bodman to Robinson, July 12, 1928, and Creed Caldwell to Robinson, folder 1, box 32, Robinson Collection.

105. Neal, "The Smith-Robinson Arkansas Campaign," 9–10; Vint Miles to Grady Miller, September 1928, folder 1, box 34, Robinson Collection; Mills, "The Presidential Campaign of 1928 in Arkansas," 55, 63.

106. Joan Hoff Wilson, *Herbert Hoover: Forgotten Progressive* (Boston: Little, Brown, and Co., 1975), 128–33; David Burner, *The Politics of Provincialism: The Democratic Party in Transition, 1918–1932* (New York: Knopf, 1968), 218; Ruth C. Silva, *Rum, Religion, and Votes: 1928 Re-Examined* (University Park: Pennsylvania State University Press, 1962), 39, 41; Lichtman, *Prejudice and the Old Politics*, 40, 46.

107. I use the official returns from the *Arkansas Democrat*, November 25, 1928; see Mills, "The Presidential Campaign of 1928 in Arkansas," 108; Ledbetter, "Joe T. Robinson and the Presidential Campaign of 1928," 122; Burner, *The Politics of Provincialism*, 230. Lichtman says that voter turnout nationally increased 8 percent from 1924 to 1928, the largest increase of any election in the twentieth century; Lichtman, *Prejudice and the Old Politics*, xvii.

108. See Strickland, "Rum, Racketeers, Rebellion, and Rascals," 67; Mills, "The Presidential Campaign of 1928 in Arkansas," 48, 116; *Arkansas Democrat*, November 25, 1928.

109. Lewis, "Ben Bogard," 86.

110. *Arkansas Gazette*, November 7, 1928; *Arkansas Democrat*, November 7, 1928.

111. Mills, "The Presidential Campaign of 1928 in Arkansas," 112; Weller, *Joe T. Robinson*, 120–21.

112. *Guardian*, November 10, 1928.

113. *Arkansas Methodist*, November 15, 1928.

114. Pratt, *The Father of Modern Landmarkism*, 112–13; "Minutes of the 27th Association of Missionary Baptist Churches of Arkansas, held at Sheridan, Nov 7–9, 1928," 34, quoted in Pratt, *The Father of Modern Landmarkism*, 112–13.

CHAPTER 6 • A Prejudice Wanes and Waxes, 1929–1960

1. Williams, *Shadow of the Pope*, 293–97.

2. Lerond Curry, *Protestant-Catholic Relations in America: World War I through Vatican II* (Lexington: University Press of Kentucky, 1972), 23–25.

3. *Arkansas Gazette*, November 23, 1932.

4. Ibid., June 7, 1933.

5. This generalization is made from a review of June–August 1933 issues of the *Baptist and Commoner*, *Arkansas Methodist*, and the *Arkansas Gazette*. Millar's recommendation is in *Arkansas Methodist*, August 10, 1933.

6. *Arkansas Gazette*, July 19, 1933. Georgia, Louisiana, Oklahoma, and South Carolina voted not to repeal. North Carolina voted not to even call a convention. For more about the end of prohibition in Arkansas, see Johnson, *John Barleycorn Must Die*, 68–75.

7. Massa, *Anti-Catholicism in America*, 35–39; Deward C. Brown, "Anti-Catholicism in Contemporary America, 1920–1960" (MA thesis, University of North Texas, 1966), 60–65. Even Frank Norris, in his later years, softened his anti-Catholicism as he began to see the Catholic Church as an ally in the fight against communism. In August 1947 Norris and three other Baptist leaders had an audience with Pope Pius XII at the papal summer residence of Castel Gandolfo, at which they discussed their common opposition to atheistic communism. See Michael E. Schepis, *J. Frank Norris: The Fascinating, Controversial Life of a Forgotten Figure of the Twentieth Century* (Bloomington, IN: WestBow Press, 2012), 189–93.

8. *Acts of Arkansas, 1937* (Little Rock, AR: Democrat Printing, 1937), 851; *Arkansas Gazette*, March 6, 1937; *Journal of the House of Representatives of the Fifty-First General Assembly of the State of Arkansas* (Newark, AR: Journal Printing, 1937), 1356; *Journal of the Senate of the Fifty-First General Assembly of the State of Arkansas* (Newark, AR: Journal Printing, 1937), 1079–80. Arkansas followed Florida and Alabama, which repealed their similar laws in 1935 and 1936, respectively. Georgia did not get around to repealing its law until 1966. *Guardian*, March 9, 1936; *Southern Cross*, July 20, 2006, 3. https://diosav.org/sites/all/files/archives/S8626p03.pdf (accessed April 6, 2015).

9. Philip Jenkins, *The New Anti-Catholicism: The Last Acceptable Prejudice* (New York: Oxford University Press, 2003), 36.

10. Herndon, *Centennial History of Arkansas*, 3:771–72; Robert R. Posey to Joe T. Robinson, July 11, 1928, folder 2, box 32, September 15, folder 1, box 34, Robinson Collection; Bob Buckman, Spring, Texas, telephone interview with author, September 18, 2012.

11. Father Boniface to Rev. P. John Nigg, OSB, January 25, 1933; Assenmacher, *A Place Called Subiaco*, 252–54.

12. *Defamers of the Church*, 60; *Salt Lake City Tribune*, September 24, 1932.

13. *Guardian*, October 6, 1923, February 23, 1924; Charles V. Heady to Rev. Msgr. J. F. Noll, January 20, 1923, Anti-Catholic Collection, Archives of the Diocese of Fort Wayne/South Bend; *Oelwein (IA) Register*, September 21, 1924.

14. *Providence News*, January 5, 1925, *State Journal*, Reno, Nevada, July 4, 1932; *Nashua (IA) Reporter*, April 15, 1942. The Liberty Party had been founded by Arkansan Coin Harvey at a 1931 convention at his home/resort Monte Ne in northwestern Arkansas. Harvey was nominated as the party's presidential candidate for 1932 with Andrea Nordskog of California as vice president. But by the fall election time he had had a falling out with other party leaders, and he left the party to run as an independent candidate. The Liberty Party was reorganized at a convention in Kansas City in July 1932, with Frank Webb nominated for president, and Nordskog as vice president. In September Spurgeon replaced Nordskog as vice presidential nominee, given that

both Webb and Nordskog were Californians. See *Lewiston Daily Sun*, July 5, 1932; and *New York Times*, September 24, 1932.

15. *Guardian*, September 29, 1934; *Arkansas Gazette*, August 5, 6, 1935; biographical information about the Comers in 1930 and Robbie Comer's death from decennial censuses, city directories, and social security death dates, available in Ancestry.com (accessed July 19, 2014). For Comer's will, see James A. Comer Probate Case File, Will Book V [as in Victor], p. 271–72, Pulaski County Courthouse, Little Rock. The probate records of 1935 show that the Comers owned seven city lots in Little Rock and North Little Rock, more than a thousand acres of farmland in Pulaski and Lonoke Counties, and more than a dozen pieces of diamond and gold jewelry.

16. Wade, *The Fiery Cross*, 264–65, 275.

17. *Gravette News Herald*, February 28, March 6, 20, April 3, 10, May 1, July 24, 31, August 7, 14, 1936, August 5, 1938; *Arkansas Gazette*, August 13, 1938.

18. J. P. Johnston to Joe T. Robinson, January 21, 1928, folder 3, box 36; J. R. Sterling to Robinson, January 19, 1928, folder 2, box 38, Robinson Collection; Weller, *Joe T. Robinson*, 130–31.

19. Weller, *Joe T. Robinson*, 131, 135–67.

20. Burner, *The Politics of Provincialism*, 204; *Arkansas Gazette*, November 6, 1930; "J. Thomas Heflin," www.EncyclopediaOfAlabama.org/face/Article.jsp?id=2952 (accessed January 14, 2015).

21. Strickland, "'Rum, Rascals, Racketeers, and Rebellion,'" 117.

22. *Baptist and Commoner*, February 20, 27, 1929, March 9, 1932.

23. Ibid., October 22, November 26, 1930.

24. Albert Garner, *The Devil's Masterpiece: The Mystery of Iniquity* (Little Rock, n.d.). Garner, a native of Wynne, Arkansas, was living in Little Rock between 1940 and 1946 as a student at Antioch Baptist Church's Seminary. He moved to Texas in 1946, and later to Lakeland, Florida. Ben Bogard, along with James "Uncle Mac" Makrell, performed Garner's wedding ceremonies. See Albert Garner, *Cabin to a Castle and Beyond: The Life and Memoirs of Albert Garner* (Lakeland, FL: Blessed Hope Foundation, 2004).

25. Pratt, *The Father of Modern Landmarkism*, 185.

26. Richard T. Hughes, *Reviving the Ancient Faith: The Story of Churches of Christ in America* (Grand Rapids, MI: William B. Eerdmans, 1996), 263–266.

27. For more information about Benson, see Hughes, *Reviving the Ancient Faith*, 154–57; Edward L. Hick, *Sometimes in the Wrong, but Never in Doubt: George S. Benson and the Education of the New Religious Right* (Knoxville: University of Tennessee Press, 1994).

28. James D. Bales, *Was Peter Pope?* (Berkeley, CA: James Bales, n.d.); James Bales, "Does the Roman Catholic Church Favor Religious Freedom," *Gospel Advocate* (Nashville, TN), January 14, 1943; James Bales, *Catholicism and Coercion* (Searcy: James Bales, 1945). In a book about his life and career as a religious debater, Bales describes how as a young Harding professor he solicited a debate with Ben Bogard, using their mutual connection with Albert Garner. Bogard turned him down saying it would not be fair for an old pro to debate a novice like Bales. James Bales, *Forty-Two Years on the Firing Line* (Shreveport, LA: Lambert Book House, 1977), 9, 20–23,

29. Everson v. Board of Education, 330 U.S. 1 (1947); Brown, "Anti-Catholicism in Contemporary America," 73–76; Curry, *Protestant-Catholic Relations in America*, 51–57.

30. Kauffman, *Faith and Fraternalism*, 371–72; Curry, *Protestant-Catholic Relations in America*, 57–59; Massa, *Anti-Catholicism in America*, 59–70.

31. Brown, "Anti-Catholicism in Contemporary America," 77–78; Curry, *Protestant-Catholic Relations in America*, 45–49.

32. Paul Blanshard, *American Freedom and Catholic Power* (Boston: Beacon Press, 1950), 59. John T. McGreevy makes the case that anti-Catholic thinking of the 1930s and 1940s, culminating in Blanshard's work, was a liberal perspective of intellectual elites, rather than a right-wing populist movement as in the 1910s and 1920s. John T. McGreevy, "Thinking on One's Own: Catholicism in the American Imagination, 1928–1960," *Journal of American History* 84, no. 1 (June 1997): 97–131

33. *Arkansas Methodist*, October 25, November 29, 1951, February 7, 1952; *Arkansas Churchman*, February 1952.

34. *Arkansas Baptist*, November 1, 8, 15; February 21, 1952.

35. *American Baptist*, November 5, December 5, 1951, January 21, February 5, 20, 1952.

36. *Gospel Light*, October 25, November 1, 8, December 20, 1951. The *Gospel Light*, edited by J. A. Copeland, was published in Delight, Arkansas, beginning in 1930.

37. James D. Bales, "The Vatican Appointment," *Gospel Advocate*, January 10, 1952.

38. Brown, "Anti-Catholicism in Contemporary America," 85–86; Shaun Casey, *Making of a Catholic President: Kennedy vs. Nixon, 1960* (New York: Oxford University Press, 2009), 7, 16–17. For more information about Kennedy's politicking for the vice presidential nomination in 1956 and his informal campaign for president before 1960, see W. J. Rorabaugh, *The Real Making of the President: Kennedy, Nixon, and the 1960 Election* (Lawrence: University Press of Kansas, 2009), 20–22, 44–57, 65–72.

39. *Time*, May 18, 1959; see also Casey's discussion of the poll, *Making of a Catholic President*, 24–25.

40. "Annual of the Arkansas Baptist State Convention in the 111st Year held at First Baptist Church, Little Rock, Arkansas, November 17–19, 1959," in folder 2, box 9, series II, Erwin L. McDonald Collection, University of Central Archives, Conway, Arkansas; *Arkansas Baptist*, May 26, 1960.

41. Brown, "Anti-Catholicism in Contemporary America," 91–92, 98; Casey, *Making of a Catholic Presidency*," 103–4; *Missionary Baptist Searchlight* (Little Rock), March 10, July 25, 1960; *Baptist Trumpet* (Little Rock), March 13, 1960.

42. *Arkansas Gazette*, July 10, 14, 1960; Casey, *Making of a Catholic President*, 151–52.

43. The entire sermon of Vaught was published in the Missionary Baptist paper, the Little Rock *Baptist Trumpet*, August 3, 1960; see also *Arkansas Gazette*, July 18, 1960; and *Arkansas Baptist* July 21, 1960.

44. *Arkansas Gazette*, September 7, 1960; *Arkansas Baptist*, September 15, 1960; Casey, *Making of a Catholic President*, 116; *Arkansas Democrat*, September 6, 7, 1960.

45. Casey, *Making of a Catholic President*, 104–10.

46. *Arkansas Gazette*, September 7, 1960; Casey, *Making of a Catholic President*, 116–20.

47. Casey, *Making of a Catholic President*, 136–46; Thomas J. Carty, *A Catholic in the White House? Religion, Politics, and John F. Kennedy's Presidential Campaign* (New York: Palgrave Macmillan, 2004), 58–61.

48. Casey, *Making of a Catholic President*, 108, 128–29.

49. See Casey's analysis of the speech, *Making of a Catholic President*, 164–76; and Rorabaugh, *The Real Making of the President*, 4, 144, 145.

50. *Arkansas Democrat*, September 9, 1960; *Arkansas Gazette*, September 10, 1960.

51. Orval Eugene Faubus, *Down from the Hills II* (Little Rock, AR: Democrat Printing, 1985), 82, 92.

52. *Arkansas Democrat*, October 3, 1960; *Arkansas Gazette*, October 4, 1960; *Guardian*, October 7, 1960. For the full text of Archer's speech, see *Arkansas Baptist*, October 6, 1960.

53. *Arkansas Gazette*, October 19, 1960; *Arkansas Baptist*, August 18, 25, September 8, 22, October 13, November 3, 1960.

54. *Missionary Baptist Searchlight*, December 25, 1960; *Guardian*, November 28, 1960; *Baptist Trumpet*, November 2, 1960.

55. *American Baptist*, August, September, October 1960.

56. *Baptist Trumpet*, August 10, 1960; see other articles in August 17 and October 5, 1960.

57. See the correspondence between Al J. Udouj, Francis Donovan, Joseph Lamb, and Luke Hart, September–October 1928, in folder 408, box 257, Bogus Oath Collection.

58. See miscellaneous correspondence in folder 408, box 257, Bogus Oath Collection.

59. *Gospel Light*, October 1960; see the discussion of Howard's challenge to Kennedy at Houston in Casey, *Making of a Catholic President*, 172–74.

60. For biographical information on Howard, see http://www.therestoration movement.com/_states/louisiana/howard,ve.htm (accessed April 15, 2015). See Casey's discussion of Church of Christ opposition to Kennedy in Casey, *Making of a Catholic President*, 181–83; and Hughes, *Reviving the Ancient Faith*, 263–65.

61. *Arkansas Democrat*, July 24, 1960.

62. See James T. Baker, *Brooks Hays* (Macon, GA: Mercer University Press, 1989), 43, 97, 116, 183–86; Brooks Hays, *Politics Is My Parish: An Autobiography* (Baton Rouge: Louisiana State University Press, 1981), 86.

63. Casey, *Making of a Catholic President*, 200–201; V. O. Key Jr., "Interpreting the Election Results," in *The Presidential Election and Transition, 1960–1961,* edited by Paul T. David (Washington, DC: Brookings Institution, 1961), 174; Gary A. Donaldson, *The First Modern Campaign: Kennedy, Nixon, and the Election of 1960* (Lanham, MD: Rowan and Littlefield, 2007), 154–56; Rorabaugh, *The Real Making of the President*, 5, 8, 139.

64. *Statistics of the Presidential and Congressional Election of November 8,* 1960 (Washington, DC: Government Printing Office, 1961), 3; Key, "Interpreting the Election Results," 156.

CHAPTER 7 • Postlude: After 1960

1. *Arkansas Gazette*, November 16, 18, 1960; *Arkansas Baptist*, December 1, 1960.

2. *Baptist Trumpet*, November 9, 1960; *American Baptist*, November, December 1960.

3. Carty, *A Catholic in the White House?*, 160; Curry, *Protestant-Catholic Relations in America*, 78–80.

4. *Arkansas Baptist*, June 7, 1972, November 28, 1963.

5. *Baptist Features*, December 1, 1963, folder 23, box 15, series II, Erwin McDonald Collection.

6. Baker, *Brooks Hays*, 186, 199–200; Hays, *Politics Is My Parish*, 200; Curry, "Protestant-Catholic Relations in America," 81. Beginning in 1969 Wake Forest University partnered with the Roman Catholic Belmont Abbey College of Belmont, North Carolina, in sponsoring the work of the institute. Hays continued to attend the annual dialogues after his retirement in the early 1970s. Anne Adkins, "Bold Venture of Faith," clipping from *Then and Now*, a magazine of Wake Forest University, Summer 1978, folder 18, box 2, sub-series 1, series 4, Lawrence Brooks Hays Supplementary Papers, Special Collections, University of Arkansas Libraries, Fayetteville.

7. Abington School District v. Schempp, 374 U.S. 203 (1963); and Epperson v. Arkansas, 393 U.S. 97 (1968).

8. Roe v. Wade, 410 U.S. 113 (1973); Daniel K. Williams, *God's Own Party: The Making of the Christian Right* (New York: Oxford University Press, 2010), 5, 80, 113–17, 156. For more information about the Baptist-Catholic dialogue on abortion in 1975, see Claude U. Broach to dialogue participants, December 8, 1975, folder 17, box 2, sub-series 1, series 4, Hays Supplementary Papers.

9. *Arkansas Gazette,* April 16, 20, 22, 1978.

10. *Arkansas Baptist*, January 5, 1984.

11. Ibid., January 5, 1984; *Baptist Trumpet*, February 22, 1984; *Arkansas Methodist*, February 24, 1984. The Episcopal paper, the *Arkansas Churchman,* made no comment about the ambassadorial appointment.

12. Carty, *A Catholic in the White House?*, 160, 170–71.

13. See the discussion of the marriage amendment in *Arkansas Baptist*, July 29, August 12, August 26, October 7, November 18, 2004; and *Baptist Trumpet*, September 15, October 13, 20, 2004. The *Missionary Baptist Searchlight* made no comment about any aspect of the election or John Kerry in 2004. The *Gospel Light* editorialized against abortion, homosexuality, and moral relativism in the fall of 2004 but never mentioned John Kerry and Catholicism.

14. Mike Huckabee, *Character Makes a Difference: Where I'm From, Where I've Been, and What I Believe* (Nashville: B&H Group, 2007), 43–44, 49, 83; for a review of resolutions passed by the Arkansas Baptist Conventions, see Williams, Granade, and Startup, *A System and Plan*, 359–69.

15. *Arkansas Gazette*, March 13, 15, 25, 1985; "Fugitive Pope" issue of Alamo's newsletter [1990], folder 2, box 1, Tony Alamo Materials, Special Collections, University of Arkansas Libraries, Fayetteville. Another example is Jack T. Chick, a writer/cartoonist in California, who has published a mass of anti-Catholic material from the 1970s onward. Chick was so extreme that he was threatened with expulsion from the evangelical Christian Booksellers Association and resigned. See Massa, *Anti-Catholicism in America*, 100–120. Massa is not sure if Chick is indeed a person, a penname, or a group of conservative Protestants using a fictional character to present their message.

16. Massa, *Anti-Catholicism in America*, 193–98; Jenkins, *The New Anti-Catholicism.*

17. I am indebted to Pagliarini's discussion of sexuality, anti-Catholicism, and Foucault in Marie Anne Pagliarini, "The Pure American Woman and the Wicked

Catholic Priest: An Analysis of Anti-Catholic Literature in Antebellum America," *Religion and American Culture: A Journal of Interpretation* 9, no. 1 (Winter 1999): 97–128. See Michel Foucault, *The History of Sexuality*, vol. 1, trans. Robert Hurley (New York: Pantheon Books, 1978).

18. *Arkansas Traveller*, October 15, 1923.

19. See Phillip E. Hammond, *The Protestant Presence in Twentieth-Century America: Religion and Political Culture* (Albany: State University of New York Press, 1992); and Martin E. Marty, *Righteous Empire: The Protestant Experience in America* (New York: Dial Press, 1970) for insightful discussions on the origins and meaning of fundamentalism. Justin Nordstrom argues strongly that anti-Catholicism was motivated by rural and small-town fears of modernity; see Nordstrom, *Danger on the Doorstep*, 66–70.

20. At the 1926 religious census, the Missionary Baptists had 41,281 members in Arkansas to the Southern Baptists membership of 103,346. Arkansas's number of Missionary Baptists was exceeded only by the 53,853 in Texas, a state with more than twice the population of Arkansas. *Census of Religious Bodies: 1926*, 2 vols. (Washington, DC: Government Printing Office, 1930), 1:146–49 and 2:225.

21. Hughes, *Reviving the Ancient Faith*, 119–45.

22. Ibid., 155–56, 163–66; Allan J. Lichtman, *White Protestant Nation: The Rise of the American Conservative Movement* (New York: Atlantic Monthly Press, 2008), 126, 136. For a longer look at Benson's career, see Hick, *Sometimes in the Wrong, but Never in Doubt.*

23. *Census of Religious Bodies: 1926*, 2:396. The Assemblies of God denomination in Arkansas has similarities to the Churches of Christ, even though evidence is lacking for the study of the views of these groups in the 1910s and 1920s. Both groups emphasize congregational sovereignty, which puts them at the opposite pole of Christianity from the hierarchical Roman Catholic Church. Pentecostals who emphasize speaking in tongues and divine healing in worship are promoting a direct communication and relationship with God that bypasses the structure, medium, and authority of a church hierarchy. Thus these groups would take a contrarian position toward the centralized authority system of a Roman Catholic Church and its theology. The Assemblies of God came out strongly against the Kennedy nomination for president in 1960. The largest white Pentecostal group, the Assemblies of God, had its beginning at an organizational meeting in Hot Springs, Arkansas, in 1914. Its world headquarters are not far away in Springfield, Missouri. Arkansas in 1926 had the highest concentration of members of the Assembly of God, ranking fourth in total numbers behind the more populous states of California, Texas, and Illinois. For this story of Pentecostalism, see Edith L. Blumhofer, *Restoring the Faith: The Assemblies of God, Pentecostalism, and American Culture* (Urbana-Champaign: University of Illinois Press, 1993.)

24. In a Gallup poll of 2013, Arkansas ranked as the eighth most religious state, behind six other southern states and Utah. The poll was based on self-reported judgments about religion as an important part of one's daily life combined with attendance at religious services every week or almost every week. Mississippi was top of the list with 61 percent very religious to Vermont's 22 percent very religious. Arkansas's percentage of very religious was 51 percent; the national average was 41 percent. See http://www.gallup.com/poll/167267/mississippi-religious-vermont-least-religious-state.aspx (accessed April 2, 2015).

25. Foucault, *History of Sexuality*, 1:43, 101.

26. See the text of the law at http://www.arkleg.state.ar.us/assembly/2015/2015R/Acts/Act1231.pdf (accessed May 19, 2015). The version used by fundamentalists and most other Protestants has the second commandment as "Thou shalt not make to thyself any graven images." This version collapses the proscription about covetousness into one final commandment. The version used by Roman Catholics, Lutherans, and most Jews omits the commandment on graven images and makes two commandments about covetousness.

BIBLIOGRAPHY

Primary Sources

Manuscript Collections

A. B. Cloud et al. v. Robbie Gill Comer et al. Pulaski County Chancery Court, No. 34369, box no. 1344, Pulaski County Courthouse, Little Rock, Arkansas.

Anti-Catholic Collection. Archives of the Diocese of Fort Wayne/South Bend, Fort Wayne, Indiana.

Anti-Catholic Printed Material Collection, 1827–1991. Notre Dame University Archives, South Bend, Indiana.

Anti-Catholicism: Bogus Oath Collection. Knights of Columbus Supreme Council Archives, New Haven, Connecticut.

Calvin W. Enders: Michigan Ku Klux Klan Research Papers. Clarke Historical Library, Central Michigan University, Mount Pleasant, Michigan.

Catholic Central Verein of America Records. Notre Dame University Archives, South Bend, Indiana.

Clifford N. Taylor Papers, Yale Collection of Western Americana. Beinecke Rare Book and Manuscript Library, Yale University, New Haven, Connecticut.

"Der Klausner von Subiako." Translated by Fr. Jerome Kodell. Archives of Subiaco Abbey, Subiaco, Arkansas.

Erwin L. McDonald Collection. University of Central Arkansas Archives, Conway, Arkansas.

Fr. Boniface Spanke Correspondence, Box XIV. Archives of Subiaco Abbey, Subiaco, Arkansas.

George S. Benson Papers. Ann Cowan Dixon Archives and Special Collections. Harding University, Searcy, Arkansas.

James A. Comer Probate Case File, Will Book V [as in Victor]. Pulaski County Courthouse, Little Rock, Arkansas.

John Francis Noll Papers, 1904–1956. Notre Dame University Archives, South Bend, Indiana.

Joseph Taylor Robinson Collection, series 5, subseries 4–5, boxes 31–39. Special Collections, University of Arkansas Libraries, Fayetteville, Arkansas.

Ku Klux Klan, Mecosta County, Michigan, Collection. Ku Klux Klan, Newago County, Michigan. Clarke Historical Library, Central Michigan University, Mount Pleasant, Michigan.

Ku Klux Klan Materials, MSS 04-30. Butler Center for Arkansas Studies, Central Arkansas Library System, Little Rock, Arkansas.

Lawrence Brooks Hays Papers, series 2, subseries 2, box 29; subseries 3, box 38. Special Collections, University of Arkansas Libraries, Fayetteville, Arkansas.

Lawrence Brooks Hays Supplementary Papers, series 4, subseries 1, box 2. Special Collections, University of Arkansas Libraries, Fayetteville, Arkansas.

"Oral Memoirs of Selsus Tull." Moody Library, Baylor University, Waco, Texas, http://digitalcollections.baylor.edu/cdm/ref/collection/buioh/id/1236. Accessed March 18, 2016.

Proceedings of Arkansas Baptist Conventions, 1900–1928. Riley-Hickingbotham Library, Special Collections, Ouachita Baptist University, Arkadelphia, Arkansas.

Sacred Heart (Morrilton) Reports. Spiritan Archives, Bethel Park, Pennsylvania.

South by Southwest Collection, box 3. Special Collections, University of Arkansas Libraries, Fayetteville, Arkansas.

Tony Alamo Materials. Special Collections, University of Arkansas Libraries, Fayetteville, Arkansas.

Published Primary Works

Autry, Allen Hill. *Grapeshot and Canister: From the Arsenal of Truth in Mission Methods*. Little Rock, AR: Doctrinal Interpreter, 1911.

———. *Warning Signals or Romanism, an American Peril*. Little Rock, AR: Doctrinal Interpreter, 1911.

Bales, James D. *Catholicism and Coercion*. Searcy, AR: James Bales, 1945.

———. *Forty-Two Years on the Firing Line*. Shreveport. LA: Lambert Book House, 1977.

———. *Was Peter Pope?* Berkeley, CA: James Bales, n.d.

Bell, Arthur H. *The Ku Klux Klan or the Knights of Columbus Klan*. Milan, IL: Rail Splitter, ca. 1924.

Blanshard, Paul. *American Freedom and Catholic Power*. Boston: Beacon Press, 1950.

———. *Communism, Democracy, and Catholic Power*. Boston: Beacon Press, 1951.

Bogard, Ben M. *Ku Klux Klan Exposed: Inside Facts Laid Bare and Explained*. Little Rock, AR, n.d.

Clark, William Lloyd. *Reminiscences of a Reformer's Life, Or Twenty-Five Years on the Skirmish Line Against Political Romanism*. Milan, IL, 1913.

Defamers of the Church: Their Character. Huntingdon, IN: Our Sunday Visitor, 1925.

Faubus, Orval Eugene. *Down from the Hills II*. Little Rock, AR: Democrat Printing, 1985.

Flowers, Benjamin O. *The Story of the Menace Trial: A Brief Sketch of This Historic Case, with Reports of the Masterly Addresses by Hon. J. L. McNatt and Hon. J. I. Sheppard*. Aurora, MO: United States Publishing, 1916.

Garner, Albert. *Cabin to a Castle and Beyond: The Life and Memoirs of Albert Garner*. Lakeland, FL: Blessed Hope Foundation, 2004.

———. *The Devil's Masterpiece: The Mystery of Iniquity*. Little Rock, AR: n.d.

Hays, Brooks. *Politics Is My Parish: An Autobiography*. Baton Rouge: Louisiana State University Press, 1981.

Huckabee, Mike. *Character Makes a Difference: Where I'm From, Where I've Been, and What I Believe*. Nashville, TN: B&H Group, 2007.

Knowles, Harry G. *Eight C's for Klanswomen*. N.p., ca. 1924.

Marshall, Charles C. "An Open Letter to Governor Smith," *Atlantic Monthly* 139 (April 1927): 540–49.

Newton, Basil E. *The K.K.K. vs. Enemies*. N.p., n.d.

Phelps, Wilbur F. *Menace Cartoons*. Aurora, MO: Menace Publishing, 1914.

Races Trust Influence Knowledge Kindling Leadership Unity Brains-Brawn-Breadth: Tri-K Klub, a Department of the Women of the Ku Klux Klan. Little Rock, AR: Women of the Ku Klux Klan, n.d.

Report of Commission on Religious Prejudices, 1915. N.p.: Knights of Columbus, 1915.

Robinson, J. P. *Why Believers Should Be Baptised and Catholicism Exposed*. Nashville, TN: National Baptist Publishing Board, 1911.

Scarboro, Joseph A. *The Bible, Baptists, and the Board System*. 1904. Reprint, Emmaus, PA: Challenge Press, 1975.

Smith, Alfred. "Catholic and Patriot: Governor Smith Replies," *Atlantic Monthly* 139 (May 1927): 721–28.

Souvenir of the dedication of St. Agnes New Church, October 16, 1922, commemorating the Silver Jubilee Year of the Ordination to Priesthood of the Very Rev. A. P. Gallagher, V.F. Mena, AR: Star Printing, 1922.

Tull, Selsus E. *Should Al Smith Be President?* Pine Bluff, AR: National Druggists Printing Supply Company, ca. 1928.

Government Documents and Statistical Directories

Acts of Arkansas, 1911, 1915, 1923, 1937. Little Rock, AR: Democrat Printing, 1911, 1915, 1923, 1937.

Biennial Report of the Attorney General of Arkansas, 1913–1914. Little Rock, AR: Democrat Printing, 1915.

Bureau of the Census. *Religious Bodies: 1926*. Washington, DC: Government Printing Office, 1930.

Bureau of the Census. *Special Reports: Religious Bodies, 1916*. Washington, DC: Government Printing Office, 1919.

Bureau of the Census. *Thirteenth Census of the United States, 1910*. Washington, DC: Government Printing Office, 1913.

Congressional Record, 68th Congress, 1st Session. Washington, DC: Government Printing Office, 1924.

Congressional Record—Senate, 70th Congress, 1st Session. Washington, DC: Government Printing Office, 1928.

Journal of the House of Representatives of the Fifty-First General Assembly of the State of Arkansas. Newark, AR: Journal Printing, 1937.

Journal of the Senate of the Fifty-First General Assembly of the State of Arkansas. Newark, AR: Journal Printing, 1937.

N. W. Ayer and Son's American Newspaper Annual and Directory, 1914–1920. Philadelphia: N. W. Ayer & Son, 1914–1920.

Interviews

Jim Bergenham, Kentwood, MI, telephone interview with author, July 5, 2012.

Bob Buckman, Spring, TX, telephone interview with author, September 12, 2012.

Newspapers and Periodicals

American Baptist (Little Rock), 1951–2004.

Arkansas Baptist (Little Rock), a Missionary Baptist publication, 1911–12, became the *Baptist* in 1912–1917, became the *Baptist and Commoner*, 1917–1939.

Arkansas Baptist (Little Rock), a publication of the Arkansas Baptist State Convention, 1947–2004.

Arkansas Democrat (Little Rock), 1915, 1924, 1928.

Arkansas Echo (Little Rock), 1914–1918, 1921.

Arkansas Gazette (Little Rock), 1913–1928.

Arkansas Methodist (Little Rock), 1914–1928.

Baptist Advance (Little Rock), 1911, 1914, 1916–1918, 1928–1930.

Baptist and Commoner (Little Rock), 1917–1939.

Baptist Trumpet (Little Rock), 1951, 1960, 2004.

Christian Chronicle (Abilene, TX), 1960.

Christian Chronicle (Oklahoma City, OK), 2004.

Conway (AR) Weekly News, 1922–1925.

Daily Graphic (Pine Bluff, AR), 1928.

Daily Texarkanian (Texarkana, AR/TX), 1915.

Dardanelle (AR) Post Dispatch, 1928.

Fayetteville (AR) Daily Democrat, 1928.

Fellowship Forum (Washington, DC), 1921–1930.

Firm Foundation (Austin, TX), 1960, 2004.

Fort Smith (AR) Times Record, 1918.

Gospel Advocate (Nashville, TN), 1943, 1960, 2004.

Gospel Light (Delight, AR), 1947–1960, 2004.

Gravette (AR) News Herald, 1912–1925.

Harrison (AR) Daily Times, 1928.

Headlight (Sheridan, AR), 1922.

Helena (AR) World, 1928.

Hot Springs (AR) New Era, 1928.

Imperial Night Hawk (Atlanta, GA), 1923.

Jonesboro (AR) Daily Tribune, 1922.

Jonesboro (AR) Evening Sun, 1922.

Kourier (Atlanta, GA), 1924–1925.

LaFayette County Democrat (Stamps, AR), 1912.

Liberator (Magnolia, AR), 1912–1915.

Log Cabin Democrat (Conway, AR), 1913–1914, 1921–1925, 1928.

Malvern (AR) Daily Record, 1928.

Marshall (TX) Messenger, 1915.

Mena (AR) Star Weekly, 1915, 1928.

Menace (Aurora, MO), 1912–1919.

Missionary Baptist Searchlight (Little Rock), 1950, 1960, 2004.

Nashville (AR) News, 1928.

New York Times, 1913, 1923, 1924, 1928.

Newark (AR) Journal, 1928.

Southern Cross (Savannah, GA), 2006.

Southern Guardian (Little Rock), became the *Guardian* in 1915 and *Arkansas Catholic* in 1986.

Southwest American (Fort Smith, AR), 1928.

Springdale (AR) News, 1928.

Washington Post, 1923.

Watson's Magazine (Hickory Hill, GA), 1910–1913.

Secondary Sources

Alexander, Charles C. "Defeat, Decline, Disintegration: The Ku Klux Klan in Arkansas, 1924 and After." *Arkansas Historical Quarterly* 22 (Winter 1963): 311.

———. *The Ku Klux Klan in the Southwest*. Lexington: University of Kentucky Press, 1966.

———. "White-Robed Reformers: The Ku Klux Klan Comes to Arkansas, 1921–1922." *Arkansas Historical Quarterly* 22 (Spring 1963): 8–23.

———. "White Robes in Politics: The Ku Klux Klan in Arkansas, 1922–1924." *Arkansas Historical Quarterly* 22 (Autumn 1963): 195–214.

Allsopp, Fred W. *History of the Arkansas Press for a Hundred Years and More*. Little Rock, AR: Parke-Harper, 1922.

Arnold, Morris S. *Colonial Arkansas, 1686–1804*. Fayetteville: University of Arkansas Press, 1991.

———. *The Rumble of a Distant Drum: The Quapaws and Old World Newcomers, 1673–1804*. Fayetteville: University of Arkansas Press, 2000.

Ashcraft, Robert, ed. *History of the American Baptist Association*. Texarkana, TX: American Baptist Association, 2000.

Assenmacher, Hugh, OSB. *A Place Called Subiaco: A History of the Benedictine Monks in Arkansas*. Little Rock. AR: Rose Publishing, 1977.

Baker, James T. *Brooks Hays*. Macon, GA: Mercer University Press, 1989.

Baker, Kelly J. *Gospel According to the Klan: The KKK's Appeal to Protestant America, 1915–1930*. Lawrence: University of Kansas Press, 2011.

Ball, Ann, with Father Leon Hutton. *Champion of the Church: The Extraordinary Life and Legacy of Archbishop Noll*. Huntingdon, IN: Our Sunday Visitor, 2006.

Barber, Christopher Bart. "The Bogard Schism: An Arkansas Baptist Agrarian Revolt." PhD dissertation, Southwestern Baptist Theological Seminary, 2006.

Berlet, Chip, and Matthew N. Lyons. *Right-Wing Populism in America: Too Close for Comfort*. New York: Guilford Press, 2000.

Billington, Ray Allen. "Maria Monk and Her Influence." *Catholic Historical Review* 22 (October 1936): 283–96.

Blee, Kathleen M. *Women of the Klan: Racism and Gender in the 1920s*. Berkeley: University of California Press, 1991.

Blevins, Brooks. "The Strike and the Still: Anti-Radical Violence and the Ku Klux Klan in the Ozarks." *Arkansas Historical Quarterly* 52 (Winter 1993): 405–25.

Blumhofer, Edith L. *Restoring the Faith: The Assemblies of God, Pentecostalism, and American Culture*. Urbana-Champaign: University of Illinois Press, 1993.

Britton, Nancy. *Two Centuries of Methodism in Arkansas, 1800–2000*. Little Rock, AR: August House, 2000.

Brown, Deward C. "Anti-Catholicism in Contemporary America, 1920–1960." MA thesis, North Texas State University, 1966.

Burner, David. *The Politics of Provincialism: The Democratic Party in Transition*. New York: Knopf, 1968.

Carruth, Joseph. "World War I Propaganda and Its Effects in Arkansas." *Arkansas Historical Quarterly* 56 (Winter 1997): 385–98.

Carty, Thomas J. *A Catholic in the White House? Religion, Politics, and John F. Kennedy's Presidential Campaign*. New York: Palgrave Macmillan, 2004.

Casey, Shaun. *Making of a Catholic President: Kennedy vs. Nixon, 1960*. New York: Oxford University Press, 2009.

Centennial History of St. Joseph's Parish (1879–1979), Paris, Arkansas. Hot Springs, AR: Hall Printers, 1979.

Chalmers, David M. *Hooded Americanism: The First Century of the Ku Klux Klan, 1865–1965*. Garden City, NY: Doubleday, 1965.

Craig, Douglas B. *After Wilson: The Struggle for the Democratic Party, 1920–1934*. Chapel Hill: University of North Carolina Press, 1992.

Curry, Lerond. *Protestant-Catholic Relations in America: World War I through Vatican II.* Lexington: University Press of Kentucky, 1972.

Daniels, Roger. *Guarding the Golden Door: American Immigration Policies and Immigrants since 1882.* New York: Hill and Wang, 2004.

David, Paul T. *The Presidential Election and Transition, 1960–1961.* Washington, DC: Brookings Institution, 1961.

Davies, Sharon. *Rising Road: A True Tale of Love, Race, and Religion in America.* New York: Oxford University Press, 2010.

Donaldson, Gary A. *The First Modern Campaign: Kennedy, Nixon, and the Election of 1960.* Lanham, MD: Rowan and Littlefield, 2007.

Donley, Paul. *Tracks to the Past: A Pictorial History of Aurora, Missouri.* Marceline, MO: D-Books, 1998.

Dougan, Michael. *Arkansas Odyssey: The Saga of Arkansas from Prehistoric Times to Present.* Little Rock. AR: Rose Publishing, 1994.

DuVal, Kathleen. *The Native Ground: Indians and Colonists in the Heart of the Continent.* Philadelphia: University of Pennsylvania Press, 2005.

Foreman, L. D., and Alta Payne. *The Life and Works of Benjamin Marcus Bogard.* 3 vols. Little Rock, AR: Foreman and Payne, 1966.

Foucault, Michel. *The History of Sexuality.* Vol 1. Translated by Robert Hurley. New York: Pantheon Books, 1978.

Fox, Craig. *Everyday Klansfolk: White Protestant Life and the Ku Klux Klan in 1920s Michigan.* East Lansing: Michigan State University Press, 2011.

Gado, Mark. *Killer Priest: The Crimes, Trial, and Execution of Father Hans Schmidt.* Westport, CT: Praeger, 2006.

The German-Americans: An Informal History. Boston: Little, Brown & Co., 1968.

Hammond, Phillip E. *The Protestant Presence in Twentieth-Century America: Religion and Political Culture.* Albany: State University of New York Press, 1992.

Harvey, Paul. *Redeeming the South: Religious Cultures and Religious Identities among Southern Baptists, 1865–1925.* Chapel Hill: University of North Carolina Press, 1997.

Hennessey S.J., James. *American Catholics: A History of the Roman Catholic Community in the United States.* New York: Oxford University Press, 1981.

Herndon, Dallas B. *Centennial History of Arkansas.* 3 vols. Chicago: S. J. Clarke, 1922.

Hick, Edward L. *Sometimes in the Wrong, but Never in Doubt: George S. Benson and the Education of the New Religious Right.* Knoxville: University of Tennessee Press, 1994.

Higham, John. *Strangers in the Land: Patterns of American Nativism, 1860–1925.* New Brunswick, NJ: Rutgers University Press, 1955.

Hinson, E. Glenn. *A History of Baptists in Arkansas, 1818–1978.* Little Rock: Arkansas Baptist State Convention, 1979.

Hockle, Sr. Henrietta. *Parish on the Ridge: A History of Blessed Sacrament Parish, 1885–2005, Jonesboro, Arkansas.* Jonesboro, AR: Pinpoint Publishing, 2007.

Holley, Donald. "A Look behind the Masks: The 1920s Ku Klux Klan in Monticello, Arkansas." *Arkansas Historical Quarterly* 60 (Summer 2001): 131–50.

Hughes, Richard T. *Reviving the Ancient Faith: The Story of Churches of Christ in America*. Grand Rapids, MI: William B. Eerdmans, 1996.

Hunt, George Murrell. "A History of the Prohibition Movement in Arkansas." MA thesis, University of Arkansas, 1933.

Hutton, Leon. "Catholicism and Civility: John Francis Noll and the Origin of *Our Sunday Visitor.*" *U.S. Catholic Historian* 15 (Summer 1997): 1–22.

Jenkins, Philip. *The New Anti-Catholicism: The Last Acceptable Prejudice*. New York: Oxford University Press, 2003.

Johnson III, Ben F. *John Barleycorn Must Die: The War against Drink in Arkansas*. Fayetteville: University of Arkansas Press, 2005.

Jones, Scott. "Monastic Missionaries in the New Wilderness: A History of Catholic Monasticism in Arkansas, 1878–1998." PhD dissertation, University of Arkansas, 1998.

Josephson, Matthew, and Hannah Josephson. *Al Smith: Hero of the Cities*. Boston: Houghton Mifflin, 1969.

Kauffman, Christopher J. *Faith and Fraternalism: The History of the Knights of Columbus, 1882–1892*. New York: Harper & Row, 1982.

Kennedy, David M. *Over Here: The First World War and American Society*. New York: Oxford University Press, 1980.

Key, V. O., Jr. "Interpreting the Election Results," in *The Presidential Election and Transition, 1960–1961*, edited by Paul T. David, 150–75. Washington, DC: Brookings Institution 1961.

Kilgore, Nettie Hicks. *History of Columbia County*. Magnolia, AR: n.p., ca. 1947.

Kinzer, Donald Louis. *An Episode in Anti-Catholicism: The American Protective Association*. Seattle: University of Washington Press, 1964.

Kodell, Jerome, OSB. "The Gospel Wagon of Father Boniface Spanke, O.S.B." *American Benedictine Review* 61 (March, June, September, 2010): 257–85.

Koren, Henry, CS Sp. *The Serpent and the Dove: A History of the Congregation of the Holy Ghost in the United States, 1745–1984*. Pittsburgh, PA: Spiritus Press, 1985.

Ledbetter, Cal, Jr. "Joe T. Robinson and the Presidential Campaign of 1928." *Arkansas Historical Quarterly* 45 (Summer 1986): 95–125.

Lewis, Todd Everett. "Ben Bogard and the Crusade against Evolution, Rum, and Romanism in Arkansas, 1926–1928." MA thesis, University of Arkansas, 1989.

———. "From Bull Mooser to Grand Dragon of the Ku Klux Klan: James A. Comer of Little Rock." *Pulaski County Historical Review* 43 (Summer 1995): 26–41.

Lichtman, Allan J. *Prejudice and the Old Politics: The Presidential Election of 1928*. Lanham, MD: Lexington Books, 2000, originally published in 1979 by University of North Carolina Press.

———. *White Protestant Nation: The Rise of the American Conservative Movement*. New York: Atlantic Monthly Press, 2008.

Lisenby, Foy. "Brough, Baptists, and Bombast: The Election of 1928." *Arkansas Historical Quarterly* 32 (Summer 1973): 120–31.

———. *Charles Hillman Brough: A Biography*. Fayetteville: University of Arkansas Press, 1996.

Luebke, Frederick C. *Bonds of Loyalty: German Americans and World War I*. Dekalb: Northern Illinois University Press 1974.

MacLean, Nancy. *Behind the Mask of Chivalry: The Making of the Second Ku Klux Klan*. New York: Oxford University Press, 1994.

Marty, Martin E. *Righteous Empire: The Protestant Experience in America*. New York: Dial Press, 1970.

Massa, Mark S. *Anti-Catholicism in America: The Last Acceptable Prejudice*. New York: Crossroads, 2003.

Maury, Reuben. *The Wars of the Godly*. New York: R. M. McBride, 1928.

Mayor, Adrienne. "Libation Titillation: Wine Goblets and Women's Breasts." *Studies in Popular Culture* 16 (April 1994): 61–71.

McGreevy, John T. "Thinking on One's Own: Catholicism in the American Intellectual Imagination, 1928–1960." *Journal of American History* 84 (June 1997): 97–131.

McVeigh, Rory. *The Rise of the Ku Klux Klan: Right-Wing Movements and National Politics*. Minneapolis: University of Minnesota Press, 2009.

Mills, Lucille Harwood. "The Presidential Campaign of 1928 in Arkansas." MA thesis, University of Arkansas, 1948.

Moore, Edmund A. *A Catholic Runs for President: The Campaign of 1928*. New York: Ronald Press Co., 1956.

Moore, Leonard J. *Citizen Klansman: The Ku Klux Klan in Indiana, 1921–1928*. Chapel Hill: University of North Carolina Press, 1991.

Murray, Robert K. *The 103rd Ballot: Democrats and the Disaster in Madison Square Garden*. New York: Harper and Row, 1976.

Myers, Gustavus. *History of Bigotry in the United States*. New York: Capricorn Books, 1943.

Neal, Nevin Emil. "A Biography of Joseph T. Robinson." PhD dissertation, University of Oklahoma, 1958.

———. "The Smith-Robinson Arkansas Campaign of 1928." *Arkansas Historical Quarterly* 19 (Spring 1960): 3–11.

Ngai, Mae M. *Impossible Subjects: Illegal Aliens and the Making of Modern America*. Princeton: Princeton University Press, 2005.

Nordstrom, Justin. *Danger on the Doorstep: Anti-Catholicism and American Print Culture in the Progressive Era*. Notre Dame, IN: University of Notre Dame Press, 2006.

O'Conner, Richard. *The First Hurrah: A Biography of Alfred E. Smith*. New York: G. P. Putnam's Sons, 1970.

The Ozark Region: Its History and Its People. 3 vols. Springfield, MO: Interstate Historical Society, 1917.

Pagliarini, Marie Anne. "The Pure American Woman and the Wicked Catholic Priest: An Analysis of Anti-Catholic Literature in Antebellum America." *Religion and American Culture: A Journal of Interpretation* 9 (Winter 1999): 97–128.

Peel, Roy V., and Thomas C. Donnelly. *The 1928 Campaign: An Analysis.* New York: Arno Press, 1974.

Pegram, Thomas R. *One Hundred Percent American: The Rebirth and Decline of the Ku Klux Klan in the 1920s.* Chicago: Ivan R. Dee, 2011.

Pioneer Faith: The History of Missionary Baptist Associations and Churches in Arkansas from 1818 to 1920. Malvern, AR: History and Archives Committee of State Association of Missionary Baptist Churches of Arkansas, 1994.

Polston, Michael D., and Guy Lancaster, eds. *To Can the Kaiser: Arkansas and the Great War.* Little Rock, AR: Butler Center Books, 2015.

Pratt, J. Kristian. *The Father of Modern Landmarkism: Life of Ben M. Bogard.* Macon, GA: Mercer University Press, 2013.

Rippley, LaVern J. *The German-Americans.* Latham, MD: University Press of America, 1984.

Rogers, J. S. *History of Arkansas Baptists.* Little Rock: Arkansas Baptist State Convention, 1948.

Rorabaugh, W. J. *The Real Making of a President: Kennedy, Nixon, and the 1960 Election.* Lawrence: University Press of Kansas, 2009.

Schepis, Michael E. *J. Frank Norris: The Fascinating, Controversial Life of a Forgotten Figure of the Twentieth Century.* Bloomingon, IN: WestBow Press, 2012.

Shelley, Thomas J. "'What the Hell Is an Encyclical?': Governor Alfred E. Smith, Charles C. Marshall, Esq., and Father Francis P. Duffy." *U.S. Catholic Historian* 15 (Spring 1997): 87–107.

Strickland, Michael Richard. "'Rum, Rebellion, Racketeers, and Rascals': Alexander Copeland Millar and the Fight to Preserve Prohibition in Arkansas, 1927–1933." MA thesis, University of Arkansas, 1993.

Taylor, Wilma Rugh. *This Train Is Bound for Glory: The Story of America's Chapel Cars.* Valley Forge, PA: Judson Press, 1999.

Thomas, William H., Jr. *Unsafe for Democracy: World War I and the U.S. Justice Department's Covert Campaign to Suppress Dissent.* Madison: University of Wisconsin Press, 2008.

Wade, Wyn Craig. *The Fiery Cross: The Ku Klux Klan in America.* New York: Oxford University Press, 1987.

Weibel, E. J. *Forty Years Missionary in Arkansas.* Translated by Sister M. Agnes, OSB, St. Meinrad, IN: Abbey Press, 1968.

Weller, Cecil Edward, Jr. *Joe T. Robinson: Always a Loyal Democrat.* Fayetteville: University of Arkansas Press, 1998.

Whayne, Jeannie M. "Caging the Blind Tiger: Race, Class, and Family in the Battle for Prohibition in Small Town Arkansas." *Arkansas Historical Quarterly* 71 (Spring 2012): 44–60.

Whayne, Jeannie M., Thomas A. DeBlack, George Sabo III, and Morris S. Arnold. *Arkansas: A Narrative History*. Fayetteville: University of Arkansas Press, 2002.

Williams, C. Fred, S. Ray Granade, and Kenneth M. Startup. *A System and Plan: Arkansas Baptist State Convention, 1848–1998*. Franklin, TN: Providence House, 1998.

Williams, Charles. "Protestant Arkansas and a Catholic President." Undergraduate paper, September 2, 2008. SMC 1640, University of Central Arkansas Archives, Conway.

Williams, Daniel K. *God's Own Party: The Making of the Christian Right*. New York: Oxford University Press, 2010.

Williams, Michael. *The Shadow of the Pope*. New York: McGraw-Hill, 1932.

Wilson, Joan Hoff. *Herbert Hoover: Forgotten Progressive*. Boston: Little, Brown and Co., 1975.

Woods, James M. *A History of the Catholic Church in the American South, 1513–1900*. Gainesville: University of Florida Press, 2011.

———. *Mission and Memory: A History of the Catholic Church in Arkansas*. Little Rock: Diocese of Little Rock, 1993.

Woodward, C. Vann. *Tom Watson: Agrarian Rebel*. New York: Oxford University Press, 1963, first published 1938.

Zeidel, Robert F. *Immigrants, Progressives, and Exclusion Politics: The Dillingham Commission, 1900–1927*. DeKalb: Northern Illinois University, 2004.

INDEX

KENNETH C. BARNES is professor of history at the University of Central Arkansas. He is the author of *Who Killed John Clayton? Political Violence and the Emergence of the New South* and *Journey of Hope: The Back-to-Africa Movement in Arkansas in the Late 1800s.*